Preschool Education Programs for Children with Autism

Preschool Education Programs for Children with Autism

Edited by Sandra L. Harris
and Jan S. Handleman

pro·ed

8700 Shoal Creek Boulevard
Austin, Texas 78757-6897

pro·ed

© 1994 by PRO-ED, Inc.
8700 Shoal Creek Boulevard
Austin, Texas 78757-6897

Library of Congress Cataloging-in-Publication Data

Preschool education programs for children with autism / Sandra L.
   Harris and Jan S. Handleman (editors).
      p.   cm.
   Includes bibliographical references.
   ISBN 0-89079-587-8
   1. Autistic children—Education (Preschool)—United States—Case
studies.   2. Classroom management—United States—Case studies.
I. Harris, Sandra L.   II. Handleman, Jan S.
LC4718.P74   1993
371.94'0973—dc20   93-9577
                                                        CIP

Production Manager: Alan Grimes
Production Coordinator: Adrienne Booth
Art Director: Lori Kopp
Reprints Buyer: Alicia Woods
Editorial Assistant: Claudette Landry

Printed in the United States of America

      3   4   5   6   7   8   9   10   98   97

Contents

Preface

In 1972 the Douglass Developmental Disabilities Center was founded on the Douglass College Campus of Rutgers University. In the 20 years since that event, we have educated hundreds of students with autism and met hundreds more children and their families. Over the course of those years, we have seen a number of fads and fancies of treatment for autism come and go. Some people have made their fame and/or fortune offering the latest in a series of "cures" or revolutionary philosophical views about the treatment of autism. Often these individuals left behind a trail of broken-hearted parents who had hoped for that bit of magic that would transform their child.

Sadly, in spite of all the claims, the cure for autism is not yet known. Nonetheless, a number of dedicated clinicians, educators, and scientists have labored over the years to develop and refine data-based procedures of proven efficacy for the treatment of autism. This steady, on-going empirical effort has led to substantial gains in our ability to educate children with autism. One of the areas where this improvement is most notable is in the education of very young children.

The educational strategies we are using today for preschool-age children with autism are quite different from those of a decade ago. However, disseminating information about these techniques has lagged behind their development. As a result, there are still many classrooms relying upon strategies more appropriate to the early 1980s than to the early 1990s. This lack of widespread sharing of information about procedures of demonstrated value makes it urgent to ensure that information about preschool education is readily available. Hence, this book was born.

We are grateful to the contributors to this book who have shared in some detail a description of their classrooms. Each of the programs described on the pages that follow relies upon data-based procedures to create its curriculum and evaluate its impact on students. We believe such rigor is the hallmark of effective education.

We wish to thank our colleagues at the Douglass Developmental Disabilities Center and the Graduate School of Applied and Professional Psychology for their ongoing support. We especially appreciate the help of Maria Arnold, Jean Burton, Lew Gantwerk, Rita Gordon, Barbara Kristoff, Ruth Schulman, and Lisa Tomchek, each of whom has offered wise counsel over the years. We also are forever indebted to those parents who have entrusted us with the education of their children. We could ask for no higher compliment than their confidence in our program. Closer to home, Lauren Handleman has been one of the most important sources of joy in lighting her father's days all these years.

Chapter 1

Preschool Programs for Children with Autism

SANDRA L. HARRIS and JAN S. HANDLEMAN

INTRODUCTION

Recently professionals have witnessed exciting reports of major progress in the treatment of very young children with autism. Early intervention programs such as those of Lovaas (1987) and Odom, Hoyson, Jamieson, and Strain (1985) have encouraged the notion that important developmental changes can occur in some young children with autism. In the most dramatic of these reports, Lovaas (1987) reported that nearly half of the young children with autism who received intensive behavior modification in his project reached normal intellectual and educational functioning at follow-up.

Odom and his colleagues documented that young children with autistic behavior can benefit socially and educationally from exposure to normally developing peers in an integrated preschool program (cf., Odom et al., 1985; Odom & Strain, 1986; Strain, Hoyson, & Jamieson, 1985). In a study at the Douglass Developmental Disabilities Center, we found a nearly 19-point increase in IQ for children with autism after 1 year of intensive work in a segregated preschool class (Harris, Handleman, Gordon, Kristoff, & Fuentes, 1991). These and other reports of measurable behavior changes in preschool-age children with autism from a number of independent settings document more substantial benefits than were thought possible a decade ago. As a result of these encouraging data, a variety of preschool projects have been developed around the country and many other educators are considering the establishment of similar programs in their own school systems.

In spite of our enthusiasm for this rapid expansion of resources for very young children with autism, we are concerned about the lack of easily available information about the organization and operation of these classes and the wide variation that is likely to develop among programs. It is important that there be communication among professionals operating these classrooms so we can compare the outcome from several different approaches and know which methods are best for which children under which conditions. There is a serious risk of drift away from the data-based treatment models toward those founded on administrative convenience, intuition, or misinterpretation unless communication among educators and administrators is kept at an optimum level and programs are challenged to document the effects on their young students. It would be a particular tragedy to offer inappropriate services at a time when the educational technology is available to provide substantial benefit to some children.

In this book we invited distinguished service providers in 10 different settings for young children with autism to describe their programs in some detail. Each author was asked to follow the same general outline, while being encouraged to embellish those areas of special relevance to his or her model. This structure offers the reader an opportunity to compare the various programs on a number of dimensions, while also giving the author the opportunity to highlight special features of the individual program.

Table 1.1 summarizes a number of important features characterizing the preschool programs described in this book. The reader will find both the differences and the similarities important in comparing programs and selecting features of potential use in creating a new preschool program. Although the level of detail in this book will not enable the reader to replicate precisely an existing program, it should serve to sensitize one to the variables that must be considered in the creation of a classroom, possible solutions to thorny problems, and methods of measuring progress to document the efficacy of one's intervention. Although many of the methods described in the following chapters are data-based, the

TABLE 1.1. Summary of Program Features

	Anderson	Bondy	Egel	Handleman	Lord	McClannahan	McGee	Powers	Romanczyk	Strain
Location	Private	Public	Public	University	Public	Private	University	Public	University	Public
University Training	Yes	Yes	Yes	Yes	Yes	Yes	Yes	No	Yes	Yes
Target Population	Aut	Aut	Aut	Aut	Aut/CH	Aut	Aut/LD	Aut	Aut/Mixed	Aut
Opportunity for Integration	Yes	Yes	Yes	Yes	Yes	Yes	Yes	Yes	Yes	Yes
CARS	Yes	No	Yes	Yes	Yes	No	No	Yes	No	Yes
IQ	Binet/Bayley	Various	Binet	Binet	Bayley	Binet	Binet	Brigance	Denver Slosson	McCarthy
DSM	No	Yes	Yes	Yes	Yes	Yes	Yes	Yes	No	Yes
Vineland	Yes	Varies	Yes	Yes	Yes	Yes	Yes	No	Yes	No
LAP/ELAP	Yes	No	Yes	No	No	No	No	No	No	Yes
Parent Training	Yes	Yes	Yes	Yes	Yes	Yes	Yes	Yes	Yes	Yes
Transitional Planning	Yes	Yes	Yes	Yes	Yes	Yes	Yes	Yes	Yes	Yes

reader will nonetheless need to measure the impact of these methods in his or her own classroom. Such accountability is an integral component of ethical educational practice.

As noted in Table 1.1, the programs showcased in this book are located in a variety of settings including public schools, private special education schools, and universities. Two of them (Bondy and Frost, Chapter 3; Lord and Schopler, Chapter 6) are models of state-wide service delivery systems. One of these state-wide systems was developed for a small state, Delaware, while the other serves a much larger state, North Carolina. Although most of the programs serve relatively densely populated areas, both Lord and Schopler's TEACCH program (Chapter 6) and the Berkshire Hills Learning Center described by Powers (Chapter 9) address the needs of children in rural settings. Some of the classrooms described in this book have been in existence for quite a while, and others are relatively new. Schopler for example, started the TEACCH program in 1972 (Chapter 6) while Powers (Chapter 9) established his new classroom in 1991. This diversity of settings and range of experiences should enable the reader to find one or more programs that are a good fit with his or her administrative context.

All of the programs in this book offer a rich ratio of adults to children. That intensity appears to be essential to the education of young children with autism. In order to meet that need, most of the preschool programs represented here buttress their full-time staff with graduate or undergraduate students from nearby colleges and universities. This is a valuable and inexpensive potential resource that every program should consider. Not only do the children benefit from the presence of energetic undergraduates, but the college students benefit as well through the opportunity for "hands-on" learning. In our own program at Rutgers University, scores of undergraduates have remained in the field of developmental disorders after their experience at our center.

Although all of the programs were selected for this book because they serve children with autism, some include other populations as well, including pervasive developmental disorder not otherwise specified, communication disabled, learning disabled, emotionally disturbed, and normally developing children. All of the programs provide opportunities for integration with normally developing children, but the degree and intensity of integration varies from those that fully integrate children with autism from the early days of schooling to those that do this later or on a less intensive or limited basis. Some programs integrate children in classes within their own physical setting, and others take the children to different facilities in the community to accomplish this goal. Each approach has its own benefits and challenges. Integration within one's own setting permits optimal flexibility and control over the experience, but integration in other settings may sometimes provide a more realistic sense of the natural environment in which the child must ultimately function. It is noteworthy that every program is attentive to the process of transition from school to the child's next educational experience. This universal concern for transitional planning highlights the importance of this aspect of program development.

This book is intended to give an educator or administrator planning to create a new classroom or reorganize an existing program a sense of the range of options currently being employed by others. We have asked the contributors to translate into relatively concrete terms what it means for their program to be "behaviorally based," "developmentally sequenced," "integrated," or "segregated." In reading the descriptions one will wish to ask such questions as: How much do the models resemble or differ from one another along these dimensions? To what extent do current data inform the operation of these programs? Given that our data base falls short of the needs for inclusive programming, how do various models fill in the knowledge gaps?

We were also interested in what these prominent service providers view as important research questions that need to be addressed before we can fully evaluate the benefits of our models for serving children with autism. We asked them what they believe are the most pressing questions confronting the field. Their response to that question may inspire those who are creating new programs to establish those programs in a way that will address some of these urgent issues. The reader will surely come away from the discussion with an appreciation of how much we still have to learn about the education of the preschool-age child with autism and a healthy skepticism about any "easy cures."

Structure and Context

Each chapter begins with an overview of the structure and context of the program. Where is it located? How long has it been in existence? How is it funded? How much does it cost to operate? This information about context helps the reader orient to the specific program and the kinds of resources available in that setting. Operating in a public school, a university campus, a hospital, or a private school may carry different implications about the structure of one's classroom (Handleman, 1988). Programs in the public schools may be required to serve every child who meets admissions criteria; those in private or university settings may be able to be more selective about whom they admit. Each setting has potential benefits. For example, being in a public school enabled Egel and his colleagues to capitalize on the presence of a Head Start Classroom as part of the integration process (Chapter 4). Similarly, Powers (Chapter 9) describes a program that draws on several groups of peers in a public school. By contrast, McGee and her colleagues (Chapter 8) and Handleman and Harris (Chapter 5) operate university-based programs that have brought the normally developing peers on campus in a kind of "reverse" mainstreaming.

Diagnosis and Assessment

We asked each of our contributors to provide considerable detail about the children being served by the program. It is often difficult to know whether the children attending one program are similar to those in another. Having this information has major implications for helping to determine to what extent differences in treatment outcome may be determined by differences in population as opposed to treatment model. The complexities of defining autism have historically lead to the inclusion of a rather heterogeneous group under this heading. The greater specificity we can bring to this task, the better the communication that will follow among us.

The diagnosis of autism has been a subject of debate for half a century. Following Kanner's (1943) initial description of infantile autism, there have been a variety of alternative definitions of precisely what constitutes autism (Schopler & Mesibov, 1988). That debate is not ended and each recent *Diagnostic and Statistical Manual of Mental Disorders* has offered somewhat different criteria for diagnosis (American Psychiatric Association, 1980, 1987). This ambiguity makes it essential that we communicate as fully as possible with one another about whom we are treating. As the reader will note in Table 1, most but not all of these programs use the DSM-III-R criteria and many also use the *Childhood Autism Rating Scale* (CARS) (Schopler, Reichler, DeVellis, & Daly, 1988). The CARS was developed by the TEACCH program staff in North Carolina. By virtue of its age and size, the TEACCH program has served more children with autism and related disorders than any of the other programs in this book, and their discussion of the complexities of diagnostic assessment is based on that rich and extensive background (Chapter 6).

In addition to the challenge of diagnosis, there is the question of how one assesses the various dimensions of the child's functioning including behavior, affect, social skills, cognition, speech and language, and so forth. Although assessment of children with autism has long been recognized as difficult (Browder, 1991; Powers & Handleman, 1984), it is also clear that the use of appropriate instruments and strategies makes it possible to conduct a meaningful, valid assessment of these youngsters (Schopler & Mesibov, 1988).

There are a variety of approaches to assessing the child with autism. One of these is the use of norm-based psychometric tests including intelligence tests, tests of developmental abilities, and speech and language assessments. For example, as evident in Table 1, most of the programs use the *Stanford–Binet IV* (Thorndike, Hagen, & Sattler, 1986) and the *Vineland Adaptive Behavior Scales* (Sparrow, Balla, & Cicchetti, 1984) as norm-based assessment devises.

Behavioral assessment of the child's skills, deficits, and behavior problems is another important strategy employed in many settings (Powers & Handleman, 1984). Assessments may be based on direct observation in the classroom, home visits, community observations, parent reports, teacher reports, and videotapes. The contributors to this book were asked to describe their own approach to this individualized assessment process. Among the innovative approaches described are Egel's care in assessing environmental variables, stimulus preference, and sensory preferences (Chapter 4). Powers (Chapter 9) makes considerable use of this approach.

Staffing and Administration

The creation of a classroom for children with autism requires a teaching staff and an administrative structure. We asked each author to describe the staff who participate in their program in terms of credentials and responsibilities. Special education teachers, speech and language specialists, and psychologists are universally involved in these programs as are teacher assistants. Other specialists such as occupational therapists or physical therapists may be part of the regular staff, or may be consulted for those children who require their services. Some of the programs have also created nontraditional job descriptions such as Egel's (Chapter 4) technical assistant who provides ongoing feedback on classroom operation and specific instructional programs, and Powers' (Chapter 9) community liaison specialist who focuses on community integration. Family coordinators or parent trainers are specifically designated in some programs.

The authors were also asked to describe the kinds of training and supervision they provide for their staff. Given the continuing changes in educational strategies for children with autism, inservice education is crucial in maintaining an effective program. McClannahan and Krantz describe in detail their systematic approach to staff training (Chapter 7).

Curriculum

Curriculum development for young children with autism is an intricate task (Handleman, 1992). Selecting appropriate goals and objectives, determining accurate levels of instruction, and identifying and creating suitable materials often present challenges for the teacher. A well balanced and orchestrated curriculum is typically the result of careful planning and the systematic organization of educational experiences (Handleman & Harris, 1986). The computerized approach to data collection, record keeping, and specialized assessment developed by Romanczyk and his colleagues (Chapter 10) will be of special interest to many readers.

An important component of each chapter of this book is an overview of the curriculum for that program. This includes the general philosophy that drives the curriculum, the major areas in the curriculum, and sources of materials used in the classroom. Sample curriculum items from the domains of social, affective, cognitive, speech and language, and self-help are described to help the reader understand specific examples of what the children are taught. A sample daily schedule is included to give one a sense of the flow of activities through the school day. Methods of assessing each child's progress are described. The reader will find considerable variation among the teaching approaches described in this book. For example, McGee and her colleagues (Chapter 8) focus on the use of incidental teaching to a greater degree than any of the other programs represented here. This work, started at the University of Massachusetts and now continuing at Emory, sets this program in contrast to many others. Another innovation of interest to many readers will be Bondy's (Chapter 3) thoughtful application of a Picture Exchange Communication system.

Integration

The development of preschool classes for children with autism and the striking progress these children have made through early intervention programs have lead to an active exploration of the value of integrating these youngsters with their normally developing peers in the classroom. Strain and Odom have been especially important in exploring this dimension of treatment (cf., Odom & Speltz, 1983; Strain, 1983). Their work and that of others raises important questions that we believed needed to be addressed. To what extent is exposure to normally developing peers viewed as essential to the child's education? If integration or mainstreaming is provided, at what point does this occur? Are children mainstreamed all day, every day from their first day in school? Is there a gradual transition? Who are the peer children? What effect does integration have on the peers? Each of the programs has its own approach to this problem. For example, Strain and Cordisco (Chapter 11) and McGee, Daly, and Jacobs (Chapter 8) present models that integrate children from their initial admission to the preschool program, while Handleman and Harris (Chapter 5) provide most of their students with 1 year of intensive segregated instruction followed by an integrated experience. Powers (Chapter 9) describes a flexible approach with integration varying according to child and task. Anderson and his colleagues (Chapter 2) first focus on home-based intervention, followed by a segregated class and then an integrated class.

Use of Aversives

Another potentially controversial question posed to each author was the use of behavior management procedures for very young children. The use of "aversive techniques" has been a topic of major debate in the treatment of life threatening or dangerous behavior for people with autism (Harris & Handleman, 1990; Repp & Singh, 1990). To what extent do these questions arise in work with very young children with autism? We asked each contributor to describe his or her philosophy concerning the use of management techniques for preschool-age children and to

indicate which specific techniques they employ when dealing with behavior problems. The reader will note that, in general, most interventions with preschool-age children involve very mild aversive interventions, with a primary focus on functional assessment and teaching of
appropriate alternative behaviors. The relatively brief learning history of
very young children offers a sense of optimism for intervening effectively
with most of their behavior problems.

Family Involvement

For more than 20 years we have known that parent and family involvement is an important factor in maintaining the behavior changes
achieved by children with autism (Lovaas, Koegel, Simmons, & Long,
1973; Schopler & Reichler, 1971). Research in the 1970s and 1980s
documented that parents can master a full range of intervention techniques and use them to facilitate their child's mastery of language, social,
self-help, and related skills (Harris, 1983; Howlin, 1981). More recently,
there has been concern expressed about the kinds of support resources
necessary to maintain optimal family functioning and ensure that the
family context remains appropriate to the needs of all of its members
(Harris, in press). The most intensive home-based program in this book
is that of Anderson and his co-workers (Chapter 2) at the May Institute
who provide 15 to 25 hours a week of direct in-home treatment during
a 6-month period. Although parents participate in that treatment, much
of it is done by professional staff in the family's home.

In recognition of the role that families can play in treatment, each
contributor was asked to consider the role of parents as teacher and the
level of family involvement and support. What do they expect of parents
and what kind of support do they provide for families? How intimately
involved are parents expected to be in their child's education? Is the
program home-based? School-based? Who trains parents? Must they
participate?

Outcome

To the extent that such data are available, each author was asked to
describe any available outcome data concerning children who have com-

pleted the program. This includes initial placement data and any systematic follow-up information the author can provide. Where have the children gone after leaving the preschool class? How have they done in those new placements? Are there any standardized measures of change for the children from admission to graduation?

Finally, each chapter concludes with recommendations from the author(s) concerning areas of special concern which he or she believes should be addressed by educators and researchers in the future. What are the limits of our intervention methods and what should we be planning to do next?

We hope this book will enable established service providers to communicate more clearly with one another about their models of intervention. We also hope it will enable the newcomer to identify those approaches most consistent with his or her own classroom goals and to adopt a teaching model most consistent with those objectives. Many of the authors who contributed to the present volume are available for consultation to other programs and the person creating a new service or revamping an old one may find dialogue with one or more of these authors a useful step in the process of change.

REFERENCES

American Psychiatric Association. (1980). *Diagnostic and statistical manual of mental disorders.* (3rd ed). Washington DC: Author.

American Psychiatric Association. (1987). *Diagnostic and statistical manual of mental disorders.* (3rd ed.—revised). Washington DC: Author.

Browder, D. (Ed.). (1991). *Assessment of individuals with severe disabilities: An applied behavior approach to life skills assessment.* Baltimore, MD: Paul Brookes.

Handleman, J. S. (1988). Educational services in the schools: Beyond the student-teacher dyad. In M. D. Powers (Ed.), *Expanding systems of service delivery for persons with developmental disabilities* (pp. 217–229). Baltimore, MD: Paul Brookes.

Handleman, J. S. (1992). Assessment for curriculum planning. In D. Berkell (Ed.), *Autism: Identification, education and treatment* (pp. 77–88). Hillsdale, NJ: Lawrence Erlbaum.

Handleman, J. S., & Harris, S. L. (1986). *Educating the developmentally disabled: Meeting the needs of children and families.* San Diego, CA: College Hill.

Harris, S. L. (1983). *Families of the developmentally disabled: A guide to behavioral intervention*. Elmsford, NY: Pergamon Press.

Harris, S. L. (in press). Treatment of family problems in autism. In E. Schopler & G. B. Mesibov (Eds.), *Assessment and management of behavior problems in autism*. New York: Plenum.

Harris, S. L., & Handleman, J. S. (Eds.). (1990). *Aversive and nonaversive interventions*. New York: Springer.

Harris, S. L., Handleman, J. S., Gordon, R., Kristoff, B., & Fuentes, F. (1991). Changes in cognitive and language functioning of preschool children with autism. *Journal of Autism and Developmental Disorders, 21,* 281–290.

Howlin, P. A. (1981). The results of a home-based language training program with autistic children. *British Journal of Disorders of Communication, 16,* 73–88.

Kanner, L. (1943). Autistic disturbances of affective contact. *Nervous Child, 2,* 217–240.

Lovaas, O. I., (1987). Behavioral treatment and normal educational and intellectual functioning in young autistic children. *Journal of Consulting and Clinical Psychology, 55,* 3–9.

Lovaas, O. I., Koegel, R. L., Simmons, J. Q., & Long, J. S. (1973). Some generalization and follow-up measures on autistic children in behavior therapy. *Journal of Applied Behavior Analysis, 6,* 131–165.

Odom, S. L., Hoyson, M., Jamieson, B., & Strain, P. S. (1985). Increasing handicapped preschoolers' peer social interactions: Cross-setting and component analysis. *Journal of Applied Behavior Analysis, 18,* 3–16.

Odom, S. L., & Speltz, M. L. (1983). Program variations in preschools for handicapped and nonhandicapped children: Mainstreamed vs. integrated special education. *Analysis and Intervention in Developmental Disabilities, 3,* 89–103.

Odom, S. L., & Strain, P. S. (1986). A comparison of peer-initiation and teacher-antecedent interventions for promoting social interactions of autistic preschoolers. *Journal of Applied Behavior Analysis, 19,* 59–71.

Powers, M. D., & Handleman, J. S. (1984). *Behavioral assessment of severe developmental disabilities*. Rockville, MD: Aspen Systems Corp.

Repp, A. C., & Singh, N. N. (Eds.). (1990). *Perspectives on the use of nonaversive and aversive interventions for persons with developmental disabilities*. Sycamore, IL: Sycamore Publishing Co.

Schopler, E., & Mesibov, G. B. (Eds.). (1988). *Diagnosis and assessment in Autism*. New York: Plenum.

Schopler, E., & Reichler, R. J. (1971). Parents as co-therapists in the treatment of psychotic children. *Journal of Autism and Childhood Schizophrenia, 1,* 87–102.

Schopler, E., Reichler, R. J., DeVellis, R. F., & Daly, K. (1988). *The Childhood Autism Rating Scale* (CARS). Los Angeles: Western Psychological Services.

Sparrow, S. S., Balla, D. A., & Cicchetti, D. V. (1984). *Vineland Adaptive Behavior Scales: Interview Edition. Survey form manual.* Circle Pines, MN: American Guidance Service.

Strain, P. S. (1983). Generalization of autistic children's social behavior change: Effects of developmentally integrated and segregated settings. *Analysis and Intervention in Developmental Disabilities, 3,* 23–34.

Strain, P. S., Hoyson, M., & Jamieson, B. (1985). Normally developing preschoolers as intervention agents for autistic-like children: Effects on class deportment and social interaction. *Journal of the Division for Early Childhood, 9,* 105–115.

Thorndike, R. L., Hagen, E. R., & Sattler, J. M. (1986). *The Stanford-Binet Intelligence Scale* (4th ed.). Chicago: The Riverside Publishing Co.

Chapter 2

The May Center for Early Childhood Education

STEPHEN R. ANDERSON, SUSAN CAMPBELL,
and BARBARA O'MALLEY CANNON

The May Center for Early Childhood Education is a program developed and operated by the May Institute, serving children in the greater Boston metropolitan area. The program actually had two beginnings. The first was the development of the Home-Based Early Intervention Program in 1983, and the second was the development of a socially integrated preschool in 1986.

The May Institute, incorporated in 1955, was for many years predominately a residential treatment program on Cape Cod serving children ages 5 to 16 years old. Although highly effective in its efforts to return children to live with their families after a period of residential intervention (Anderson & Schwartz, 1986; Christian, 1984), staff of the institute recognized the need to develop outreach services that might prevent the need for out-of-home placement.

Impressed by the accomplishments of Ivar Lovaas (1987) and encouraged by our own success at outreach parent training (Czyzewski, Christian, & Norris, 1984), we wrote and received several private foundation and federal grants to develop home-based services for young children with autism and their families. Despite success with home-based training, our earliest efforts often seemed thwarted by the poorly de-signed and managed school programs that also served the students. Al-though some positive impact on these schools was achieved through consultation by institute staff, the results were substantially less than what was desired to maintain treatment gains and to set the stage for further learning.

As an alternative to the school-based options available, the institute received a small private foundation grant to develop a socially integrated preschool classroom for children with and without autism. Since that time the program has grown to three classes for preschoolers and three classes for children ages 6 to 12 years old. This chapter will describe the program and students who attend the preschool program only.

The May Center for Early Childhood Education is located in a for-mer parochial school building in an urban setting on the outskirts of Boston. It is a private, not-for-profit school licensed by the Massachu-setts State Department of Education. The tuition for the 1992–93 school year was $26,362 for a 12-month school year. The tuition was higher ($32,056) for children who participated in a program of combined home-based and center-based services.

Under Massachusetts state law (Chapter 766), local school districts are required to develop special education services that provide the child with "maximum feasible benefit" (a slightly higher standard than P.L. 94-142). If unable to meet this standard, a local school district may contract with another approved agency (like the May Center) to provide appropriate educational services for an individual child.

The May Center must meet the licensing requirements of the State Department of Education, which has lead responsibility to ensure that all provisions of state and federal special education laws are met, and the Massachusetts Office for Children (OFC), which approves "group day-care" programs that serve children with and without developmental disabilities.

GENERAL STRUCTURE OF THE PROGRAM

The program includes the following basic service components: (1) in-tensive home-based special education and behavior therapy, (2) com-prehensive parent training and family support, (3) socially integrated preschool programming, and (4) transitional programming into kindergarten. Although variations of the model occur, children typically enter the center's home-based training program simultaneously with, or prior to, entering the preschool program. A comprehensive description of the home-based program and its results have been reported elsewhere (Anderson, Avery, DiPietro, Edwards, & Christian, 1987; Anderson, 1989) and will be briefly described later. In short, the program provides 15 to 25 hours (including the parents' participation) of direct, in-home training each week across a 6-month intervention period.

Turning to the preschool program, the May Center consists of two socially integrated classes and one segregated classroom setting (First Step). The children typically enter the First Step classroom initially, where the ratio is three teachers with a group of eight students. The instructional format includes work in small groups of two or three students to one teacher, as well as large group activities with one teacher serving in a lead role and the other teachers providing support. The curriculum emphasizes the development of skills important for the children's successful transition into one of the socially integrated classes (e.g., ability to follow simple instructions, imitation, parallel play, working in large groups). The transition to one of the socially integrated classrooms can be accomplished within 12 months for most of the children. In the socially integrated classrooms, the ratio is three teachers to six students who have developmental disabilities plus seven students who are typically developing. The curriculum (described later) targets the skills needed by the children to successfully move into regular kindergarten.

While children are receiving the combined home-based and preschool services, they attend school 3 hours a day (either mornings or afternoons) and participate in home-based services the other half of the day. After the home-based program has been completed, the children participate in a 30-hour per week preschool program.

POPULATION SERVED

Forty-two children have participated in the combined home–preschool program and met the following criteria: (1) were under 6 years old at the time of admission, (2) participated in at least 6 months of home-based training, and (3) completed at least 1 year of preschool services. Eighty additional children have participated in a broad range of services but did not meet these criteria. Currently 24 children are enrolled, not including the typically developing children who also attend the preschool program. The majority of referrals are by parents, although school systems, diagnostic hospitals, and early intervention programs also make referrals. Our mission is to serve children with autism or pervasive developmental disorder, or other developmentally disabled children who exhibit significant behavior disorders. If a diagnosis of autism is unconfirmed, an experienced member of the team completes the *Childhood Autism Rating Scale* (CARS) (Schopler, Reichler, & Renner, 1990). Only a small number of students are accepted who do not meet the diagnostic criteria for autism.

The mean age at admission for children who have entered the combined home-preschool program is 3.9 years (range: 3.0 years–5.2 years). Of the 42 children that have entered the program, 35 were male and 7 were female. The ethnic breakdown is as follows: 33 Caucasian, 5 African-American, 2 Asian, and 2 other.

Although standardized tests were initially used to assess all children who entered the home-based program (prior to the development of preschool services), the practice was discontinued as the number of students served grew too large to maintain a regimen of pre-, post-, and follow-up assessments. Recently, however we have reintroduced norm-referenced assessments for all new students entering the program. Using the *Bayley Scales of Infant Development* (Bayley, 1969) or the *Stanford–Binet Intelligence Scale* (Form L-M) (Terman & Merrill, 1972), and most recently the *Stanford–Binet Intelligence Scale IV* (Thorndike, Hagen, & Sattler, 1986), IQ scores available for 10 children range from 37 to 71 with a mean of 49. This group appears to be representative of the type of children served in our early childhood program.

SCREENING AND ASSESSMENT PROCEDURES

An initial screening is conducted to determine each child's eligibility for admission to the program. The screening process consists of a detailed application, review of relevant records, parent interview, informal evaluation of the child, and in some cases, a home visit. The process is designed to: (1) assess whether the child exhibits deficits and behavior characteristic of children with autism, and (2) determine whether the child's parents are willing to commit to the level of involvement that will be required of them. During the parent interview, a developmental and behavioral profile of the child is obtained as well as a summary of the parents' expectations and commitment to participate. The evaluation of the child involves a variety of staged activities designed to assess their social responsiveness, play skills, school readiness, response to obligatory teaching situations, and general level of functioning. Once all of the steps have been completed, an admissions team meets to consider acceptability for admission. Only two formal instruments are completed prior to admission, the *Vineland Adaptive Behavior Scales* (Sparrow, Balla, & Cicchetti, 1984) and the *Developmental Play Assessment Instrument* (DPA) (Lifter, Sulzer-Azaroff, Anderson, & Edwards-Cowdery, 1993). The DPA is an instrument used to assess the play development of children with disabilities relative to the play of nondisabled children. The developmental quality of toy play is evaluated according to the level of pretend play and the frequency and variety of play activities within the level identified.

Once a child is admitted into the program, formal assessments are completed during the child's first month of placement. These assessments are used as a baseline against which future development is measured. As indicated previously, this battery of assessments has been recently reintroduced and has been completed on only a small number of students to date. We project that 15 to 20 children of preschool age will be assessed this year at admission and again after 1 year of participation in the program. The specific evaluation instruments being used are as follows:

- *Bayley Scales of Infant Development* (Bayley, 1969) or *Stanford–Binet Intelligence Scale* (4th ed.) (Thorndike, Hagen, & Sattler, 1986)

- *Vineland Adaptive Behavior Scales* (Sparrow, Balla, & Cicchetti, 1984)

- *Early Learning Accomplishments Profile* (ELAP) (Glover, Priminger, & Sanford, 1988) or *Learning Accomplishments Profile* (LAP) (Sanford & Zelman, 1981)

- *Sequenced Inventory of Communication Development* (Hedrick, Prathre, & Tobin, 1975)

- *Developmental Play Assessment Instrument* (Lifter et al., 1988)

A variety of family assessments also are completed at the time of admission and 1 year later. At this time, these instruments are used only to determine any pre- and posttest changes and are not specifically used to tailor the course of individual programming for a family or child. The instruments include: (1) *Behavioral Vignettes Test* (Baker, 1989), (2) *Parent Stress Index* (Abidin, 1983), (3) *Family Assessment Devise* (Epstein, Baldwin, & Bishop, 1982), (4) *Questionnaire on Resources and Stress* (Holroyd, 1987), (5) *Family Adaptability and Cohesion Evaluation Scales III* (FACES III) (Olson, Portner, & Lavee, 1985), and (6) *Child Improvement Locus of Control* (Devellis, Devellis, Revicki, Lurie, Runyan, & Bristol, 1985).

TEACHING AND ADMINISTRATIVE STAFF

Each preschool classroom has a senior teacher and two assistant teachers. The senior teacher is typically certified in early childhood education or special education for young children with special needs. Assistant teachers may hold credentials of certification as well. All other staff, including the home-based therapists, have bachelor's or master's-level education in psychology, special education, speech, or early childhood education. The center employs a full-time speech and language pathologist and part-time consultants in occupational and physical therapy.

The approach to the training and supervision of classroom and home personnel consists of several basic steps beginning with the identification of important areas of competency (e.g., assessment, defining behaviors, measurement, case management). Each new staff member completes approximately 30 hours of didactic instruction to familiarize them with the philosophy of the program and to impart general information about the important areas of competency. Each individual also is given an opportunity to demonstrate individual competencies on the job while his or her supervisor provides feedback. Checklists (Larsson, Luce, & Christian, 1989) are used to evaluate many important competencies and to provide an extra level of training when the individual is struggling to acquire a relevant skill. In addition, each staff member receives a clear set of job performance standards prior to employment that delineate their specific job responsibilities and serve as part of their employment contract. Each employee's supervisor conducts an evaluation of the individual's performance against the specific job performance standards at 3, 6, and 12 months for new employees and annually thereafter.

Each senior teacher and assistant teacher (hereinafter, both groups will be referred to as teachers or case managers) serve as a case manager for at least two children. The case manager's duties include: completing behavioral and criterion-referred assessments, developing education/treatment objectives, writing detailed programs, designing evaluation systems and tracking progress, documenting education and treatment progress in the student's case record (e.g., graphs, progress notes), assisting in transitional planning, communicating with parents, and generally monitoring the student's program to ensure that his or her needs are being met and that the child's rights are being protected.

The home-based program and the preschool are each managed by a master's-level individual with significant experience in the education and treatment of children with autism and related disabilities. These two individuals have ultimate responsibility for the selection and training of staff and the supervision of the day-to-day operations of the program.

Related services of speech, occupational therapy, and physical therapy are almost entirely integrated into the classroom curriculum. It is unusual for the ancillary staff to remove the child for any services or to provide direct services themselves (some physical therapy may be the exception). For example, in the case of communication training, the speech pathologist completes a formal assessment, then consults with the case manager to develop specific goals, objectives, and programs for training. The speech pathologist then trains the classroom and home-based staff to provide direct, individualized instruction and to use incidental language teaching strategies to promote generalization (Dyer & Kohland, 1990). In the case of occupational therapy, relevant objectives are imbedded within the regular classroom curriculum.

The program has three part-time secretaries (2.0 full-time equivalents), a social service coordinator who is responsible for admission and discharge, and an outreach coordinator who consults to individual families and public schools. One part-time psychologist has responsibilities for program administration, clinical support, and research and dissemination.

The May Center maintains affiliations with colleges and universities in greater Boston that prepare students for teaching, speech and occupational therapy, and special education administration for children with autism and other developmental disabilities. During the last year, the center served as a practicum and training site for 10 individuals completing requirements for undergraduate or graduate degrees.

CURRICULUM

The curriculum addresses each of the major skill areas of language, social/behavioral, play, fine and gross motor, self-help, and preacademic. A broad range of materials are used to teach specific skills, but no single instructional curriculum is used exclusively. In short, the curriculum is individually developed based on the results of behavioral and criterion-referenced assessments including: (1) an interview or survey of parents, (2) direct observation of the child during natural times, (3) administration of the ELAP or LAP, and (4) direct observation during structured tasks or activities designed to assess levels of functioning within specific skill areas. A basic skills curriculum (see Table 2.1) that identifies specific competencies believed to be important for every child in the program is directly assessed and becomes part of the child's individual curriculum if needed.

The case manager, in cooperation with other staff, identifies 15 to 25 objectives to be conducted at home and at school. At home, the training involves one-to-one instruction with the child's parents as active participants. The education plan is weighted to reflect deficits and behavior excesses identified by the child's parents to be most important. The objectives typically emphasize play, self-care, and language skills as well as the reduction of problem behaviors.

On the other hand, instruction at school primarily occurs in small and large groups. The schedules and activities differ from the segregated and integrated settings (see Table 2.2 for an example of classroom schedules). In the segregated classroom, children work almost exclusively in small groups within highly structured, teacher-directed activities. Instructional trials for each child on targeted objectives are interspersed within and across activities.

In contrast, children in the integrated classroom are capable of successfully working both in small and large group activities, thus the schedule is reflective of their abilities. For example, the schedule (see Table 2.2) includes two discovery learning periods (Allen & Hart, 1984) that encompass those parts of the curriculum most often referred to as "free play." Although it appears to be free play, discovery learning periods are

TABLE 2.1.   An Example of a Basic Skills Curriculum for a New Admission to the Program

Communication	Social/Attending
Requesting assistance	Eye contact
Following instructions	Appropriate sitting
Indicating preference	Working in a group
Indicating termination	Motor imitation
Appropriate protest	Waiting appropriately
Receptive object identification	
Indicating recurrence	
Appropriate requesting	
Self-Care	**Play/Motor**
Toileting	Tricycle riding
Handwashing	Independent play
Dressing	Ball play
Toothbrushing	
Eating	
Preacademics	**Aberrant Behavior**
Matching	Tantrums
Puzzle completion	Aggression
Coloring	Noncompliance

thoroughly planned and arranged by the teachers. These periods provide opportunities for the teachers to arrange and support social interactions, conduct incidental language teaching, and actively program the generalization of skills acquired in more individual and small group sessions.

The teachers organize three or four learning centers within the classroom (e.g., dramatic play, manipulative, and creative arts) and the children are free to move among areas as they choose. Specific training objectives for individual children are imbedded into these play activities, often using task analyses so that teaching occurs at each child's current skill level and gradually increases in complexity. While these activities are occurring, students are removed individually for brief periods of time (10–15 minutes) for instruction on educational objectives that are less easily imbedded into the play curriculum (e.g., self-care) or that require significant repetition or practice in the initial acquisition phase.

Although criterion-referenced assessments help to identify specific

TABLE 2.2. A Contrast of Schedules for the Integrated and Segregated Classes

INTEGRATED		SEGREGATED	
Time	*Activity*	*Time*	*Activity*
9:00–10:00	Discovery Period 1 Individual Objectives	9:00–9:20	Free Play
		9:20–9:40	Circle
10:00–10:30	Circle/Snack	9:40–9:50	Bathroom
10:30–11:00	Small Group/Music	9:50–10:15	Individual/Small Group
11:00–11:15	Large Group	10:15–10:35	Large Group
11:15–11:45	Playground/Gym	10:35–10:45	Snack
11:45–12:30	Lunch	10:45–11:20	Individual/Small Group
12:30–1:00	Rest Period	11:20–11:30	Bathroom
1:00–1:45	Discovery Period 2 Individual Objectives	11:30–12:00	Lunch
		12:00–12:30	Playground/Gym
1:45–2:00	Snack	12:30–1:00	Rest Period
2:00–2:25	Small Group/Music	1:00–1:45	Individual/Small Group
2:25–2:45	Circle	1:45–2:05	Large Group
2:45–3:00	Gross Motor	2:05–2:15	Snack
		2:15–2:35	Bathroom/Self-Care
		2:35–2:50	Circle
		2:50–3:00	Gross Motor

deficits and help to organize the objectives developmentally, the specific approach to instruction is clearly behaviorally-based and involves detailed lesson plans (referred to as a Short-Term-Objective Sheet or STO) that provide a behaviorally-stated objective with acquisition criteria; outline methods of evaluation; identify the baseline and teaching procedures; specify reinforcers; provide a task analysis; and indicate generalization and maintenance criteria (see Figure 2.1). An STO Sheet is completed by the case manager for every educational objective specified for each child.

**Program Description for
Short-Term Objective**

Child: _____   Case Manager: _____

Objective: _____

_____

Day/Times to be Conducted: _____ Materials Needed: _____

Possible Reinforcers: _____

Measurement: Form _____   Day _____   Time _____

Instruction or Cue: _____

Teaching Procedure: _____

Step Criterion: _____

Steps of Program (Task Analysis)

Step No.   Description

_____   _____

_____   _____

_____   _____

_____   _____

_____   _____

_____   _____

_____   _____

_____   _____

_____   _____

Programming Generalization:

Persons   Setting   Materials   Inst./Cues

_____   _____   _____   _____

_____   _____   _____   _____

_____   _____   _____   _____

Postchecks: Day/Time   Criterion Met?

Week 1   _____   Yes   No

Week 2   _____   Yes   No

Week 3   _____   Yes   No

Figure 2.1.   An example of a Short-Term Objective Sheet (STO) completed by the case manager for each targeted objective.

Methods for completing ongoing assessment of each child's progress and for making data-based clinical decisions are built directly into the case-management system. The basic format includes four important components: (1) a clearly defined behavior or skill, (2) a baseline assessment of the behavior, (3) systematic introduction of education or treatment procedures, and (4) ongoing evaluation and assessment (data obtained daily or several times weekly) for each child on each targeted objective (a total of approximately 160 objectives per class). This baseline assessment followed by treatment design (AB) is used for the introduction and evaluation of all programs (Baer, Wolf, & Risley, 1968). Problem behaviors are addressed in the same manner, and on occasion, reversal designs (i.e., a brief return to baseline conditions followed by a return to treatment) are used to evaluate specific intervention strategies.

Data obtained in the classroom and at home are summarized and graphed for each education/treatment objective. Case managers also are responsible for ensuring that every program includes agreement between independent observers (i.e., inter-observer reliability) conducted during each condition or step of the program. Figure 2.2 provides a flow chart of procedures for curriculum design, training, and evaluation.

INTEGRATION VERSUS SEGREGATION

The program emphasizes the acquisition of skills and behaviors that will allow each child to benefit from integration and ultimately mainstreaming experiences. The program provides a natural progression from individual (home-based) to small group (segregated classroom) to small and large group (integrated setting) to large group (kindergarten) instruction. As the children move along this continuum, the complexity of skills and behaviors required gradually increases. This graduated approach seems consistent with the learning style of children with autism (e.g., the need for individual and small group instruction initially) and appears to ensure that important skills (e.g., attention to task and imitation) are acquired.

Once it has been determined that a child is ready for transition into a mainstream public school setting, a plan is developed. The plan is crafted individually to address the specific needs of each child, the family, and the characteristics of the school setting. Although many variations have been used, the general steps are as follows: (1) obtain the commitment of all members of the education team including parents and public school officials; (2) assess possible kindergarten placement options so that an appropriate match can be made between the child's learning characteristics, the teacher's instructional style, and the curriculum; (3) refine the skills that the child may need for public school transition (based upon observations in the future environment); (4) train

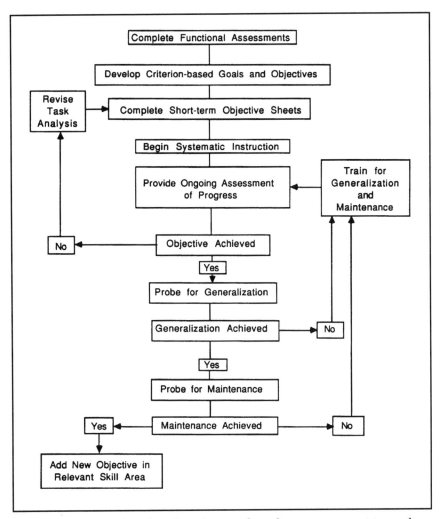

Figure 2.2.   A flow chart describing the procedures for assessment, training, and evaluation of each child's educational program.

relevant public school personnel; and (5) develop a detailed transition plan.

Our success in mainstreaming has relied heavily upon our ability to develop practical plans, successfully advocate for the child, and effectively train teacher and support staff. In many cases, the local school has agreed to select and have us train one individual who will serve as an instructional aide or facilitator in the kindergarten classroom. Rather than providing one-to-one instruction, the facilitator is available to help the regular education teacher to develop instructional goals, modify the curriculum, perform case-management duties, and provide direct support to the student as needed. Each summer we conduct an 8-day teacher-training institute that focuses on the skills needed by teachers and facilitators to successfully integrate children with autism.

BEHAVIOR MANAGEMENT

Children who enter the program often display challenging behaviors that interfere with learning. Two particular areas of difficulty that affect most of the students served are noncompliance and poor generalized instruction-following. Thus, initial efforts at controlling serious behavior problems start with simple compliance training that occurs both in structured and natural situations. In structured situations, compliance training may occur within the context of lessons for motor imitation (e.g., "Do this" followed by a demonstration such as clapping hands) and/or lessons for simple instruction following (e.g., "Come here," "Sit down," "Fold your hands"). Compliance training also occurs naturally throughout the day whenever the teacher, the home-therapist, or the parent makes a simple request of the child (e.g., "Pick up your coat, please"). In both the structured or natural situations, a discrete trial format is employed (Koegel, Russo, & Rincover, 1977) involving a clear and concise presentation of the request, an effective prompt or cue (e.g., a physical prompt), and an immediate consequence (e.g., praise for correctly responding). Many problem behaviors decrease as the child's ability to respond to simple instructions improves (Luiselli, 1990). Some behavior problems continue to be resistant to simple compliance training and extinction procedures and other intervention efforts are needed.

A multidimensional approach to behavior management that relies upon functional assessment and positive instructional strategies is used. A variety of instruments may be used to complete a functional assessment including a simple analysis of antecedents and consequences (A-B-C), parent interviews, and direct observation (e.g., O'Neill, Horner, Albin, Storey, & Sprague, 1990). Based on the results of the functional assessment, an individualized program is prepared emphasizing the development of alternative skills (e.g., functional communication) and employing positive reinforcement strategies (e.g., frequent praise when the

TABLE 2.3.   Potential Planned Consequences for Problem Behavior

Brief verbal reprimand ("NO")

Ignore behavior and continue with task

Ignore behavior and redirect child

Timeout from positive reinforcement

Simple correction

Overcorrection

Brief positive practice

Contingent effort*

Brief physical restraint*

---

*Unlikely to be used in one of our socially integrated classrooms

undesired behavior does not occur). Planned consequences for the problem behavior may also be introduced beginning with the least restrictive (e.g., ignoring a child's aggression and gently prompting his or her hands back to a task). Table 2.3 provides a brief summary of consequences sometimes used to control aberrant behavior in addition to other positive intervention strategies.

As in the case of teaching adaptive skills, the child's case manager completes a Short-Term-Objective sheet (STO) that specifies a behavioral objective, defines the target behavior in objective terms, establishes a measurement system and contains the instructions for establishing a baseline. It also is the responsibility of the case manager to complete the functional assessment of the problem behavior that may help identify the child's source of motivation and will ultimately assist in the selection of treatment procedures. Finally, the case manager, in cooperation with other program staff, develops a blueprint for treatment that includes preventive strategies (e.g., gradually introducing a difficult task), a plan for differential reinforcement and the teaching of adaptive alternatives (e.g., functional communication), and immediate consequences (see Table 2.3).

The May Institute has a human rights committee that reviews restrictive treatment programs and serves as a barometer of public opinion. Treatments are assigned to levels based upon the potential for abuse, the length of the intervention, the degree of resistance demonstrated by the student, professional acceptance, and similar assignments made in the professional literature. The most restrictive procedures require the permission of the Human Rights Committee (HRC) and the child's parents prior to implementation. The HRC reviews the utilization of all procedures twice a year and receives quarterly reports on the utilization of the most restrictive procedures.

PARENTAL AND FAMILY INVOLVEMENT

As indicated previously, a major focus of parent involvement is their participation in the home-based training program. The primary goals of the program are to: (1) provide direct instruction to the children that will facilitate the acquisition of skills and behaviors that enable them to participate in normal family activities, (2) prepare the children for entry into a preschool program, and (3) improve the parents' ability to effectively apply education and treatment practices across a variety of situations with their children. The parents' involvement proceeds gradually from observer to primary teacher for their child at home and in the community. The parents agree to participate 80% of the time that the therapist is in the home (15 hours/week) and to devote another 10 hours per week to training at other times. Parents also receive the training manuals *Steps to Independence* (Baker & Brightman, 1989) and/or *Teaching Developmentally Disabled Children* (Lovaas, 1981). These manuals help to acquaint parents with basic principles of learning theory, relevant terms, and specific strategies. Parent training groups also are conducted periodically on such topics as Managing Behavior Problems, Teaching New Skills, and Incidental Language Teaching. There is no specific requirement for parents to attend these groups.

Generally speaking, parent compliance with participation in the home-based training program is good. During the initial screening and again prior to admission, it is stated verbally and in writing that their child's placement at the May Center is contingent upon the parents' full participation in home-based training. Accommodations are sometimes made in special circumstances such as when both parents work or when there are several very young children living in the home (e.g., fewer hours of participation may be required for these parents). In most cases, the child's mother is the primary participant. It has been our experience that parents are less consistent in the application of behavioral procedures once the home-based training program is completed.

After 6 months of home-based training, periodic (approximately monthly) visits are made by the child's case manager from the school. During these visits, the case manager reviews the child's progress and makes suggestions and recommendations for effective programming. Parents continue to be very active in the development of annual goals and objectives and are required to make monthly visits to observe their child at the school. If the parents have a particular problem that cannot be resolved during monthly visits, home-based staff will conduct "booster" sessions designed to intensively address the problem.

A parent advisory board meets quarterly to help shape the direction of the program. Parent support groups and topic-oriented discussions occur monthly as well. Furthermore, the May Institute (in cooperation with the Association for Retarded Citizens) operates the Autism Support Center which provides an array of supportive services to assist families of children and young adults with autism. The program provides respite to many families served at the May Center, training and consultation to public schools and community groups, and information and referral.

OUTCOME MEASURES

Figure 2.3 provides a summary of transitions from the preschool program since its beginning. Twenty-six children have been discharged from the preschool program after at least 1 year of participation. This includes 19 children who participated in the socially integrated preschool program and seven children who never achieved the skills believed to be important for transition from the First Step program into one of the integrated classrooms.

Fourteen students were mainstreamed into regular kindergarten (54%); two students were placed in resource rooms within their home

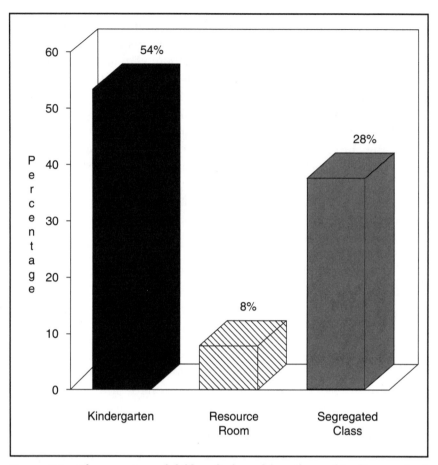

Figure 2.3.   The percentage of children discharged from the combined home-school program who entered kindergarten, a resource room within the public school, or a segregated classroom within a public or private school.

schools (8%); and 10 students moved into segregated placements within private schools (38%). It should be noted, however, that many of the students (57%) who were fully mainstreamed required specialized supports (e.g., an instructional aide) within the regular education classroom.

As indicated, only recently have we begun to regularly obtain pre- and follow-up measures on the children's developmental progress. A previous report (Anderson, Avery, DiPietro, Edwards, & Christian, 1987) provided pre- and posttreatment data on 14 students served in the home-based program and provided strong indications that substantial growth had occurred for most of the children served. In the future we intend to establish whether children exhibit significantly accelerated learning during a combined home-preschool training program.

The program has demonstrated substantial treatment change for individual children based upon a large number of baseline-treatment (AB) designs. This large accumulation of single-subject designs provides some evidence to support that the program's intervention, not other uncontrolled variables, resulted in the treatment gains.

MAJOR ISSUES FOR FUTURE EFFORT

The development of an empirically-based technology for effectively educating children with autism in an integrated classroom setting is still very limited. The staff of the May Center hope to have a direct impact upon the development and expansion of this technology by refining and expanding our current model of service delivery, as well as attempting to answer a number of relevant research questions.

First, most studies have focused on one important variable, namely positive social interactions. However, children with autism often demonstrate a myriad of behavior excesses and skill deficits across all developmental domains. Thus, the field needs to expand its perspective to examine the potential beneficial effects of integration across a broad range of skills and behavior.

Second, studies have suggested that integration may not occur without active and direct programming (Jenkins, Speltz, & Odom, 1985). Therefore, we need to continue to refine and empirically validate practical and easily disseminated methods for increasing the interactions between children with and without autism.

Third, our current model typically includes a period of individual and small group instruction in a segregated setting prior to full integration. Our hypothesis is that there are prerequisite skills that a child must acquire in order to substantially benefit from integration. It is our intent to investigate this hypothesis through ongoing and future research.

On a different level, we plan to continue to formalize and expand methods for predicting and evaluating program effectiveness. We have a unique opportunity to track a large group of students who will be entering the combined home-preschool program this year. And we have a similar opportunity to conduct a longitudinal assessment of the students that are being mainstreamed into kindergarten this year. These students demonstrate a broad range of abilities and could provide valuable information about the characteristics of children who succeed and those who may not.

Another area of interest will be to expand current efforts of consulting to public schools. During the last 3 years, the May Institute has been actively involved in helping public schools design and develop effective preschool programs. At this time, we fully operate one classroom in a public school and we are largely responsible for the development of classes in two other school systems. It is our goal to expand outreach services and to meet the challenge of how to better educate children with autism in mainstream and special education classes in public school settings.

Obviously, autism is a complex disorder and a great many questions remain. At times it seems like our desire to give children the opportunities for integration exceeds our understanding of how to obtain the best results. Nevertheless, the achievements that have been made during the last 10 years can only be perceived as positive, and they provide substantial hope for every teacher, parent, professional, and child involved.

REFERENCES

Abidin, R. R. (1983). *Parenting Stress Index (PSI)*. Charlottesville, VA: Pediatric Psychology Press.

Allen, K. B., & Hart, B. (1984). *The early years.* Englewood Cliffs, NJ: Prentice Hall.

Anderson, S. R. (1989). Autism. In B. L. Baker (Ed.), Parent training and developmental disabilities (pp. 137–153). *Monograph of the American Association on Mental Retardation, 13.*

Anderson, S. R., Avery, D. L., DiPietro, E. K., Edwards, G. L., & Christian, W. P. (1987). Intensive home-based early intervention with autistic children. *Education and Treatment of Children, 10,* 352–366.

Anderson, S. R., & Schwartz, I. (1986). Transitional programming. In F. I. Fuoco and W. P. Christian (Eds.), *Behavior therapy in residential treatment environments* (pp. 76–100). New York: Van Nostrand Reinhold Company, Inc.

Baer, D. M., Wolf, M. M., & Risley, T. R. (1968). Some current dimensions of applied behavior analysis. *Journal of Applied Behavior Analysis, 1*, 91–97.

Baker, B. (1989). Parent training and developmental disabilities (pp. 230–233). *Monograph of the American Association on Mental Retardation, 13.*

Baker, B., & Brightman, A. J. (1989). *Steps to independence.* Baltimore: Paul H. Brookes Publishing Co.

Bayley, N. (1969). *Bayley Scales of Infant Development.* San Antonio, TX: The Psychological Corporation.

Christian, W. P. (1984). The effects of institutional change: A case study. In W. P. Christian, G. T. Hannah, and T. J. Glahn (Eds.), *Programming effective human services* (pp. 83–103). New York: Plenum Press, Inc.

Czyzewski, M. J., Christian, W. P., & Norris, M. B. (1984). Preparing the family for client transition: Outreach parent training. In W. P. Christian, G. T. Hannah, and T. J. Glahn (Eds.), *Programming effective human services* (pp. 177–199). New York: Plenum Press, Inc.

Devellis, R. F., Devellis, B. M., Revicki, D. A., Lurie, S. J., Runyan, D. K., & Bristol, M. (1985). Development and validation of the child improvement locus of control (CILC) scales. *Journal of Social and Clinical Psychology, 3*, 307–324.

Dyer, K., & Kohland, K. (1990). Communication training at the May Center's preschool: Assessment, structured teaching, and naturalistic generalization strategies. In E. Cipani (Ed.), *A guide for developing language competence in preschool children with severe and moderate handicaps* (pp. 162–200). Springfield, IL: Charles C. Thomas.

Epstein, N. B., Baldwin, L. M., & Bishop D. S. (1982). *McMaster Family Assessment Device (FAD).* Providence, RI: The Brown University / Butler Hospital Family Research Program.

Glover, M. E., Priminger, J. L., & Sanford, A. R. (1988). *Early Learning Accomplishments Profile.* Winston-Salem, NC: Kaplan Press.

Hedrick, D. L., Prather, E. M, & Tobin, A. R. (1975). *Sequenced Inventory of Communication Development.* Seattle, WA: University of Washington Press.

Holroyd, J. (1987). *Questionnaire on Resources and Stress.* Brandon, VT: Clinical Psychology Publishing Company, Inc.

Jenkins, J. R., Speltz, M. L., & Odom, S. L. (1985). Integrating normal and handicapped preschoolers: Effects on child development and social integration. *Exceptional Children, 52*, 7–17.

Koegel, R. L., Russo, D. C., & Rincover, A. (1977). Assessing and training teachers in the generalized use of behavior modification with autistic children. *Journal of Applied Behavior Analysis, 10*, 197–205.

Larsson, D. G., Luce, S. C., & Christian, W. P. (1989). Attaining clinical competence at the May Institute. *The Behavior Therapist, 12*, 219–222.

Lifter, K., Sulzer-Azaroff, B., Anderson, S., Edwards-Cowdery (1993). Teaching play activities to preschool children with disabilities: The importance of developmental considerations. *Journal of Early Interventions, 17,* 1–21.

Lovaas, I. O. (1981). *Teaching developmentally disabled children: The me book.* Baltimore: University Park Press.

Lovaas, I. O. (1987). Behavioral treatment and normal educational and intellectual functioning in young autistic children. *Journal of Consulting and Clinical Psychology, 55,* 3–9.

Luiselli, J. K. (1990). Recent developments in nonaversive treatment: A review of rationale, methods, and recommendations. In A. C. Repp and N. N. Singh (Eds.), *Perspectives on the use of nonaversive and aversive interventions for persons with developmental disabilities* (pp. 73–86). Sycamore, IL: Sycamore Publishing Co.

Olson, D. H., Portner, J., & Lovee, Y. (1985). *Family Adaptability and Cohesion Evaluation Scales III.* St. Paul, MN: Department of Family Social Science, University of Minnesota.

O'Neill, E., Horner, R. H., Albin, R. W., Storey, K., & Sprague, J. R. (1990). *Functional analysis of problem behavior: A practical assessment guide.* Sycamore, IL: Sycamore Publishing Company.

Sanford, A. R., & Zelman, J. G. (1981). *Learning Accomplishments Profile.* Winston-Salem, NC: Kaplan Press.

Schopler, E., Reichler, R. J., & Renner, B. R. (1990). *The Childhood Autism Rating Scale.* Los Angeles: Western Psychological Services.

Sparrow, S. S., Balla, D. A., & Cicchetti, D. V. (1984). *Vineland Adaptive Behavior Scales: Interview Edition.* Circle Pines, MN: American Guidance Service.

Terman, L. M., & Merrill, M. A. (1972). *Stanford-Binet Intelligence Scale: Manual for the Third Revision, Form L-M.* Boston: Houghton Mifflin Company.

Thorndike, R. L., Hagen, E. P., & Sattler, J. M. (1986). *Stanford-Binet Intelligence Scale: Fourth Edition.* Chicago: The Riverside Publishing Company.

Chapter 3

The Delaware Autistic Program

ANDREW S. BONDY and LORI A. FROST

The Delaware Autistic Program (DAP), founded in 1980, is a public school program serving children throughout Delaware. The DAP serves children from the earliest ages of identification through age 21. There are three principal center-based sites within Delaware, all containing preschool components. The largest center, based in Newark, serves the northern, more populous part of the state.[1]

Preschool children identified with autism typically attend a center-based classroom that contains three to five autistic students with one teacher and an assistant. Because almost 80% of entering preschoolers display no functional speech, an alternative communication system—the *Picture-Exchange Communication System* (PECS) (Bondy, 1989; Frost & Bondy, 1992; Ryan & Bondy, 1988)—is frequently used within each preschool classroom. The DAP's early emphasis is upon developing communication skills within a context of appropriate play and social activities wherein the child is the initiator. As a child's communication skills improve and generalize to other children, additional part- or full-time placement options are developed. For example, because there are no preschool programs for nondisabled children operated by the public school, when staff decide a child would benefit from increased peer-modeling and interaction, part-time placement (with staff support) can be arranged in local private daycare or preschool programs.[2]

As with other public school programs, funds for DAP are derived largely from state (approximately 70%) and local tuition (30%) with some specific federal support. State levels of support for professional and paraprofessional staff are set by legislative bills. The DAP, administered by the Christina School District, serves all districts within the state, is designed for all school-aged children, and has no separate funding for preschoolers. (Some of the expense for DAP that may influence local tuition costs does not directly influence preschool children.) The total cost per student per year in 1992–93 (12 months plus additional respite days) was approximately $40,000 with local tuition contributing around $12,000.[3]

Several oversight groups have been created by legislative action specifically for the DAP. These include a Statewide Monitoring Review Board whose purpose is to review the identification, placement, Individualized Education Program (IEP) development, and implementation for all students with autism. Members include school staff from around the state, representatives from nonschool child service agencies (e.g., Department of Mental Retardation, Department of Vocational Rehabilitation, a local children's hospital) and a lay representative. In addition, Peer Review and Human Rights Committees were created to review all behavior management interventions. Finally, a Statewide Parent Advisory Council represents parents from all state sites and meets with the statewide director at least four times a year.

POPULATION SERVED

All students have an educational classification of autism consistent with Delaware's educational system. During the 1992 school year there were 33 preschoolers enrolled in DAP. During 1987–1992, a total of 56 preschoolers have attended DAP (not including preschoolers who moved out of the state within a year of enrollment). The classification criteria are virtually identical to those used to diagnose Autistic Disorder or Pervasive Developmental Disorder, Not Otherwise Specified (American Psychiatric Association, 1987). Classification is established by the child's IEP team, including a school or clinical psychologist and is reviewed by the Statewide Monitoring Review Board.

Of the 33 students enrolled during 1992, 28 were male (85%); this is consistent with national figures. Of this group 18% were African-American and one was Asian. When they started school, the youngest was 27 months and the mean age was 46 months. Upon enrollment, almost half (47%) of these students had assessed developmental quotients below 50 or displayed sufficient behavior-management problems to render reliable estimates suspect. Only 21% had developmental quotients above 80 upon entry into DAP.

ASSESSMENT PROCEDURES

Any parent or medical/educational professional with parental permission can refer a child directly to DAP. As part of the public school system, the child's home school district must participate in identification and placement decisions. Parents are asked to forward any existing medical or educational records for their child and to complete a lengthy survey prior to bringing the child to DAP. Occasionally, due to the child's age or other circumstances, the DAP staff's initial contact with a child may occur in the child's home or some other setting. The intake team minimally consists of a psychologist, a speech and language pathologist, a teacher, and an educational diagnostician. While the child interacts with team members, the parents are interviewed, given a tour of the program, and shown potential classrooms for their child.

The initial observation focuses upon two key issues: communicative functioning and social orientation. The team assesses the child's primary mode of communication (e.g., speech, gesture, crying) and identifies what functional communication skills the child displays (e.g., requests, rejects, comments). If the child has speech, the presence of unusual features such as echolalia or perseveration is assessed. In terms of social orientation, the child is placed in a variety of situations designed to probe reactions to adult approaches, social initiations by peers, mild demand situations from adults (both parents and staff), and reactions to being left alone and then rejoined by adults. During this intake session, staff also note the display of any unusual self-stimulatory behaviors or other actions that may interfere with routine educational techniques.

Placement in the DAP is contingent upon the completion of an IEP. Therefore, the intake team, upon recommendation and acceptance of the educational classification, must write appropriate objectives for the IEP. These initial objectives are reviewed and usually revised after the child's first 30 days of school. There is no waiting period for placement into this public school program.

During the first month or so, the IEP team reviews existing educational records and accepts or supplements that record. For example, if a complete psychological battery has been provided by another school or a nonschool agency, that assessment may be accepted as accurately reflecting the child's skills. On the other hand, if the record includes statements such as "untestable," the team will proceed with a more thorough assessment.

Attendance in any public school is contingent upon parents supplying standard medical records. Furthermore, although we offer information to parents regarding agencies in the community that provide a full spectrum of pediatric services, we do not provide direct medical assessments or services.

TEACHING AND ADMINISTRATIVE STAFF

All teachers in the DAP must hold or obtain within 3 years a certificate as Teacher of Autistic/Severely Handicapped Students. This certificate is contingent upon certification as a Teacher of Exceptional Children, and completion of three required courses (an introductory course in autism and severe disabilities, a methods and curriculum course, and a course in functional communication) and two electives in related areas for a total of 15 graduate credits. Although teachers are encouraged to take electives in the area of preschool education, such course work is not mandatory. Paraprofessionals with high school diplomas must satisfactorily complete comprehensive in-house training in a variety of teaching, communicative, and behavior management procedures.

Speech and language pathologists (SLPs) must have a master's degree, state licensure, and certification from the American Speech and Hearing Association. The SLPs provide their services within a collaborative framework, integrating their work with children in classrooms or in the community. A significant SLP responsibility is to assure that other staff continuously implement each communication system as designed for each child. A psychologist (school or clinical, at a master's or doctoral level) is part of each IEP team and assists in the area of instructional design (e.g., prompting and error correction strategies, reinforcement strategies, curriculum content) and behavior management. The team psychologist also coordinates efforts to work with all family members.

Each child receives 30 minutes per day of adaptive physical education from two certified staff. The DAP contracts for necessary occupational and physical therapy which is provided during school hours. In these areas, as in the communication area, services are provided within a collaborative framework. Students are removed from their class for services only when there are distinct apparatus requirements or the activity could negatively impact upon other students. A certified music specialist works weekly with the children.

The DAP director, a doctoral level behavior analyst and child psychologist, is responsible for coordinating all educational services within Delaware for students with autism and their families. The director oversees the school program, a residential program, respite services for families (in- and out-of-home), an after-school recreational program, and other aspects of DAP. The director also works with the administering school district and others within Delaware. The director is responsible for organizing ongoing inservice training of DAP staff and for bringing outside experts in the area of autism to the program. He or she also serves on each of the program's oversight committees.

An administrative intern functions as a building assistant principal, addressing various program needs including transportation, supplies, and maintenance, as well as staffing and scheduling issues for the recreation and residential programs. Two full-time secretaries and one clerk address associated needs of staff and families throughout the year. A program coordinator (with a master's degree in psychology) coordinates the intake process, assures that staff have adequately addressed various student and parental rights, and reviews the transitioning of students into other programs or other schools.

The program often has served as a training site for undergraduate student-teachers, several of whom have joined the staff upon their graduation. The DAP does not have a systematic research program affiliated with the local university. However, staff have presented over 80 papers and poster presentations at several major regional and national conventions during 1986–1992 describing the work accomplished and originated at the DAP. The research by staff has focused on the Picture-Exchange Communication System, error-correction strategies, novel behavior management procedures, and community-based training (including preschoolers). Staff are supported for continuing their own educational pursuits via tuition reimbursement for university-level course work. Furthermore, staff are encouraged to visit other prominent programs in the northeast and to participate in regional workshops and conventions regarding autism and related issues.

CURRICULUM

The central curriculum issue for preschool children is based upon improving communicative competence within functionally relevant activities. The IEP is organized around significant functional domains (Brown, Nietupski, & Hamre-Nietupski, 1976), including domestic skills (e.g., eating, dressing, grooming, area cleaning), school-based skills (e.g., potential academic areas or school-building routines), and recreation/leisure skills (e.g., solitary and interactive play skills, body-movement activities). In addition, all communication concerns not addressed within the other domains are grouped within one area as are any behavior management targets that may occur across domains. Activities and associated materials must be deemed age-appropriate.

Teachers are encouraged to use a variety of curriculum source guides as opposed to using a single curriculum description. Sources include curriculum materials used within the school district and various checklists and guidelines developed for children with disabilities (e.g., *The Integrated Preschool Curriculum*, Odom et al., 1988; *Individualized Assessment and Treatment for Autistic and Developmentally Disabled Children, Volume I, Psychoeducational Profile Revised*, Schopler et al., 1990).

Instructional format is as important to the DAP staff as instructional content. Staff view the preschool years as a critical time to prepare students in "learning-to-learn" skills as well as a time to develop specific skills. For example, when a child begins preschool, he or she is generally relatively insensitive to socially-based reinforcers, such as praise, smiles, winks, etc. With such restrictions in mind, staff must initially use whatever concrete rewards effectively motivate a child during instructional activities.[4] However, for children to succeed in the long run within public school settings, they must be able to learn in a teaching environment that relies upon social rewards (often on a spartan schedule). Therefore, staff must institute a program that will help the child change from requiring frequent concrete rewards to responding appropriately to fewer and more socially-oriented rewards.

Teachers accomplish this long-term goal by starting every lesson with "let's make a deal." The "deal" always begins by identifying what the child currently desires. Teachers use one of several techniques to identify what a child wants depending upon the level of the child's verbal skills. For example, this step could begin with the teacher asking the child what he or she wants via spoken words, objects, or pictures. Furthermore, the teacher could observe the most common activities for a child (e.g., rocking in a particular chair, playing with a particular item) and use these items as potential rewards. However, if staff cannot determine what the child wants, the lesson cannot begin.

Once a selection is made, the object or a corresponding picture (or some other symbolic representation of the desired object) is placed on a small card that is put in view of the child. The card also contains several circles (from two to five, depending upon how "new" the system is to the child) within which small items (e.g., small toy bears, pom-poms, stickers) can be placed. As the child completes the lesson (or, as described later, behaves appropriately) the circles are filled in as staff remind the child that they are getting closer to receiving their selected reward. When all the circles are filled in (the child need not be able to count) the child exchanges the card for the reward. After the reward is "consumed" (literally or figuratively), a new "deal" is set and the lesson continues. This system is used by all students in DAP, including adolescents in the vocational program. As the children get older, rewards are provided less frequently (i.e., the schedule is "thinned") and require more effort to be earned. This system also helps teachers focus on what the child can earn rather than what the child "must" do when the child's attention wanes (i.e., "Do you want the cookie?" as opposed to "Get back to work!").

Other aspects of instruction involve systematic attention to prompting procedures designed to minimize teacher repetition and the development of child prompt dependency. The DAP also has developed a number of error correction strategies (Bondy, 1990) wherein staff focus on teaching rather than "fixing" when students err. For example, if a preschooler walks out of a bathroom without having washed his hands, the teacher would not just prompt him to go wash his hands. Rather, the teacher would recognize that the "error" took place in the bathroom before the boy walked into the classroom and that the corrected lesson must take place in the bathroom at a point in the sequence just before the error. Different error correction strategies are associated with different prompting and teaching protocols (cf. Bondy, Peterson, Tarleton, & Frangia, 1990).

Children with autism often respond to seemingly unimportant aspects of a lesson (cf. "stimulus over selectivity," Lovaas, Schreibman, Koegel, & Rehm, 1971). Therefore, lessons must be accurately described in a manner understood by all staff (e.g., teachers, paraprofessionals, specialists). Such attention to procedural detail requires a strong data base upon which decisions to maintain or modify lesson plans can be made. Although it is not necessary to collect data on every lesson trial, each teacher is responsible for designing a system to collect sufficient data for periodic team review. Parents are provided two-part comprehensive progress reports four times a year. The data-based reports detail the student's performance on each IEP objective in a manner that is sensitive to each type of lesson format. For example, on certain lessons, progress may be described in terms of the frequency of an action while for another lesson, the level of prompt support required would be reported. The narrative report provides a description (organized by the major domains described earlier) written in lay terms that integrates progress across objectives.

In each preschool classroom, one or more children use the *Picture-Exchange Communication System* (PECS) as their primary communication system. Training on the PECS (Frost & Bondy, 1992) begins by noting what a child wants in the immediate environment. Then, as the child is reaching for that item (e.g., a cookie), staff physically guide the child to place a picture of a cookie into the open hand of another teacher. Upon receipt of the picture, staff say, "Oh! You want a cookie! Here it is!" and give the child the cookie. Over ensuing trials, the child is taught to pick up the picture and give it to a teacher. It is very important that the teacher avoid verbally prompting the child (e.g., "What do you want?," "Show me what you want"). Such prompts tend to develop prompt dependency wherein the child would only "ask" for a cookie when someone asks him or her what is wanted. Gradually, the teacher moves further away from the child, compelling the child to actively seek out the teacher in order to give a picture of a desired item. Over time, additional objects and their associated pictures are taught to the child.

This exchange develops certain critical skills. The child initiates the exchange within a social context, gaining the teacher's attention and referring to a particular item in the immediate environment. Furthermore, these skills are acquired without substantial prerequisite training. The child does not have to make eye-contact nor does the child have to be able to imitate hand motions (as in sign-language training) or vocal productions (as in direct speech training). PECS has been taught to over 85 autistic children in Delaware and many of these children learned the first step during their first day in school (Bondy & Peterson, 1990; Frost & Bondy, 1992).

We believe it is extremely important to distinguish between requesting an item and labeling that item. Requests are learned because they are followed by receipt of the requested item. Labeling, on the other hand, is learned in large part because the child receives general praise or attention for "knowing the name of something." For example, if we ask a child "What is this?", we respond "That's right" or "Good!" or "Yes!" when the child answers correctly. For preschoolers with autism, it is precisely this type of social reward that is extremely weak in its educational effect (Bondy, 1988). Therefore, we begin communication training by having the child learn a behavior (e.g., requesting via the picture-exchange) that is rewarded by the receipt of the concrete item requested. Similarly, skills related to imitation and eye-contact—acquired by typically developing children due principally to their social consequences supplied by adults—are difficult to teach preschoolers with autism who are not responsive to those types of rewards. Training in the PECS does not require that these skills be acquired prior to training functional communication skills.

Of course, good communicators eventually need to learn functions other than requesting and the PECS provides for teaching these other skills as well (Ryan, Bondy, & Finnegan, 1990). An important aspect in the development of labeling, commenting, or answering teacher questions is the introduction of a "sentence strip." This part of PECS permits children to create "sentences" while maintaining the use of pictures and the exchange of the pictures for particular items or other educational rewards. Children first learn to create the sentence "I want X" (with "I want" as a single picture/symbol) and then learn to create "I see X" or "I have X." In this manner, we have been able to teach children to distinguish between requesting and labeling (Bondy, Ryan, & Hayes, 1991) and to maintain spontaneous requests while being able to answer "What do you want?" versus "What do you see?".[5]

Pictures are also used to teach the children to follow schedules of activities (Ryan, 1990). Pictures (or concrete objects) may also be used as transitional objects (Kanter, 1991) during transitions between lessons or transitions from area to area (within the room or the school building). These systems are designed to augment feedback to the child regarding adult expectations and other systematic changes in the child's daily routine. The use of pictures and similar systems also helps reduce the number of verbal prompts that teachers must use to change activities and thus promotes greater student independence.[6]

Daily and weekly schedules are prepared by the classroom teacher in conjunction with the specialists. For the preschoolers, the morning schedules tend to focus on one-to-one or small-group instruction in the

school-based and domestic areas. The afternoons tend to address recreational activities in small or large group situations. Activities may con-
tain elements from several aspects of the child's educational needs. For
example, during a cut-and-paste activity, the teacher may address particular communicative skills (e.g., asking for more paper, specifying the
color, size, or shape of the paper), motor coordination skills (e.g., cutting
along a line, putting a stick into the glue jar), and direction following
(via verbal or modeled prompting) while concurrently attending to compliance issues or other behavior management concerns. During group
instruction (e.g., morning-circle activities) when following global
prompts is emphasized, the focus may be on generalizing skills acquired
during one-to-one instruction or on learning new routines or new skills
(e.g., a new song, the name of a new classmate). At least weekly, each
preschool class goes into the community. These trips are not "field-trips"
designed to expose children to the real world (or to entertain them) but
are designed to teach specific skills (Squittiere, 1990). For example, stay-
ing with a group or holding onto a shopping cart may be addressed in
one setting, while eating appropriately may be focused upon in a fast-
food restaurant. Teachers maintain the same instructional procedures
and data base in the community as provided within the school.

INTEGRATION VERSUS SEGREGATION

We believe that in order to provide a free and appropriate education to
preschool children with autism, a school must assure that the principles
associated with the least restrictive effective environment are addressed.
Thus, we seek to maximize the number of placement options available
to students with autism and not force a placement by a classification
assignment. We believe that a center-based option should be available
in the continuum of services mandated. Such centers must maximize to
the extent appropriate a disabled child's interaction with peers and access to services available to all students. Our center-based option provides students with autism experiences initially in segregated classrooms.
We believe that many of these experiences, including PECS training
and continuous reward and behavior management systems, would not
be replicable in fully integrated settings.

As preschoolers progress, staff arrange for a variety of mainstream
and reverse-mainstream opportunities (i.e., activities in our location

joined by nondisabled peers). DAP is located adjacent to an elementary school that affords many opportunities for our students to interact with typically developing peers. However, as public schools do not routinely provide educational services to preschoolers, DAP has sought solutions in the community. For children whose verbal skills and social orientation skills have sufficiently advanced, time in local day-care or preschool programs is arranged. Staff accompany the child as infrequently as two weekly part-day sessions to as often as full-time placement. The schedule of activities in such settings is selected by the staff of the local service provider. The focus for our students in these settings is on social skills with peers (i.e., responding to social approaches and initiating social interactions) with group instruction following.

Another option that has been created for kindergarten-age children is an integrated team-taught class with a group of children with mild disabilities. A class of three to five students with autism, with a teacher and an assistant, are team taught with a group of 12 or so students with mild disabilities (e.g., learning disabilities, language delays) with their teacher and assistant. The students are grouped according to abilities not by classification. This team arrangement has been extended into first and second grades and into a middle school as well.

We also have individually placed several children by kindergarten or first grade into classes for students with mild disabilities or into regular classes with specialist support. For these students, DAP continues to monitor their IEPs and progress and offers consultative support when necessary.

BEHAVIOR MANAGEMENT

Virtually all of the preschoolers who enter DAP display behaviors that parents and staff would prefer to reduce in frequency, intensity, or severity. All interventions designed to reduce behavior management targets are viewed as behavior management procedures (regardless of how benign or intrusive the procedure appears). All such procedures must be reviewed by DAP's Peer Review and Human Rights Committees. Furthermore, these committees are responsible for identifying particular procedures for which prior approval is necessary (e.g., isolated time-out exceeding 15 minutes per day across a week's time). All procedures must be consistent with the current clinical literature on behavior interventions. During 1986–1992, no intervention requiring prior committee approval was recommended for any preschool student. Interventions that have been used were generally considered mild in terms of intrusiveness such as in-area or in-chair time-out, verbal reprimand, various differential reinforcement-based procedures, brief immobilization of hands (e.g., 5 seconds), or brief contingent activities (e.g., putting 10 toothpicks into a container).

Our behavior management plans are team developed. We do not believe that any one person should have responsibility for designing behavior interventions. The team minimally consists of the teacher, the psychologist, and the SLP. Each perspective is necessary because behavior management targets may arise from diverse factors such as inappropriate expectations for skill development, inappropriate teaching techniques, or deficiencies in communication skills (Bondy, 1992).

There are four key issues addressed by each behavior management plan (Bondy & Battaglini, 1992). The first area addresses assessment factors yielding information regarding a functional analysis of the target behavior. Appropriate issues include identifying common circumstances under which the target occurs, what environmental or social changes follow the target, and what biomedical factors may be associated with the behavior.

The second area focuses on the development of functionally equivalent (and appropriate) alternative responses. For example, if a child likes to run around the room, an activity with an equivalent function would not include having the child sit quietly in a chair. The selected alternative would need to involve some aspect with regard to what the child enjoys about running around (e.g., allowing the child to run or play tag at designated times). On the other hand, a child's running across a room may be related to the lack of skill in requesting a specific item, a "break" from work, or going to the bathroom. In such a case, an alternative communication skill would need to be developed, again rather than teaching quiet sitting.

The third area involves descriptions of the actions staff are to take upon the occurrence of the behavior target. These are the consequences that are reviewed by the oversight committees. The final area concerns identifying criteria for data collection and setting guidelines (i.e., how often, by whom, how summarized) for team review of data.

Our orientation to behavior management views behavior targets as occurring within a specific educational context. Behavior management interventions will be successful in the long run only if certain base issues are satisfactorily addressed (Bondy, 1992). Students must be (a) working on functionally selected activities, (b) taught via appropriate teaching procedures, (c) supported by powerful reinforcement systems, and (d) taught within an environment where the child has access to a functional communication system. If any of these core concerns is lacking, behavior management interventions will be found wanting.

PARENTAL AND FAMILY INVOLVEMENT

Skills that children attending DAP acquire must transfer to the child's home if true progress is to be made. With this goal in mind, parents play a key role in supporting and developing functional skills within the home.

There are four broad types of parental involvement (Bondy & Battaglini, 1992). The first is associated with the preparation of the IEP and its objectives. Parental input is critical in assessing the child's domestic and community needs. The second area involves sharing information about autism with parents. This area is addressed through monthly meetings with staff regarding specific topics and often involves special speakers. Although broad meetings are held for all parents associated with DAP, there are special groups focused on issues pertinent to parents of the very youngest children in the program. The third area focuses on parents getting to know other parents of students with autism. The school organizes a monthly parent-staff meeting. Parents are also encouraged to participate in state-level advocacy organizations that pertain both to autism as a unique disability and to special education in its broadest terms. The final area involves directly training parents (and other willing family members) in the use of effective procedures with their children.

Direct parental training may take place in school or in the home. Each IEP team is given the responsibility of developing a home-based program with parental input. The IEP team may recommend in-home training with current team members or request additional support if warranted. For example, one preschooler had the habit of waking up at approximately 3 a.m. and insisting that his mother prepare oatmeal. A variety of efforts to help his mother change her routines proved unsuccessful. To deal with the problem when it occurred, a staff member was assigned to be in the child's home for about one week at the critical time and instituted an intervention whenever the child left his room. The parents were able to maintain this new pattern and staff did not have to continue with such an unusual work schedule.

When parents request help with in-home behavior management problems, they first are taught how to reward their child for appropriate actions and to use whatever communication system has been designed for their child. Upon successfully using these procedures, staff train parents in direct consequences for particular target behaviors.

OUTCOME MEASURES

We believe that changes in communication skills are the critical outcomes for preschoolers with autism. Therefore, outcome measures for children using PECS as their initial communication system are first described. During 1987–1992, 26 preschoolers have attended DAP for more than 2 years. Of these students, 20 started on PECS. For these students, 14 (70%) have developed speech and now use speech as their sole communication modality. Three other students use both speech and PECS.

Our statewide experience with over 85 students begun on PECS during 1986–1992 has yielded comparable outcomes. There are 66 children who were started on PECS in 1991. For this group, 41 now speak without any augmentative aides and an additional 13 use a picture or word-based system to augment their speech. Thus, 82% of children started on PECS have acquired speech and now use it either independently or augmented. Results from one small group study (Bondy, 1989) indicated that for children who come to speak following PECS training, they did so on an average of 11 months of PECS training and having acquired an average of 70 pictures in their PECS repertoire. We also have found that children who develop speech following the introduction of PECS demonstrate significant reductions in the overall number of autistic features (Bondy & Peterson, 1990) as measured by the *Autism Behavior Checklist* (Krug, Arick, & Almond, 1980).

Another type of success measure for early intervention programs is the number of students who no longer require intense educational services. Of the 26 preschoolers who attended DAP for 2 or more years, 10 (38%) have been declassified or reclassified as learning disabled, with five students changing their status during the 1991 school year. Of these 10 children, seven started school with the PECS system, further supporting the overall success of this communication system with very young children with autism. In addition to the de- or reclassified students, eight other children have been placed individually or in team-taught classes for children with a variety of mild disabilities. Thus 69% of this total group no longer receives services from a center-based program. It should be noted that preschool children with severe retardation as well as autism are included in the DAP and for some of these children, the degree of retardation appears to be a greater impediment to their growth and development than are their autistic features.

MAJOR ISSUES FOR FUTURE EFFORT

In comparison to other major programs for children with autism, the DAP is unique in being a public school program that directly provides a full range of services for preschoolers (as well as all other student age groups) including respite, recreational, and residential components. As part of a public school system, the DAP has been able to create the placement options that preschool children need in order to maximize their likelihood of academic success. One critical effort for further study is to determine the conditions under which other school districts will recognize the advantages of pooling resources for low incidence populations while maintaining a broad range of placement options. A center-based option within a public school does not run counter to the principles of the least restrictive placement as long as placement is not based upon "classification" and a continuum of placements is available (and promoted).

The development of functional communication and its concomitant influence on social orientation and interaction must remain a central focus for programs serving preschool children with autism. One of our prime questions is seeking prognosticators for future communicative growth. Our earliest efforts suggest that the rate at which autistic children learn to make requests via PECS does not differentiate those who achieve speech versus those who remain on a picture-base system (Finnegan & Bondy, 1989). On the other hand, those children who learn relatively easily to label objects appear to have a high probability of achieving functional speaking skills. Further research into the learning patterns displayed during the early aspects of PECS training and their relationship to long-term communication development is warranted (cf.

Bondy & Ryan, 1991; Bondy & Frost, 1992; Frost, 1992). Finally, further research is needed concerning how PECS acquisition and its rapid development of child approaches to teaching adults influence peer-oriented interactions and interactive play skills.

Continued efforts in the area of family training within a public school context are necessary to maximize intervention efforts. Full inclusion of family and community members, from siblings and extended family members to neighbors, would enhance the social and communicative development of these children. Finally, research concerning staff development, both for those who work directly with these children upon entrance into special programs and those who teach after transition programming, must continue for the early child centered benefits not to dissipate over time.

ACKNOWLEDGMENTS

We would like to thank the staff of the Delaware Autistic Program for making possible all that is reported in this chapter. We also thank the Christina School District and the state of Delaware for supporting students with autism in the manner described. Finally, we wish to thank Kate vanHorn for her assistance in preparing the statistical descriptions cited in this chapter.

NOTES

1. All statistical descriptions are based upon the Newark site. The instructional components are comparable at all program sites.

2. The DAP arranges for such placements by paying tuition fees for the slots students fill on a part- or full-time basis.

3. The DAP operates a residential program; however no preschool children have participated in this service.

4. While staff should use socially-based rewards with students with autism, they should be certain to pair their praise with currently effective reinforcers.

5. The impact that PECS has upon the development of speech will be reviewed in the section on outcome measures.

6. It should be noted that we do not seek to develop complete independ-

ence in preschool children with regard to their daily routine. Rather, the goal is part of the long-term process of reducing dependence upon teacher prompts while providing systematic information regarding "What comes next?"

REFERENCES

American Psychiatric Association. (1987). *Diagnostic and statistical manual of mental disorders* (3rd ed.) Washington, DC: Author.

Bondy, A. (1988, May). *Autism and initial communication training: How long have we been wrong?* Paper presented at the Association for Behavior Analysis convention, Philadelphia, PA.

Bondy, A. (1989, May). *The development of language via a picture exchange system with very young autistic children.* Paper presented at the annual Association for Behavior Analysis convention, Milwaukee, WI.

Bondy, A. (1990, May). *Error correction: Three novel approaches.* Symposium presented at the Association for Behavior Analysis convention, Nashville, TN.

Bondy, A. (1992, April). *The pyramid of educational power.* Paper presented at the annual Delaware State Council for Exceptional Children convention, Dover, DE.

Bondy, A., & Battaglini, K. (1992). Strengthening the home-school-community interface for students with severe disabilities. In S. Christenson & J. C. Conoley (Eds.) *Home-school collaboration: Building a fundamental educational resource* (pp. 1–19). Washington, DC: NASP Publishers.

Bondy, A., & Frost, L. (1992, May). *Autism as an autoclitic disorder.* Paper presented at the annual Association for Behavior Analysis convention, San Francisco, CA.

Bondy, A., & Peterson, S. (1990, May). *The point is not to point: Picture-exchange communication system with young students with autism.* Paper presented at the Association for Behavior Analysis convention, Nashville, TN.

Bondy, A., Peterson, S., Tarleton, R., & Frangia, S. (1990, May). *Error correction: Summary.* Paper presented at the Association for Behavior Analysis convention, Nashville, TN.

Bondy, A., & Ryan, L. (1991, May). *Picture-exchange communication system: Its relationship to verbal behavior.* Paper presented at the Association for Behavior Analysis convention, Atlanta, GA.

Bondy, A., Ryan, L., & Hayes, M. (1991, May). *Tact training following mand training using the picture-exchange communication system.* Paper presented at the annual Association for Behavior Analysis convention, Atlanta, GA.

Brown, L., Nietupski, J., & Hamre-Nietupski, S. (1976). The criterion of ultimate functioning and public school services for severely handicapped students. In M. A. Thomas (Ed.), *Hey, don't forget about me: Education's investment in the severely, profoundly, and multiply handicapped* (pp. 2–15). Reston, VA: Council for Exceptional Children.

Frost, L. (1992, May). *Discourse analysis vs. behavior analysis: A follow-up.* Paper presented at the Association for Behavior Analysis convention, San Francisco, CA.

Frost, L., & Bondy, A. (1992, August). *The picture-exchange communication system: An interactive communication system for nonverbal children.* Paper presented at the International Society for Augmentative and Alternative Communication, Philadelphia, PA.

Kanter, E. (1991). *Transitional objects.* Document prepared for the staff manual of the Delaware Autistic Program. Newark, DE.

Krug, D. A., Arick, J. R., & Almond, P. J. (1980). Behavior checklist for identifying severely handicapped individuals with high levels of autistic behavior. *Journal of Child Psychology and Psychiatry, 21,* 221–229.

Odom, S., Bender, M., Stein, M., Doran, L., Houden, P., McInnes, M., Gilbert, M., Deklyen, M., Speltz, M., & Jenkins, J. (1988). *The integrated preschool curriculum.* Seattle, WA: University of Washington Press.

Ryan, L. (1990, April). *Picture-based augmentative communication systems for autistic students.* Paper presented at the Mid-South Conference on Communicative Disorders, Memphis, TN.

Ryan, L., & Bondy, A. (1988, May). *Beginning picture-based communication systems with very young autistic children.* Paper presented at the Association for Behavior Analysis convention, Philadephia, PA.

Ryan, L., Bondy, A., & Finnegan, C. (1990, November). *Please don't point! Interactive augmentative communication systems for young children.* Paper presented at the American Speech-Language-Hearing Association, Seattle, WA.

Schopler, E., Reichler, R., Bashford, A., Lansing, M., & Marcus, L. (1990). *Individualized assessment and treatment for autistic and developmentally disabled children: Volume I, psychoeducational profile–revised.* Austin, TX: PRO-ED.

Squittiere, D. (1990, May). *The community is not just a big classroom: The new role for teachers.* Paper presented at the Association for Behavior Analysis convention, Nashville, TN.

Chapter 4

The Montgomery County Public School System Preschool for Children with Autism

ANDREW L. EGEL

CONTENT AND STRUCTURE OF THE PROGRAM

The Montgomery County Public School System (MCPS) preschool classrooms for children with autism began in 1986 as part of an ongoing collaborative effort between this chapter's author and MCPS. The program was funded in part by a 3-year grant awarded to the author from the U.S. Office of Special Education and Related Services / Handicapped Children's Early Education Program (OSERS/HCEEP). MCPS provided teachers, assistants, and any related service personnel (e.g., speech pathologists, psychologists, occupational therapists) identified as necessary, a location for the classroom, and classroom supplies. The grant funded project staff (e.g., director, coordinator, technical assistants, parent educator), provided intensive training experiences, and engaged in a variety of other demonstration and dissemination activities. When the grant expired, MCPS continued the funding noted above as well as provided county-funded positions for the technical assistants and parent educator and established an administrative, "teacher-in-charge" position. The educational model developed during the grant funding cycle was also adopted by county administrators and continues today. At this time, the preschool classrooms for children with autism are funded completely by MCPS.

The two preschool classrooms are part of a comprehensive elementary school situated in a large, suburban county. The school serves children in Headstart and grades K–6. The Headstart classrooms are the main integration site for children with autism.

POPULATION SERVED BY THE CLASSROOMS

Thirty-three children have been enrolled in the preschool between Winter, 1987 and the 1991–1992 school year. All children had been diagnosed as having autism or Pervasive Developmental Disorder—Not Otherwise Specified (PDD–NOS) (American Psychiatric Association, 1987). The male to female ratio of the students in the classrooms is nearly 4:1, and the majority of children have been Caucasian or of African-American descent.

The students served in the preschool classrooms are identified through a variety of sources. For example, some children are referred by public and non-public school programs within the county, County Child Find staff, and/or local medical personnel. Once a student has been referred to the placement office, a teacher specialist in that office is assigned to the family. Typically, this person will contact one of the technical assistants and request that a particular child be observed, his/her records reviewed, and a recommendation be made as to the child's appropriateness for the preschool classrooms.

The staff member observes the student in activities typically occurring at that time and discusses the student's behavior and learning characteristics with the teacher, program representative, and/or the parent. The technical assistant's questions and discussion are guided by the criteria for autism and PDD–NOS as established by DSM-III-R (American Psychiatric Association, 1987). In addition, the technical assistant completes the *Autism Behavior Checklist* (ABC) (Krug, Arick, & Almond,

1980). The ABC is a screening instrument designed to identify students for whom a diagnosis of autism may be appropriate. If the child's behavior meets the criteria for autism, the technical assistant will also use the *Childhood Autism Rating Scale* (CARS) (Schopler, Reichler, DeVellis, & Daly, 1988) to determine the severity of autism. The majority of students placed in the preschool classrooms have met the criteria of autism as established by DSM-III-R and have received scores on the CARS placing them in the moderate to severe range.

All of this information is presented to the MCPS Central Area Review and Dismissal Committee together with a recommendation of the preschool autism program if such a placement is appropriate. Actual placement decisions are made by the committee based on the report from the autism program staff and a variety of other factors (e.g., input from parents and other relevant professionals, space availability, transportation).

Efforts are also made to ensure that children in each classroom reflect a heterogenous grouping of individuals within the autism category. Providing variation in terms of the degree of autism and cognitive impairment is important for both students (e.g., higher functioning children can serve as models) and teaching staff (e.g., mixture of cognitive levels and rates of behavior problems may prevent staff burnout).

ASSESSMENT PROCEDURES

A variety of methods are used to assess students initially. As mentioned above, the ABC, CARS, and direct observation are used to provide a general indication as to whether or not a student is appropriate for the preschool classrooms. The County Offfice of Special Education and Related Services also requires criterion-based assessments from the instructional staff and each of the related service providers (e.g., psychologist, speech-language pathologist, occupational therapist, physical therapist) at the end of every year. Comprehensive, standardized assessments by these individuals are required every 3 years or when a change in placement is necessary. The specific instruments selected vary both within and across disciplines and are determined separately for each child depending on their behavioral repertoires. The psychologist, for example, observes children in different settings (e.g., structured group, free play, integrated activities) and uses standardized measures such as the *Stanford–Binet IV* (Thorndike, Hagen, & Sattler, 1986), *Vineland Adaptive Behavior Scales* (Sparrow, Balla, & Cicchetti, 1984), and/or the *Columbia Mental Maturity Scale* (Burgemeister, Blum, & Lorge, 1972) to develop a broad perspective on a child's overall level of performance. The speech-language pathologists have relied on direct observation and a variety of instruments designed to measure a child's functional use of language.

The classroom staff utilize a variety of methods to assess aspects of the environment that might enhance the effectiveness of instruction. *Environmental assessment,* for example, is used to determine the skills necessary for students to function most effectively in his or her current and subsequent environments. Teachers obtain such information through direct observation of the students, interviews with parents and previous teaching staff, and determination of skills critical to survival in following environments (e.g., Headstart classrooms). The information obtained by teachers from these assessments is then used to develop both short- and long-range goals and objectives for individual children.

Teachers also conduct *stimulus preference assessments* to determine the types of stimuli, events, and/or activities that can be used to teach new skills and maintain existing ones. For example, teachers can identify individual preferences for some children by noting the amount of time a child engages in certain behaviors or activities and the frequency with which the child chooses a specific event, toy, or behavior. This information is then used to generate individualized lists of highly preferred items that are provided contingent on appropriate behavior.

Children's *sensory preferences* are also assessed to determine their most preferred sensory modalities (cf. Pace, Ivancic, Edwards, Iwata, & Page, 1985). These modalities include visual, auditory, gustatory, olfactory, tactile, vestibular, thermal, and social. If a child indicates preference in any one category more than 80% of the time, a list is compiled of objects, activities, and events that represent the preferred sensory modalities. For example, a child who exhibited a preference for visual stimulation might be given bubbles or a kaleidoscope as reinforcers because each provides visual feedback. Similarly, a child who preferred auditory stimuli might be reinforced with music from records or tapes or any particular musical instrument. The assumption is that by identifying stimulus preferences, a teacher should be able to select materials that are highly reinforcing.

Once teachers have identified potential reinforcers using either of the methods noted above, a daily mini-reinforcer assessment is conducted (Mason, McGee, Farmer-Dougan, & Risley, 1989; Mason & Egel, in press) to increase the likelihood that teachers have access to highly preferred reinforcers when presenting a given task.

The above are examples of assessment strategies that teachers use in addition to the ongoing collection of data on student performance. Globally, the *Early Language Accomplishment Profile* or *Language Accomplishment Profile* (E-LAP or LAP) (Sanford & Zelman, 1981) is the primary standardized measure used to evaluate child progress. This measure was chosen for several reasons. First, it assesses relevant and diverse developmental domains (e.g., language, social, cognitive, self-help, gross and fine motor). In addition, it is sensitive to fairly small changes in child functioning due to the relatively large number of items at each age level.

Several additional measures were obtained when the preschool classrooms were funded by OSERS (1986–1989). These measures focused primarily on aspects of the family and included: the *Parent Stress Index* (PSI) (Abidin, 1983), the *Family Environmental Scale* (FES) (Moos & Moos, 1981), and the *Child Improvement Locus of Control Scale* (CILC) (DeVellis et al., 1985). The PSI assesses stress related to child characteristics, parent characteristics, and life events. The FES measures social climate within the family in the areas of family relationships, personal growth, and family system maintenance. The CILC evaluates parental perceptions about improvement across five dimensions: chance, divine influence, parent, professional, and child. These measures were not continued once the funding period ended.

TEACHING AND ADMINISTRATIVE STAFF

A teacher and two instructional assistants instruct five to six children in each classroom. This ratio allows staff the flexibility to provide instruction in a variety of contexts, with group instruction (2:1, 3:1, and 4:1) the most frequent format. Each classroom is supported by a technical assistant and a parent educator. We view the technical assistant position as critical because that person provides teaching staff with continuous feedback on overall classroom management and structure as well as on specific instructional programs (e.g., delivery, rate of reinforcement, use of prompting systems, error correction strategies). In addition, the technical assistant is often designated by the principal to chair annual review meetings and is responsible for reviewing students who are potential candidates (see description under "Population Served"). The persons who have filled this position typically have had considerable training in Applied Behavior Analysis and systematic instruction, as well as training and supervisory experience.

Related services from a speech-language pathologist, occupational and/or physical therapist, psychologist, etc., are provided by the County School System to each individual child based on needs identified through initial assessments. These services are given in group and individual sessions with teaching staff serving as assistants. In this way, recommendations from related service personnel can be implemented across the school day.

Overall responsibility for administration of the preschool classrooms rests with the school principal. Programmatic administration is conducted at several different levels. For example, the technical assistant provides teachers with ongoing feedback on their instructional programs, while also maintaining responsibility for reviewing potential candidates, attending placement meetings to present program recommendations, coordinating IEP meetings at the school-level, etc. The technical assistant reports primarily to the teacher in charge. The person in this position has administrative responsibility for all of the classrooms in the county program for children with autism, pre- through middle school. The teacher in charge meets with senior staff on at least a weekly basis to resolve any administrative or programmatic issues and provides overall direction to the program.

The preschool classrooms also serve as practicum placement sites for undergraduate and graduate students of several universities (e.g., Department of Special Education at the University of Maryland, Johns Hopkins University Department of Special Education). These students typically spend a semester in the classrooms for two to four half-days per week and are involved in all aspects of the instructional program. Supervision is provided by the classroom teacher and a university-based supervisor.

Staff are provided with inservice training throughout the school year. Some of these training programs focus on topics appropriate for the entire school (e.g., identification and response to child abuse, motivating student response, preventing staff burnout, multicultural programming); others are specific to providing instruction to preschool children with autism (e.g., development of augmentative communication programs, incidental teaching strategies, strategies for promoting social integration). In addition, staff occasionally attend relevant state and national conferences and provide inservice sessions on the most important topics to staff who did not attend.

CURRICULUM

Individual curricula are developed in several instructional domains by the classroom teacher together with the technical assistant and parents. For example, instruction occurs in areas such as receptive and expressive language (e.g., concept acquisition and functional communication skills), pre-academics (e.g., counting and number recognition, sound-symbol identification, fine motor activities), social and recreational skills (e.g., peer interaction, social exchanges, appropriate toy play), self-care (e.g., dressing, toilet training, hygiene, meals, safety), behavior deficits (e.g., independent work, attention skills, responding during large group instruction, following instructions delivered to an entire group, responding when schedules of reinforcement are lean), and excesses (e.g., remediation of stereotypic, perseverative, aggressive, and/or noncompliant behaviors). A strong emphasis is placed on teaching skills most essential for the student's independent functioning in current and future environments (e.g., Headstart, kindergarten) within a broad developmental framework.

To ascertain student's needs in each domain, an ecological inventory (cf. Vincent, Salisbury, Walter, Brown, Gruenewald, & Powers, 1980; Salisbury & Vincent, 1990) is conducted by the classroom teacher or technical assistant. This inventory yields a listing of all present and predicted environments and sub-environments that students will need to function, as well as the activities that must routinely be performed in each. A list of the skills needed to perform these activities is subsequently generated. This information helps to identify strengths and weaknesses that need to be addressed as objectives and taught in the context of next environment teaching activities.

Once specific objectives have been identified for each student, a program protocol is developed. These protocols delineate all aspects of the child's instructional program including behavioral objectives, baseline and intervention procedures, methods of data collection, evaluation design, and procedures for programming generalization and maintenance. Teachers are responsible for collecting and analyzing performance data for each student both prior to and throughout all stages of instruction. This is a particularly critical component of the instructional model used in the preschool classrooms because it is the only means for accurately measuring program effectiveness. In selecting a data collection system, teachers ensure that it corresponds to the performance statements in the IEP. For example, a duration measure would be most appropriate if it is specified that a student will play independently for 3 consecutive minutes. Likewise, a goal requiring a student to read 8 out of 10 sight words correctly would suggest that the teacher collect data on correct versus incorrect responses to each word. Finally, the data are graphed in order to determine whether or not the instructional procedure(s) is (are) effective and to subsequently revise the program as needed to assure continued progress.

Instruction is presented in a variety of formats (e.g., individualized instruction within a group of two to six children; one-to-one; independent work) and in various school/home settings such as classroom, school hallway, outdoors (recess), kitchen, bedroom, bathroom, family room, etc. The format and location of instruction is selected on the basis of a systematic analyses of both the skills required to perform the task and the format/location under which a student learns most efficiently. Instruction is conducted using both discrete trial (Koegel, Russo, & Rincover, 1977) and naturalistic teaching strategies (Halle, 1982).

A weekly schedule of classroom activities is posted for all staff (see Table 4.1). Integration activities occur throughout the day primarily with children from the Headstart classrooms. Related services (e.g., speech/language therapy) are provided within the context of the classroom activities so that classroom staff may employ the same instructional strategies for targeted behaviors.

INTEGRATION VERSUS SEGREGATION

From our perspective, the evidence is quite clear that integrated educational programs for preschool children with autism offer opportunities that are unavailable for children attending segregated schools (Egel & Gradel, 1988). The primary advantage in an integrated setting is the availability of nondisabled peers to encourage attempts at social behavior by children with autism; attempts that are very unlikely to be reinforced by students in a segregated classroom. Furthermore, integration enables

TABLE 4.1. Classroom Schedule

9:00–9:15	Classroom arrival / toilet training / greetings
9:15–9:30	Fine motor (writing, cutting, coloring)
9:30–10:00	Circle
10:00–10:20	Work session I
10:20–10:40	Work session II
10:40–11:00	Snack
11:00–11:20	Work group session III / language activities
11:20–11:30	Self-care (toilet training)
11:30–12:00	Interactive play groups
12:00–12:15	Music
12:15–12:45	Lunch
12:45–1:00	Clean-up / free play
1:00–1:15	Small group
1:15–1:35	Art centers
1:35–2:00	Work session IV / Language
2:00–2:10	Self-care
2:10–2:30	Recess
2:30–3:00	Structured play / release

nondisabled students to gain a better understanding of children with autism and other disabling conditions.

Integration activities for children in the MCPS preschool program occur primarily in Headstart classrooms adjacent to the classrooms for children with autism. Integration activities and instruction are conducted primarily in the context of naturally-occurring situations including circle and storytime, free play, lunch, recess, and snack. In order to maximize the likelihood that integration activities are effective, each environment is carefully assessed in order to identify the skills necessary for success. For example, particular attention may be given to variables such as group composition (e.g., student-teacher ratio), rate of teacher attention and praise, rules that govern the activity, and type of materials typically used in the integrated setting. Such information is then used to change the children's classroom program so that activities are similar to those conducted in Headstart.

Students in the classrooms are integrated early in the program with their nondisabled peers. The specific activity and amount of time is determined on an individual basis by the staff from each program. Staff from the autism classrooms subsequently attend the activities with their students. These individuals prompt and reinforce interactive behaviors of the peers and children with autism and subsequently fade their presence as interactions increase. Nondisabled peers serve occasionally as peer tutors. In this situation, teachers ask peers to model an appropriate behavior (e.g., climbing bars, riding a scooter) after which children with autism are either reinforced for imitating the response independently or prompted to imitate.

MANAGEMENT OF DISRUPTIVE BEHAVIORS

Children with autism have been identified historically as exhibiting disruptive behaviors at a rate that seriously interfere with teaching efforts. Teachers and researchers responded most frequently to these behaviors with a variety of procedures designed to reduce their rate of occurrence. More recently, the literature has reflected a growing consensus that it may be possible to assess the function(s) of these behaviors and consequently develop programs to teach alternative responses that serve the same purpose (e.g., Harris & Handleman, 1990; Iwata, Dorsey, Slifer, Bauman, & Richman, 1982; Repp & Singh, 1990).

As noted previously, the staff of the MCPS preschool classrooms for children with autism respond to disruptive behaviors by identifying antecedent and/or consequent stimuli that may be maintaining problematic behavior. Specifically, teachers initially identify the time of day in which the behavior occurs most frequently, whether a particular activity is more likely to evoke it, the number of other children and staff taking part in the activity, and the events that preceded and followed the occurrence of a behavior. Following careful analyses of patterns, staff generate hypotheses and develop related interventions. For example, if the data showed that the behavior occurred most frequently in demand situations, and the most consistent consequence was halting the task, the

Functional Analysis

intervention would focus on teaching the student how to ask for help (lower task difficulty) and increasing the availability of more preferred reinforcers. Thus, the interventions are most frequently reinforcement-based (DRO, DRA); although, teachers on occasion use brief timeout and/or verbal reprimands. Regardless of the procedure selected, program implementation and student performance are staff monitored continuously throughout the process.

PARENTAL AND FAMILY INVOLVEMENT

Parental involvement is considered an integral part of the preschool autism program. All families receive daily notes from the classroom teacher describing their child's accomplishments across the day as well as information on their child's behavior programs (when applicable). Parents are encouraged to respond by describing their child's day from the time they return home until they leave for school the next day, respond to comments written by the teacher, and communicate general information. This type of system provides parents and teachers with an immediate, ongoing, and efficient source of valuable information.

A parent educator provides specific training, focusing most intensely on families whose children initially entering the preschool classrooms each year. The parent educator begins the process by providing families with a 4-week parent training group. This group combines didactic and experiential methods and lays the foundation for a social learning approach to modifying the behavior of preschool children with autism. Topics covered include reinforcement principles and techniques, assessment of motivation, generalization and maintenance, functional assessment and treatment of behaviors that interfere with learning, data collection techniques, and graphing. More family-based issues including community resources, family life-cycle issues, and related concerns are addressed as they are brought up by parents.

When the group ends, the parent educator provides each family with individual home-based parent training from 1 to 1½ hours per week. The home-based sessions focus on teaching families how to teach their children in naturally occurring situations. The parent training program is noteworthy in that parents are not asked to set aside a period of time daily for teaching their child. Rather, parents are taught to identify teaching opportunities that present themselves during everyday activi-

Different from the 15 min. extended diagnostic sessions designed by TEACCH

ties (e.g., dressing, mealtime, bathtime, shopping) and to use those times to teach various language and social skills. For example, during breakfast a child may be provided a bowl of cereal with no milk and no spoon, thus requiring him to ask for both. Parents are encouraged to keep highly preferred toys out of reach, requiring the child to make specific requests for that toy. It is also noted that bathtime can be used to teach relationships among objects (e.g., under, over, behind) as well as body parts. By teaching parents to use naturally occurring teaching opportunities, we hope to contextualize the learning task for both the parent and child and, in the process, increase the number of teaching opportunities between the parent and child during a day.

OUTCOME MEASURES

Child and family progress data have been analyzed most extensively for the children and families who were enrolled in the classrooms during the initial implementation of the project (i.e., during support by the federal grant). As mentioned previously, the E-LAP or LAP was used as a primary measure of child performance. Change between intake and follow-up scores on these measures was evaluated using the *Proportional Change Index* (PCI) (Wolery, 1983). The PCI provides a comparison of child progress over time, with the passage of time held constant. PCI rates represent proportional gains made during treatment as compared to gains made by the child pretreatment. Thus, a follow-up PCI of 1.5 indicates that a child's progress in treatment was one and one-half times greater than his pretreatment progress. Data on the first 12 children who completed 1 full year in the classroom showed that all but one of the children made substantial progress. For these students, the PCI scores averaged 3.53, with a range of 1.52–6.03. Although this type of analysis was not completed in subsequent years (due to the expiration of federal funding), comparison of pre- and 1-year scores on the E-LAP suggest that the majority of children made substantial gains. Initial analyses have also been completed on the parent data in an effort to identify predictive factors related to child outcome. Powers and Egel (1988) reported a significant relationship ($p < .05$) between the father's perceptions of higher levels of family cohesion on the FES at intake and greater child progress at follow-up. There was also a significant relationship ($p < .05$) between the father's perceptions of reduced family conflict on the FES at intake and greater child progress at the end of the year. Parental perception of chance (on the CILC) as a factor influencing their child's future was significantly correlated with greater child progress. Finally, there was a significant relationship ($p < .05$) between parental perceptions of the need for increased professional involvement on the CILC and lower child progress at follow-up.

Several noteworthy trends were observed that did not reach significance at the .05 level due to one outlying score in each analysis (always the same family). For example, initial scores on the FES suggested that the mother's perception of high levels of family conflict and her view that family life was not rule-governed may be related to slower child progress at follow-up. The FES scores also suggested that higher levels of parental disagreement on the overall family environment may be related to slower child progress when measured at the end of the school year. Finally, higher levels of maternal stress on the PSI at intake may have been related to lower child progress at follow-up. These results, however, must be interpreted cautiously due to the very small sample size ($N = 13$). Even when viewed as preliminary data, the results suggest that family variables may contribute in important ways to the educational progress of preschool children with autism.

MAJOR ISSUES FOR FUTURE RESEARCH

The importance of providing intensive services to very young children with autism has been highlighted by the growing number of programs reporting substantial gains (e.g., Harris, Handleman, Gordon, Kristoff, & Fuentes, 1991; Hoyson, Jamieson, & Strain, 1984; Lovaas, 1987; McGee, Almeida, Sulzer-Azaroff, & Feldman, 1992). Particularly interesting are the programmatic differences that exist and the different levels of "success" that have been reported. For example, Strain and his colleagues (Hoyson et al., 1984; Strain, 1986) noted that the majority of graduates from their integrated preschool program were participating on a full-time basis in classrooms for nondisabled children. Conversely, Handleman and Harris (1994) wrote that, despite substantial gains, only a few graduates of their program had been completely integrated in classrooms for nondisabled children. These differences raise questions that must be addressed in order to understand individual program results in a broader context. For example, it is important to determine whether there are specific child characteristics that are related to the degree of improvement and subsequent level of placement. We also must determine whether there are unique aspects of programs and/or child-program interactions that influence the rate of child progress and participation in integrated settings following graduation from preschool. This seems especially important given that programs have had differing levels of success although important aspects of the instructional program were similar.

A related area that needs investigation is replication. We need information at three levels: (a) variables that influence upper level school administrators' agreement to adopt a particular model, (b) variables that influence replication of procedural components of highly successful programs for preschool children with autism, and (c) whether or not the same magnitude of effect can be obtained across programs. One issue that has substantially influenced our ability to replicate our model has been the training of available teaching staff. Prior to being selected by the school principal, teachers at replication sites have generally not had training in the use of systematic instruction, including the ability to collect and analyze data; conduct environmental, motivational, or preference assessments; or provide consequences contingent on behavior. Although intensive staff training in the above areas can alleviate some of these problems, continuous consultation and feedback is necessary to assure successful implementation of specific program components. Our experience suggests that this position should be filled by a person who can provide technical assistance in the manner described previously.

Other issues such as improving methodologies for training parents and other family members (e.g, Egel & Powers, 1989) and programming more effectively for generalization and maintenance of reported changes are two more of the many areas requiring attention. Fortunately, the literature shows that the development of effective programs for preschool children with autism continues to receive substantial attention.

REFERENCES

Abidin, R. R. (1983). *Parenting Stress Index*. Charlottesville, VA: Pediatric Psychology Press.

American Psychiatric Association. (1987). *Diagnostic and statistical manual of mental disorders* (3rd ed.–Revised). Washington, DC: Author.

Burgemeister, B. B., Blum, L. H., & Lorge, I. (1972). *Columbia Mental Maturity Scale* (3rd ed.). New York: Harcourt Brace.

Egel, A. L., & Gradel, K. (1988). Social integration of autistic children: Evaluation and recommendations. *Behavior Therapist, 11,* 7–11.

Egel, A. L., & Powers, M.P. (1989). Behavioral parent training: A view of the past and suggestions for the future. In E. Cipani (Ed.), *The treatment of severe behavior disorders: Behavior analysis approaches* (pp. 153–173). Washington, DC: American Association on Mental Retardation.

Halle, J. W. (1982). Teaching functional language to the handicapped: An integrative model of natural environment teaching techniques. *Journal of the Association for the Severely Handicapped, 7,* 29–43.

Handleman, J. S., & Harris, S. L. (1994). The Douglass Developmental Disabilities Center. In J. S. Handleman and S. L. Harris (Eds.), *Autism: The preschool years,* (pp. 71–86). Austin, TX: PRO-ED.

Harris, S. L., & Handleman, J. S. (1990). *Aversive and nonaversive interventions: Controlling life-threatening behavior by the developmentally disabled.* New York: Springer Publishing Company.

Harris, S. L., Handleman, J. S., Gordon, R., Kristoff, B., & Fuentes, F. (1991). Changes in cognitive and language functioning of preschool children with autism. *Journal of Autism and Developmental Disorders, 21,* 281–290.

Hoyson, M., Jamieson, B., & Strain, P. S. (1984). Individualized group instruction of normally developing and autistic-like children: A description and evaluation of the LEAP curriculum model. *Journal of the Division for Early Childhood, 8,* 157–172.

Iwata, B. A., Dorsey, M. F., Slifer, K. J., Bauman, K. E., & Richman, G. S. (1982). Toward a functional analysis of self-injury. *Analysis and Intervention in Developmental Disabilities, 2,* 1–20.

Koegel, R. L., Russo, D. C., & Rincover, A. (1977). Assessing and training teachers in the generalized use of behavior modification with autistic children. *Journal of Applied Behavior Analysis, 10,* 197–206.

Krug, D. A., Arick, J. R., & Almond, P. J. (1980). *Autism Screening Instrument for Educational Planning.* Austin, TX: PRO-ED.

Lovaas, O. I. (1987). Behavioral treatment and normal educational and intellectual functioning in young autistic children. *Journal of Consulting and Clinical Psychology, 55,* 3–9.

Mason, S. A., & Egel, A. L. (In press). Using a mini-reinforcer assessment to increase student participation in instructional activities. *Teaching Exceptional Children.*

Mason, S. A., McGee, G. G., Farmer-Dougan, V., & Risley, T. R. (1989). A practical strategy for ongoing reinforcer assessment. *Journal of Applied Behavior Analysis, 22,* 171–180.

McGee, G. G., Almeida, M. C., Sulzer-Azaroff, B. & Feldman, R. (1992). Promoting reciprocal interaction via peer incidental teaching. *Journal of Applied Behavior Analysis, 25,* 117–126.

Moos, R. H., & Moos, B. S. (1981). *Family Environment Scale.* Palo Alto, CA: Consulting Psychologist Press.

Pace, G. M., Ivancic, M. T., Edwards, G. L., Iwata, B. A., & Page, T. J. (1985). Assessment of stimulus preference and reinforcer value with profoundly retarded individuals. *Journal of Applied Behavior Analysis, 18,* 249–255.

Powers, M. D., & Egel, A. L. (1988, May). *Child and family factors in preschoolers with autism.* Paper presented at the Association for Behavior Analysis meeting, Philadelphia, PA.

Repp, A. C., & Singh, N. N. (1990). *Perspectives on the use of nonaversive and aversive interventions for persons with developmental disabilities.* Sycamore, IL: Sycamore Publishing Company.

Salisbury, C. L., & Vincent, L. J. (1990). Criterion of the next environment and best practices: Mainstreaming and integration ten years later. *Topics in Early Childhood Special Education, 10,* 78–89.

Sanford, A. R., & Zelman, J. G. (1981). *The Learning Accomplishment Profile.* Winston-Salem, NC: Kaplan.

Schopler, E., Reichler, R. J., DeVellis, R. F., & Daly, K. (1980). Toward objective classification of childhood autism: Childhood Autism Rating Scale (CARS). *Journal of Autism and Developmental Disabilities, 10,* 91–103.

Sparrow, S. S., Balla, D. A., & Cicchetti, D. V. (1984). *Vineland Adaptive Behavior Scales.* Circle Pines, MN: American Guidance Service.

Strain, P. S. (1986). *National Institute of Mental Health Renewal Grant.*

Thorndike, R. L., Hagen, E. R., & Sattler, J. M. (1986). *The Stanford-Binet Intelligence Scale: 4th ed.* Chicago IL: The Riverside Publishing Company.

Vincent, L., Salisbury, C., Walter, G., Brown, P., Gruenewald, L., & Powers, M. (1980). Program evaluation and curriculum development in early childhood special education: Criteria of the next environment. In N. Certo, N. Haring, and R. York (Eds.), *Public school integration of severely handicapped students* (pp. 259–301). Baltimore, MD: Paul Brooks Publishing Company.

Wolery, M. (1983). Proportional change index: An alternative for comparing child change data. *Exceptional Children, 50,* 167–170.

Chapter 5

The Douglass Developmental Disabilities Center

JAN S. HANDLEMAN and SANDRA L. HARRIS

The Douglass Developmental Disabilities Center (DDDC) was founded in 1972 by the authority of the Board of Governors of Rutgers, The State University of New Jersey. Initially established to serve children of all ages with autism, the center did not create a specialized preschool component until 1987 when a Small Group Preschool class and an Integrated Preschool class called "Small Wonders" were opened. Three years later, in 1990, a third preschool class, designated the "Prep" class was introduced.

Both the Integrated and Small Group preschool classes rely primarily upon group instruction. In the Small Group class, consisting entirely of children with autism, the instructional ratio ranges from two children and one adult to six children with one adult leader and the remaining staff in a support role as needed to help the children maintain themselves in the group. Along with the overall preschool curriculum, this class emphasizes increasing the children's awareness of other people in the environment and learning to be independent in a group setting.

In the Integrated class with eight normally developing peers and six children with autism, the youngsters are exposed to groups as large as 14 students. In this room, children with autism and their friends, who serve as social and language role models, are carefully blended in the large and small group activities. A systematic program is used to teach the peers to act as socialization agents through structured interactions and modeling. An important emphasis of this specialized programming is to teach the peers to persist in their efforts to interact with their often unresponsive classmates.

Typically, children are admitted to the Small Group class and move to the Integrated class after 1 to 2 years. The physical and organizational structure in both of these classes closely resembles that of a very good regular preschool classroom, with a curriculum adapted to meet the needs of the children with autism. Our development of these classes followed our visit to Phillip Strain's integrated preschool program in Pittsburgh in 1986.

Our Prep class was created after we visited Ivar Lovass at UCLA in 1989 and observed the impressive progress he was making with preschool aged children. Following that visit we established a class that emphasizes one-to-one instruction during the initial phases of treatment, provides 25 hours a week of at-school instruction supplemented by an additional 15 hours of parent effort within the home, and offers intensive home support. The Prep program stresses an individualized curriculum and fast-paced instruction to maximize stimulation. Children move from individual to group work as they develop necessary skills and are eligible to move to the integrated preschool. In theory, movement is possible among any of the preschool classes, but in practice the Small Group and Prep classes are "feeders" for the Integrated class.

The DDDC is located on the Douglass College campus of Rutgers University, in a former college recreation center now converted into a school building that serves all of the center's programs from preschool through adolescence. It is a state operated school supported almost exclusively by tuition money paid by local school districts for individual pupils. In 1992–93 the 12-month tuition was $37,417. This rate increases at a rate roughly consistent with the annual cost of living.

Special education in New Jersey is mandated by a series of important legislation. In 1951, the Beedleston Law required local school districts to provide education to children with disabilities from ages 5 to 21. The age range was extended in 1981 to include children 3 to 5 years old by the passing of the Individuals With Disabilities Education Act. Services to children with autism, in particular, were enhanced with the 1991 amendment to the Quality Education Act, establishing autism as a separate educational classification.

POPULATION SERVED

Thirty-six children have been enrolled in the preschool programs between 1987 and 1992. In 1992–93 there were six children with autism and eight normally developing peers in the Integrated Preschool, six children with autism in the Small Group Preschool class, and six in the Prep class. With the exception of the peers, who have no known developmental or behavioral difficulties, all of these children were referred to the center with a diagnosis of Autistic Disorder or Pervasive Developmental Disorder, Not Otherwise Specified (American Psychiatric Association, 1987). A diagnosis of autism was confirmed or (in the case of a PDD–NOS referral, established) at the center by an experienced clinical psychologist using the criteria of *DSM-III-R* (American Psychiatric Association, 1987) and the *Childhood Autism Rating Scale (CARS)* (Schopler, Reichler, DeVellis, & Daly, 1988). No child is accepted who does not fall within the category of autism on the CARS and the range of scores to date has been 30 to 40, with most children in the mild to moderate range (Mean = 34).

Consistent with the general literature (e.g., Lord & Schopler, 1987), most of the the children admitted to the center are boys. Among the 36 children who have attended, 29 were male, 7 female; 32 Caucasian, 2 African-American, and 2 Asian. Their age range at admission was from 30 months to 62 months (Mean = 50 months). Their Stanford–Binet IQ's at admission have ranged broadly from below 36 to 105 (Mean = 61). For the first 2 years these IQ scores were based on the earlier *Stanford–Binet* (Thorndike, 1972) and since then on the *Stanford–Binet IV* (Thorndike, Hagen, & Sattler, 1986).

ASSESSMENT PROCEDURES

Following a review of their medical and educational records, children who appear suitable for admission to our preschool programs are invited to the center for a screening evaluation. During this visit parents are encouraged to observe the several classes in the preschool program so that they will be able to make an informed decision about whether the available opening is suitable for their child.

The initial screening interview is conducted for roughly 45 minutes during which two or three children are observed in a semi-structured setting by several staff members who expose the children to a variety of social and academic stimuli and observe the children with one another. This preliminary screening is helpful in ruling out children whose paper credentials sound consistent with the diagnosis of Autistic Disorder, but whose actual observed behavior is too social and responsive to support this diagnosis or whose profound degree of mental retardation make a diagnosis of Autistic Disorder ambiguous.

Following the initial visit, children who appear appropriate, are asked to return for an in-depth evaluation. This entails obtaining a developmental history from the parents by a clinical psychologist, classroom observations and assessment of the child's response to a range of our curriculum items by a special education teacher, and a speech and language assessment by a speech and language specialist using the *Preschool Language Scale* (Zimmerman, Steiner, & Pond, 1979). At the conclusion of this assessment the intake staff—which includes the executive director, director, assistant director, a speech therapist, and one or more teachers—meet to decide if the child is suitable for admission. If the diagnosis of Autistic Disorder is clear and the child's suitability for the program and the specific classroom opening available is agreed upon, the decision about admission will be made at this meeting. Alternatively, if more data are needed, a home visit, school visit, or conference with the child's present teacher will be arranged to address remaining questions.

Following admission the child is tested by an experienced examiner with the *Stanford–Binet IV* (Thorndike et al., 1986), *Peabody Picture Vocabulary Test* (Dunn & Dunn, 1981), and the *Vineland Adaptive Behavior Scales: Survey Form* (Sparrow, Balla & Cicchetti, 1984). Results from the assessment battery provide a profile of development in the major curricular areas and a baseline against which to measure progress. This testing is repeated once a year to track the child's developmental gains. In addition, a standardized videotape assessment is conducted each year.

Every child who is admitted must have a complete medical examination, and most children come to us with detailed pediatric and neurological evaluations as well as audiometric assessment, and other related tests. We are not a medical facility and do not provide these kinds of assessments.

TEACHING AND ADMINISTRATIVE STAFF

All of the teachers in the center's preschool programs are certified in special education and have preschool credentials as well. There is one teacher and three full-time assistants in each classroom. In addition, there is a speech and language specialist in each class half-time providing group and individual services and consulting regularly with the teacher. The center does not employ occupational or physical therapists and children who require these services receive them in other settings after school hours.

The executive director of the center, a clinical psychologist, in addition to his or her administrative tasks, supervises the delivery of psychological services at the center. The director, who holds a doctorate in special education, is a certified principal as well and supervises the overall administration of the center. The assistant director is a master's level special educator who coordinates and oversees all educational activities. The supervisor of educational services, who has a master's degree in special education, oversees activities related to the children's programs such as curriculum planning, monitoring of progress, and supervision of teaching staff. In a parallel role, the supervisor of speech and communication services, is a master's level person who has a Certification of Clinical Competence in Speech and Language Programming. This supervisor oversees the activities of the speech therapists and coordinates and plans the communication curriculum. Three full-time secretarial personnel provide support for the teaching and administrative staff.

Five doctoral students from the University's Graduate School of Applied and Professional Psychology or the Graduate Program of the Department of Psychology are also employed at the center. One of them serves as research coordinator and the other four provide home support services for parents of children in the three preschool classes.

Another important source of person power at the center is the undergraduate students who enroll in a psychology course titled Field Work in Psychology. Through the mechanism of this course, the students work one full day a week under supervision as individual tutors for children. One of the DDDC's special roles is that of training students from several disciplines including psychology, speech, and special education. A one-semester placement at the center is required for all special education majors at the university.

The center is a place where everyone is always learning. All staff are required to participate in regular inservice presentations on topics such as the use of medication in the treatment of autism, identification and response to child abuse, the use of augmentative systems in teaching communication, first aid for children, the use of non-aversive procedures in managing disruptive behavior, and so forth. In addition, the entire staff is expected to attend the annual Berkshire Conference on Behavior Analysis and Therapy in Amherst, Massachusetts where they are exposed to some of the most sophisticated work on developmental disabilities in the north eastern states. We also co-sponsor with New Jersey's autism advocacy agency (COSAC) an annual state-wide conference on autism. Many staff members have co-authored research papers and presented at regional and national conferences.

The undergraduate students and teaching assistants are under the immediate direction of the classroom teacher, who, in turn, receives regular supervision from the supervisor of educational services. It is this supervisor's responsibility to formally observe and provide written feedback to each teacher at least once a month. New teachers and those who are mastering new techniques are supervised on a frequent basis until they demonstrate mastery of the necessary skills. In her or his first months at the center, a teacher receives intensive daily observation and supervision. Similar supervision is provided for all speech therapists by the supervisor of speech and communication services. Both of these supervisors in turn report to the assistant director.

The director has oversight responsibility for the management of the center, meets regularly with staff, and consults with the executive director in planning and implementing major policy decisions. The doctoral students receive psychological supervision from the executive director and procedural supervision from the assistant director and supervisor of educational services. They collaborate closely with the classroom teacher in the development and implementation of home programming.

CURRICULUM

The curriculum for the preschool programs is developmentally-organized and language-focused and includes the areas of receptive and expressive language, cognition, fine and gross motor ability, affect, socialization, and self-help skills. For example, goals and objectives in the area of cognitive development emphasize pre-academic tasks, and those in the area of social development focus on peer and adult interaction, self-concept, and classroom behavior.

Curriculum planning progresses from relatively narrow and intensive fundamental skills training to instruction in all developmental areas. For example, initially a child is taught to attend to a task and to comply with instructional demands and then, once these skills are established, programming expands to include a balance of activities in the areas of communication, social and cognitive development, and so forth. Table 5.1 provides examples of developmentally sequenced objectives in each of the curricular areas.

Teaching materials include a blend of some commercial offerings with an extensive library of teacher-made workbooks, activity sheets, and folders. For example, some activities in the areas of cognitive and communication development are drawn from the *AIMS* (An Instructional Manipulative Series: Continental Press, Earlley, 1986) and *TOTAL* (Teacher Organized Training for Acquisition of Language: Communication Skill Builders, Witt & Boose, 1984) programs. In addition, a number of materials published by the Developmental Learning Materials Company (DLM) are used to reinforce instruction in the areas of fine motor development and concept formation. Individual Educational Plans (IEPs) and quarterly progress reports are based on the *I.G.S. Curriculum* (Romanczyk & Lockshin, 1982).

Individual speech and language services are provided for all children with autism twice each week. During these sessions, each student's individual communication needs are addressed and the speech therapist's assessment of progress is integrated into recommendations to the teacher for comprehensive speech and language instruction during the coming week. Goals for individual lessons, as well as for classroom programming are determined according to the results of formal and informal assessment measures; classroom observation; and input from parents, teachers and other support staff. Both a child's strengths and weaknesses are considered when planning instructional experiences. Along with individual sessions by the speech specialist, a classroom language group is conducted weekly by this same therapist to facilitate carry-over of skills and to promote total program integration. In addition to being a useful experience for the children, this in-class group session allows the teacher and teaching assistants to observe the specific instructional techniques of the speech therapist and thus enhances coordination

TABLE 5.1. Examples of Objectives According to Curricular Area

LANGUAGE: *Receptive*
Points to 1 body part
Follows 8, 1-step directions
Follows 5, related 2-step directions
Selects 2 items from a category
Solves 2 problems involving "if . . . then" situations

LANGUAGE: *Expressive*
Uses 10 simple words
Names 3 body parts
Refers to self by pronoun
Adds "ing" to 5 words
Names 3 pictures of actions

COGNITIVE
Matches 5 objects
Names primary colors
Points to circle, square, triangle
Counts 3 objects
Tells time by hour

SOCIALIZATION
Plays beside another child for 5 minutes
Takes turn when playing simple board game
Selects playmate during activity time
Expresses ownership when asked about item
Names 2 emotions

MOTOR
Puts cube in cup
Laces yarn through holes on sewing card
Copies 3 pegboard designs from card
Prints first name
Catches bean bag with two hands

SELF-HELP
Takes off socks when requested
Pours from pitcher without spilling
Sleeps through night without soiling
Washes/dries hands after snack
Ties shoes

TABLE 5.2.   Classroom Schedules

	Prep	*SGp*	*Int*
9:30–10:00	Group	Group	Group
10:00–10:30	Work Session	Circle	Circle
10:30–11:00	Work Session	Small Group	Small Group
11:00–11:30	Work Session	Centers Group	Centers Social
11:30–12:00	Lunch	Lunch	Lunch
12:00–12:30	Work Session	Sensory Motor	Fine Motor
12:30–1:00	Gross Motor	Gross Motor	Gross Motor
1:00–1:30	Work Session	Small Group	Small Group
1:30–2:00	Work Session	Snack Centers	Snack Centers
2:00–2:30	Group	Group	Group

among staff members. The presence of the speech therapist in the classroom for half of each school day helps to ensure a close link between educational and communication programming.

Classroom activities are planned according to weekly schedules. Time for small and large group instruction, independent work sessions, and speech lessons are carefully balanced. Table 5.2 provides examples of typical classroom schedules for each of the three classes. During "work sessions" the children in the prep class work on their programs in the areas of cognition, language, and self-help skills. The small and large groups in the preschool classes involve similar material.

INTEGRATION VERSUS SEGREGATION

We believe that experiences that promote mainstreaming and integration are important components of educational programming for children with autism. It is however our hypothesis that for some children an initially segregated experience may increase their ability to benefit from the subsequent integrated experiences. For all classes, objectives and activities are planned with the goal of teaching the fundamental skills that will eventually promote responsiveness to normalized and community-based living. This effort is most apparent in the integrated preschool class which provides daily opportunities for interacting with normally-developing classmates. However, both the small group and prep classes employ educational strategies that will ultimately enable the child to learn the more advanced skills available in the integrated setting. Thus, there is a careful progression of skills that begins with mastering basic compliance and self-control skills and advances to learning sensitivity to others and the ability to maintain one's self in a group. The transition policy of the center is guided by the highly individualized and increasingly complex curriculum that sets the framework for mainstreaming efforts.

The actual transition process from the center to another school is carefully planned and implemented in a highly systematic fashion. For example, by initially visiting various public and private settings, a preliminary student/placement match can be identified by the teacher. After a comprehensive assessment of the skills needed in the new setting, requisite skills can then be assessed and the child's existing deficits corrected. The teacher's assessment of the potential placement includes variables such as staff/student ratio, contingencies, school-life activities, and classroom structure. Our programming efforts at the center are directed toward approximating the new placement in order to facilitate the student's optimal adjustment. This transition process is further enhanced by having the student attend the new school for increasing periods of time prior to enrollment and by providing formal follow-up services after graduation. Parents are encouraged to be full participants in the transition process, visiting prospective placements, making the decision about a preferred setting, and working at home to facilitate the process of change.

BEHAVIOR MANAGEMENT

Because some of our children pose challenging behavior problems, it is essential that we bring to bear the best of current behavior management technology. Behavior management policies at the DDDC reflect the broad spectrum of empirically based options. Our choices of specialized intervention strategies are consistent with the standards of appropriate clinical practice as determined by treatment effectiveness and the results of efficacy research. The ongoing monitoring and evaluation of these policies ensures adherence to changing professional and legal guidelines.

As the field changes, policies regarding behavior management continue to evolve and are guided by current research and documented innovations in educational technology. For example, traditional techniques such as discrete trial teaching and systematic reinforcement are blended with incidental teaching, functional communication training, and community involvement experiences. Rigorous performance and procedural monitoring and close communication among staff, parents, and referring agencies promote accountability and treatment effectiveness.

Behavior reduction concerns are viewed within the context of a student's total educational program. Functional analysis of behavior, communication training efforts, and the application of naturalistic contingencies are some of the important strategies that are considered when planning specialized procedures.

Informed parental consent, agreement by case managers, and careful monitoring are among the procedural safeguards that guide the implementation of a range of programming options. Table 5.3 outlines those behavior reduction procedures that are currently used; it is rare that anything other than a verbal reprimand, differential reinforcement, or a brief time out is employed in the preschool classes.

PARENTAL AND FAMILY INVOLVEMENT

The role of parents as teachers and advocates is central to the operation of the center. A variety of services are provided for parents to enhance their skills as child managers, to increase the comfort of family life, and to help parents function as effective collaborators with the professional staff.

Every parent in the preschool programs receives at least two home visits a month from the doctoral student assigned to that class. These visits cover the broad range of parenting concerns and integrate the teaching of general psychological principles of child management with the specific ongoing needs of the child. Parents are asked to read *Teaching Developmentally Disabled Children* (Lovaas, 1981) and to use it as

TABLE 5.3. Behavior Reduction Procedures

Verbal reprimand

Differential reinforcement

Time out

Overcorrection

Mild restraint

a reference book in preparing home programs. Specific behavioral concepts are introduced in the context of home programming.

In the course of consulting about home programming, the doctoral students are encouraged to be sensitive to the needs of the family as a system. For example, they look for constructive ways to engage older and younger siblings in home programming, encourage families to find equitable ways to distribute child care and other responsibilities, and in general, try to be respectful of the family unit while helping families explore new ways to organize family routines. A continuing clinical challenge is that of meshing a behavioral approach with the complexities of the individual family structure. Every family is asked to spend at least 2 hours a day on home programming, especially self-help, socialization, and behavior management activities as these arise in the course of family life.

In the prep and small group classes, parents are invited to "Clinics" twice monthly where all of the persons who work with the child are urged to participate, exchange ideas, and watch one another carry out programs. These clinics, which we first observed being used by Lovaas' staff at UCLA, facilitate communication among the several people working with a child, ensure that everyone is demanding the same level of performance, and stimulate the development of new programming ideas. In the integrated preschool, similar meetings are conducted once a month. Home and school communication is also enhanced by regular phone contact and by a notebook that goes home with the child each day.

In addition to the parent training and involvement of parents in the educational needs of the child, the center also provides support services for families. These include evening discussion groups during which parents are encouraged to share with one another their feelings about the special stresses in their lives and methods of coping with these demands. For example, group members might discuss their reactions to their child's diagnosis, their fears about their child's long-term needs, the responses of their extended family to the child's special needs, the stresses they experience in their marriage, and so forth. These voluntary groups provide a useful source of support and often form the basis for new friendships among families. Similar age-appropriate support groups for siblings have also been a useful adjunct service. These "sib" groups typically meet on a Saturday morning or Sunday afternoon, combine play with discussion, and encourage children to share their experiences growing up with a sibling with autism.

Approximately six times a year all of the parents at the center, including those in the preschool programs, come together for an evening meeting. These meetings include a session with the classroom teacher as well as an invited speaker discussing a topic of general concern. These topics have included such things as advocating for one's child within the school system, the expression of sexuality by children with special needs, genetic counseling, the needs of siblings, preparing a will that meets the needs of the child with autism, and so forth.

OUTCOME MEASURES

Among the 21 children who have completed the preschool program, 16 went to other less restrictive placements for neurologically impaired and communication disabled children and two were promoted to classes for older children within the center. Two children have been fully integrated into regular kindergartens and one into a first grade in the public schools. We provide ongoing consultation to families and schools after the children leave us, and so far none of the youngsters has been returned to us for additional intervention.

We have been obtaining regular psychometric measures on the children's developmental progress for the past several years. In terms of speech and language changes, our work shows that although functioning at a lower developmental level than the normal peers both before and after treatment, the children with autism show an accelerated rate of language acquisition after one year at the center (Harris, Handleman, Gordon, Kristoff, & Fuentes, 1991; Harris, Handleman, Kristoff, Bass, & Gordon, 1990).

In a recent study of gains in intellectual ability as measured by the *Stanford–Binet IV* (Thorndike, Hagen, & Sattler, 1986) we found a nearly 19-point increase in IQ after 1 year of treatment (Harris et al., 1991). In another study (Handleman, Harris, Celiberti, Lilleleht, & Tomchek, 1991) we found significant gains on the *Battelle Developmental Inventory* (Newborg, Stock, Wnek, Guidubaldi, & Svinicki, 1984) and the *Learning Accomplishment Profile* (Lemay, Griffin, & Sanford, 1977). Thus, standard psychometric measures have consistently indicated that the children make measurable progress in speech and language, developmental skills, and intelligence over the course of their enrollment at the center. Our data also suggest significant benefits to the normally developing peers when compared to normally developing youngsters at a university day care center (Harris et al., 1991).

MAJOR ISSUES FOR FUTURE EFFORT

As members of a university-based facility, the staff of the DDDC is committed to ongoing program evaluation and development. This commitment has contributed to the evolutionary nature of the program and continues to result in innovations in programming for the range of children being served at the center. Current interests focus on issues related to the nature of autism and the specialized needs of these students.

Among the issues we believe need to be addressed is clarification of diagnostic and assessment criteria, particularly for the preschooler with autism. It is not yet clear to us to what extent symptoms of autism in early childhood are predictive of Autistic Disorder at later ages. It is important to know how many of the changes seen in very young children with autistic behavior, especially "higher functioning" youngsters, reflect developmental change rather than response to treatment. It is also important to know how consistently the diagnosis of autism is being used across educational and research settings. Some of our own work is aimed at assessing the differing models of preschool intervention. We are interested, for example in comparing our small group preschool and prep class in terms of their relative advantages as an initial preschool placement.

There are also a number of issues that relate to the needs of children with autism regardless of age. For example, meeting the special needs of families, particularly siblings, remains a focus of research and programming for us. In addition, addressing the challenging behaviors of the students with autism is an ongoing concern of our staff as it is for the field in general. We hope that our early intervention efforts will diminish the severity of disruptive behavior problems at later ages.

A great deal remains to be learned about optimal educational strategies for young children with autism. To the extent that diagnostic criteria are clearly agreed upon and intervention strategies well defined, it will be increasingly possible to move on to more complex questions.

REFERENCES

American Psychiatric Association. (1987). *Diagnostic and statistical manual of mental disorders* (3rd ed.–revised). Washington, DC: Author.

Dunn, L. M., & Dunn, L. M. (1981). *Peabody Picture Vocabulary Test–Revised*. Circle Pines, MN: American Guidance Service.

Earlley, E.C. (1986). *AIMS: Pre-reading Kit*. Elizabethtown, PA: The Continental Press.

Handleman, J. S., Harris, S. L., Celiberti, D., Lilleleht, E., & Tomchek, L. (1991). Developmental changes of preschool children with autism and normally developing peers. *Infants–Toddler Intervention, 1*, 137–143.

Harris, S. L., Handleman, J. S., Gordon, R., Kristoff, B., & Fuentes, F. (1991). Changes in cognitive and language functioning of preschool children with autism. *Journal of Autism and Developmental Disorders, 21*, 137–143.

Harris, S. L., Handleman, J. S., Kristoff, B., Bass, L., & Gordon, R. (1990). Changes in language development among autistic and peer children in segregated preschool settings. *Journal of Autism and Developmental Disorders, 20*, 23–31.

LeMay, D., Griffin, P., & Sanford, A. (1977). *Learning accomplishment profile—Diagnostic edition*. Chapel Hill, NC: Chapel Hill Training-Outreach Project.

Lord, C., & Schopler, E. (1987). Neurobiological implications of sex differences in autism. In E. Schopler & G. B. Mesibov (Eds.), *Neurobiological issues in autism* (pp. 191–211). New York: Plenum.

Lovaas, O. I. (1981). *Teaching developmentally disabled children: The me book*. Baltimore, MD: University Park Press.

Newborg, J., Stock, J. R., Wnek, L., Guidubaldi, J., & Svinicki, J. (1984). *Battelle Developmental Inventory. Examiner's manual.* Allen, TX: DLM Teaching Resources.

Romanczyk, R. G., & Lockshin, S. (1982). *The I.G.S. Curriculum.* Vestal, NY: C.B.T.A.

Schopler, E., Reichler, R. J., DeVellis, R. F., & Daly, K. (1988). *The Childhood Autism Rating Scale.* Los Angeles: Western Psychological Services.

Sparrow, S. S., Balla, D. A., & Cicchetti, D. V. (1984). *Vineland Adaptive Behavior Scales. Interview Edition. Survey form manual.* Circle Pines, MN: American Guidance Service.

Thorndike, R. L. (1972). *Manual for Stanford-Binet intelligence scale.* Boston: Houghton-Mifflin.

Thorndike, R. L., Hagen, E. R., & Sattler, J. M. (1986). *The Stanford-Binet Intelligence Scale: 4th Ed.* Chicago: The Riverside Publishing Co.

Witt, B., & Boose, J. (1984). *Teacher Organized Training for Acquisition of Language.* Tucson, AZ: Communication Skill Builders.

Zimmerman, I. L., Steiner, V. G., & Pond, R. E. (1979). *Preschool language scale manual.* Columbus, OH: Charles E. Merrill.

Chapter 6

TEACCH Services for Preschool Children

CATHERINE LORD and ERIC SCHOPLER

Division TEACCH (**T**reatment and **E**ducation of **A**utistic and Related **C**ommunication Handicapped **CH**ildren) was founded in 1972 as a division of the Department of Psychiatry, University of North Carolina at Chapel Hill. TEACCH is a statewide, comprehensive, community-based program in North Carolina dedicated to improving the understanding and services for children with autism and communication disabilities and their families. As of 1992, there were six TEACCH centers distributed across the state, as well as an administration and research section located in the School of Medicine in Chapel Hill and a Community Living and Learning Center for adults located near campus. TEACCH's services are both center- and outreach-based. There is one demonstration preschool classroom located in the medical school in Chapel Hill; however other educational services are provided within schools and programs in the communities in which children and adults with autism live. Because one of the mandates of TEACCH is to provide services that best meet the needs of individual communities, these services range in conceptualization and focus. However, the overriding goal is to provide continuity of services from preschool to school age and adult life. This chapter will describe general characteristics of the services provided by TEACCH centers to preschool children across the state and, in some cases, offer specific examples from the Greensboro–High Point TEACCH Center in order to illustrate particular points.

87

North Carolina is predominately a rural state with several small to mid-size cities. TEACCH centers are placed in cities where branches of the University of North Carolina are located in order to provide TEACCH staff access to educational support while providing students and researchers access to TEACCH. Each center serves 6 to 11 counties. Educational and early intervention services for preschool children in these areas are funded primarily by state and county resources; school systems are now providing services for children down to age 3 years. TEACCH provides training and consultation for teachers and staff in these programs.

TEACCH is funded by state monies allocated through the university budget with funds of about $2.6 million to cover costs of all centers and programs. There are also several projects carried out through TEACCH jointly with the Autism Society of North Carolina and with state vocational rehabilitation services. Federal and state grants provide money for training; federal grants and funds from private foundations provide money for research. In addition, some of the activities of TEACCH are self-supporting, including teaching materials, conferences, and workshops.

A total of about 250 new preschool children are seen at the six TEACCH centers each year. This means that at any given time, about 650–700 preschool children are receiving TEACCH services. Most children receive a standard assessment that will be described below. However, this assessment and the kinds of services that the children receive are individualized according to families' needs and the services available in the community. TEACCH's goal is to provide appropriate services for every child with autism and severe communication disability in North Carolina, regardless of his or her parents' ability to pay or to participate in particular clinical activities. Each TEACCH center has regular contracts with specific classrooms and programs offered by school systems and county agencies; TEACCH also "follows" children into other placements their parents have selected for consultation. Because of the size of the TEACCH system and the fact that preschool children do not receive services separable in kind from older children, adolescents, or adults, it is not possible to provide an estimate of costs per preschool student per school year. For the Greensboro–High Point Center, costs are estimated at under $1,200 per year per active case, including children and adults.

Autism/communication-disability is a classification recognized by the Department of Public Instruction in North Carolina. There is a specific mandate that no more than six school age children in this category will be placed with a teacher and an assistant in a classroom specifically designated for children with autism. Separate guidelines are not available for preschool children and, because of the very high student-teacher ratio allowed in North Carolina for preschool children, this has been a source of concern.

POPULATION SERVED

Over 4,500 children, adults, and their families have been served by TEACCH in the 20 years it has been in existence. By far, the majority of these children were first seen during the preschool years and have grown up with the program, although there are also children identified at later ages or those who have moved to North Carolina at older ages. One of the most important changes in TEACCH services over the last 10 years has been the decreasing age at which children are first referred. In the 1970s, children were most often seen entering or getting ready to enter kindergarten or first grade. Now, as early intervention and screening programs have become more active, the model age for first referral is 3, with substantial numbers of 2-year-olds referred as well. TEACCH serves children who receive formal diagnoses of autism, as well as children with pervasive developmental disorder (American Psychiatric Association, 1987) or severe communication disability, a category consistent with state educational regulations. In the 20 years TEACCH has been in existence, a variety of different diagnostic schemes have been proposed. All children are given the *Childhood Autism Rating* Scale (Schopler, Reichler, & Renner, 1988) and currently, clinical diagnoses using DSM-III-R (American Psychiatric Association, 1987) and ICD-10 draft (World Health Organization, 1987) criteria are employed in the clinics. Children are not accepted or rejected into the program on the basis of formal diagnostic criteria. Once a child has been accepted for assessment, follow-up is available to any child and family for whom TEACCH is deemed to be the most appropriate agency to provide services; otherwise children are referred elsewhere.

Recent statistics suggest that about 65% of newly diagnosed children at TEACCH meet formal diagnostic criteria for autism (American Psychiatric Association, 1987; World Health Organization, 1987), with the majority of remaining children meeting criteria for pervasive developmental disorders or language disorders, with or without mental disability. However, the preschool age level presents some special diagnostic problems discussed below.

Ethnic distribution is equivalent to that of the State of North Carolina with most recent estimates of the TEACCH population as 66% Caucasian, 31% African-American, and 3% other ethnic groups. Estimates of the intellectual abilities of the preschool children, separate from all older children in all the TEACCH centers, are not available. However, using the Greensboro–High Point TEACCH Center as an example, mean IQ / developmental quotients for children under 6 seen for initial assessment in the last 3 years averaged from 55 to 60, with a range of 10 to 146. These scores are generally based on the mental scale of the *Bayley Scales of Infant Development* (Bayley, 1969) or performance tests such as the *Merrill-Palmer Scale of Mental Tests* (Stutsman, 1931). The sex ratio is 3:1 males to females.

ASSESSMENT PROCEDURES

The diagnosis of autism is more difficult at the preschool age level than at later ages. For example, social behaviors of both normal children and children with mental retardation are relatively limited at very young ages. Moreover, mothers often develop repetitive routines like pat-a-cake that can mask the lack of spontaneous interaction. A mother's automatic response to a young child's distress masks the extent to which a child does not seek comfort. Likewise, there is less language at an early age, even in normal children, and so it becomes more difficult to observe pronoun reversal; delayed echolalia; or abnormal pitch, rate, and rhythm. Repetitive behavior also presents special diagnostic consideration. Both normal and mentally retarded preschool children have attachments to objects like blankets. For these considerations, special emphasis is given to diagnostic assessment at the preschool level both formally and informally, and a research project on early identification was initiated at the Greensboro–High Point TEACCH Center (Lord, 1991).

A standard structured diagnostic assessment is consistently used across all of the TEACCH centers; additional aspects of the assessment vary according to the center and the individual child's needs. As an example, the assessment procedure followed at the Greensboro–High Point TEACCH Center will be described. When a child is referred to the center, a TEACCH psychoeducational therapist contacts the source of referral, the child's parent, and the child's teacher or intervention worker, to determine the appropriateness of the referral. Children are accepted for whom there is some suspicion of autistic behaviors or who have a combination of severe language delay and social impairment not accounted for by mental disability. If the child is accepted for a full assessment, the assessment begins with a home visit by a therapist in which a standard diagnostic interview, the *Autism Diagnostic Interview–Revised* (ADI–R) (Rutter, Lord, & LeCouteur, in press), is given to the parents. In addition, this visit provides a chance to meet the child and to get a sense of the parents' priorities. In other centers, this interview may be scheduled as part of the in-clinic assessment. At the beginning of each diagnostic session, parents are asked to identify questions and concerns they would like to be considered in the context of the evaluation.

A standard assessment involves a team of three people: a clinical psychologist (the clinical director of the center) and two psychoeducational therapists, one of whom works with the child, while the other, who has already interviewed the parent(s) in their home, assumes the role of parent consultant and serves as the primary family contact. The child's teachers and other professionals working with the child are invited to a staff meeting before the assessment begins. They can then observe the assessment through a one-way mirror. The *Psychoeducational Profile–Revised* (PEP–R) (Schopler, Reichler, Bashford, Lansing, & Marcus, 1990) is always given first by a psychoeducational therapist. This instrument establishes developmental levels in seven areas and allows the therapist to observe the child during a variety of tasks that vary in structure and social communicative demands. During this time, the parents are given the *Vineland Adaptive Behavior Scales* (Sparrow, Balla, & Cicchetti, 1984) and the parent consultant discusses with them any new concerns. During this time, the parents watch the testing through a one-way mirror or may join the child in the testing room if necessary. Parents are asked to keep the staff informed about how typical their child's behavior has been during the clinic day.

After the Psychoeducational Profile is administered, nonverbal intelligence, standard intelligence, or developmental scales and language tests are given by the psychologist. The language tests most frequently used are the *Sequenced Inventory of Communication Development* (Hedrick, Prather, & Tobin, 1975) and *Peabody Picture Vocabulary Test–Revised* (Dunn & Dunn, 1981). Because many of the children who we see are young and not verbal, infant assessments are used frequently, including the *Bayley Scales of Mental and Motor Development* (Bayley,

1969) and the *Mullen Infant and Early Learning Scales* (Mullen, 1989). The *Merrill-Palmer Scale of Mental Tests* (Stutsman, 1931) scored as a nonverbal test, the *Wechsler Preschool and Primary Scale–Revised* (Wechsler, 1989), and the *Differential Abilities Scale* (Elliott, 1990) are used with higher functioning children. If appropriate, a structured observational schedule of social and communicative behavior [*Prelinguistic Autism Diagnostic Observation Schedule* (PL-ADOS) (DiLavore, Lord, & Rutter, 1993)] is administered to the child with the help of a parent. This instrument provides an opportunity to observe specific aspects of the child's social behavior such as joint attention, imitation, and sharing of affect with the examiner and with the parent. Parents are then asked to play with their child with toys they have brought from home. The clinical psychologist uses the *Childhood Autism Rating Scale* (CARS) (Schopler, Reichler, & Renner, 1986) to formalize observations of the child's behavior throughout the day.

While families are at lunch, a second staff meeting, including visiting professionals and teachers, takes place to discuss test results and parents' concerns. At the end of this meeting, results are conveyed to the parents by the therapists and clinical director. Parents and professionals whom parents identify are later provided with written reports by the psycho-educational therapist and the psychologist and a letter from the parent consultant summarizing the final conference. A second session is scheduled approximately 1 month later after the parents have received the reports to discuss the meeting and to provide another opportunity for the TEACCH staff to work with and observe the child. If the child is placed in a day program or receiving individual therapy, a school visit or a further consultation is also generally arranged at this time.

Treatment options at TEACCH are discussed in the section on curriculum. As part of the referral process, parents are encouraged to have a recent audiological assessment and a comprehensive pediatric examination of their child before the TEACCH assessment, if possible. If other medical concerns arise during the assessment, children are referred to different medical consultants.

TEACHING AND ADMINISTRATIVE STAFF

Each TEACCH center has five to seven psychoeducational therapists. In most centers, one of the therapists is identified as the person who works with adults and adolescents and supervises job coaches. The remaining therapists serve as "generalists," taking on all the different roles of therapist/consultant. These therapists, in most cases, have master's degrees or bachelor's degrees and substantial amounts of experience with children with autism. They come from a range of disciplines, including special education, speech therapy, and social work. For individual treatment cases and assessments, therapists are often assigned to a particular child or placed in a particular role because of their expertise; however, the expectation is that each therapist will be able to work in a variety of different content areas with children of different ages and ability levels and to serve as a consultant to classrooms, as a support to parents, and to provide direct treatment to children and families. Each TEACCH center is headed by a clinical psychologist and is provided support by one or more secretaries. Most centers have graduate interns from psychology, social work, psychiatry and/or pediatric residents, and psychology and special education graduate students who rotate through practica. In the last few years, TEACCH has also had an increasing number of international visitors. Several of the clinics have research projects that employ full-time research associates.

Staff at TEACCH are hired through an intensive process in which they are asked, as part of the interview, to work with a child and to talk to a parent. Both situations are observed by the clinic staff from one-way mirrored observations rooms. Candidates are asked to formulate impressions of the child's learning problems and of the parents' primary concerns. They are asked to write a description of their brief interview, document their impressions and observations of the child, and then write a description of their experience. Even though psychoeducational therapists are required to have at least 2 years experience working with persons with autism or a related disorder, this procedure allows staff to be selected on the basis of their flexibility and clinical skill to a degree not possible without this process. Using this mini-work sample provides a high degree of staff consensus for hiring decisions. Training of staff continues throughout all aspects of the job. For the first 6 months to a year of employment, psychoeducational therapists are supported by another therapist or the clinical director in consultation, treatment, and work with parents. TEACCH is also involved in educational training for internal staff and others. Week-long summer training, a day-long fall workshop, a 2-day winter inservice, and a 2-day spring conference are part of the formal educational opportunities offered each staff member as well as teachers in TEACCH-affiliated community schools. Clinic and research staff are also encouraged to attend other conferences and meetings.

CURRICULUM

A long established and central aspect of the TEACCH curriculum is structured teaching. It provides educational continuity from preschool age to adult years (Schopler, Mesibov, & Hersey, in press) and also prevents many behavior problems. When we first showed that children with autism learned better in a structured rather than an unstructured learning situation (Schopler et al., 1971), we also noted that children at earlier developmental levels needed structure more than children at higher levels of functioning. However, just as the diagnosis of autism is more obscure and requires more special consideration at the preschool age than at later ages, so does the use of structured teaching.

In addition to resolving diagnostic ambiguities, the emphasis in the preschool class is on learning to be students and developing appropriate social and communicative behavior. Compared with school-age children, preschoolers are exposed to a wider range of skills. Due to their shorter attention span, preschoolers' daily schedules are changed more frequently. Children spend more time learning in small groups, fine and gross motor skills need more practice, and parents are more often involved in the classroom than with the later ages. These activities contribute to the greater emphasis on the physical structure aspect of the curriculum and the layout of the classroom. This is illustrated in a depiction of a preschool class in Raleigh in Figure 6.1.

In this figure, there are clear indications of where each activity will occur in order to help the student learn to stay in certain areas. Work tasks for teaching cognitive, fine motor, eye/hand integration, and organizational skills occur at the tables. Self-help skills such as toileting, eating habits, washing hands, wiping tables, and hanging up coats are taught in the lower lefthand corner. Expressive communication, receptive language, and social interaction are formally taught in another marked area but also occur as part of other activities. Daily schedules clearly help the child learn directions, and those with better visual processing skills can be helped to understand schedules as illustrated in Figure 6.2. Such schedules can be adapted according to levels of communication and can help to prevent frustration and behavior problems.

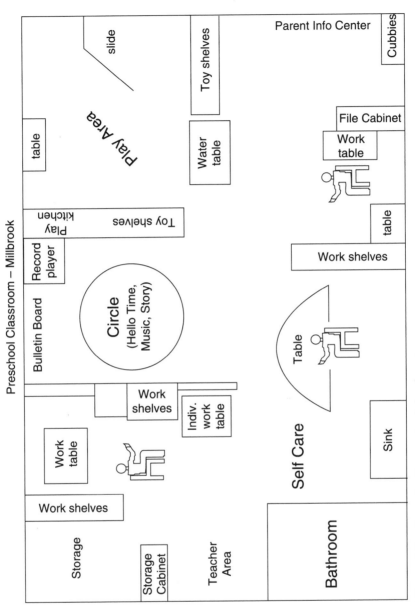

Figure 6.1. Example of a preschool class layout.

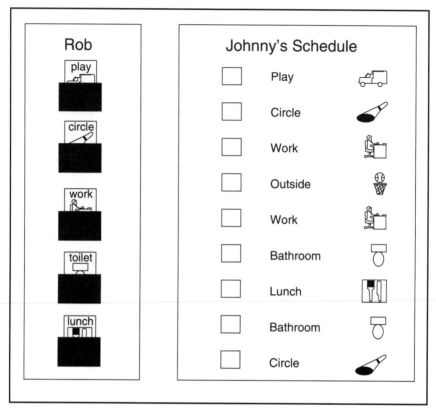

Figure 6.2. Example of a daily schedule.

The TEACCH philosophy includes the recognition that each family and each child with autism is unique and require a continuum of services individualized for diverse family situations and differences in the cognitive, social, and language levels of each child. Very young children are reevaluated annually or on the basis of new concerns. Parents are offered a number of treatment options in the TEACCH centers and are encouraged to maintain some contact with TEACCH after an assessment, even if they do not participate in a formal treatment program.

Available to parents are "extended diagnostic" sessions in which parents return to the clinic for six to eight 1-hour sessions over the course of several months to work as co-therapists with their child on goals that they choose (e.g., anything from toilet training to increasing communication to creating activities for a child while a parent cooks dinner).

Families are directed to family support groups, both specifically for autism such as local chapters of the Autism Society of North Carolina, or groups for developmental disorders in general such as "Parent-to-Parent" organizations run from local hospitals. Each clinic also provides different support groups for parents, depending on the particular needs of the clients at the time.

Suggested teaching activities and strategies for parents and teachers are published in *Individualized Assessment and Treatment for Autistic and Developmentally Disabled Children: Teaching Strategies for Parents and Professionals, Volume II* (Schopler, Reichler, & Lansing, 1980) and *Teaching Activities for Autistic Children, Volume III* (Schopler, Lansing, & Waters, 1983). There is also a TEACCH communication curriculum that can be used both in school and at home (Watson, Lord, Schaffer, & Schopler, 1988). Two central aspects of each of these curricula are structuring the environment and facilitating independence at all levels of functioning. The importance of observing and assessing each child's current repertoire of spontaneous and practiced behavior is emphasized in order to design a truly individualized program that will facilitate the most rapid and generalizable progress.

Each TEACCH clinic has contractual relationships with a variety of educational programs. These contracts are not financial but consist of regular consultation provided to classrooms in return for school systems sending teachers to summer training and releasing them to attend inservice training and clinic-based assessments of their students during the year. In the Greensboro–High Point TEACCH cachement area, for example, there is one categorical preschool program for children with autism run in a special school, there are 13 noncategorical preschool programs for children with disabilities run by school districts and mental health consortiums, and there are eight integrated programs in which children with disabilities participate with their own teacher in a regular day care center. Other children are at home with mothers who are fulltime homemakers working with home programs or are placed in other child care settings to which the TEACCH staff may provide consultation as needed.

Older children with autism served by TEACCH centers participate in a similar range of placements though there are regional differences in what is available. Within each of these contexts, the primary role of the TEACCH consultant is to help teachers and other professionals understand the special learning needs associated with autism and individual children and to help them distinguish between skills that can be taught directly from learning deficits that require environmental accommodation. The latter frequently requires structured teaching and understanding of how structure reduces behavior problems and provides demonstration of appropriate teaching techniques and environmental manipulations appropriate for children of preschool age and older. Consultants also support an emphasis on spontaneous communication and social skills, whether within an integrated situation or using reverse mainstreaming. Children are followed throughout the year with regular visits to their educational placements, and parents may elect to return to the clinic for follow-up sessions at any time.

INTEGRATION VERSUS SEGREGATION

The TEACCH philosophy is that a continuum of services from complete inclusion to highly specialized, structured programming by teachers specifically trained in autism should be available. Families and professionals should be able to select the most appropriate service for each child from this continuum. Least restricted environments are supported, but there is also a commitment to providing highly structured intensive treatment for children who need this level of service. TEACCH attempts to support services developed in each community. In one community in which there are very good categorical classrooms for autism, TEACCH may provide consultation to preschool classes and serve as an advocate for reverse mainstreaming and a greater focus on spontaneous communication and social interaction. In another community, the TEACCH therapist may work with a group of mothers who are homemakers joining together in biweekly sessions with their children. The therapist may consult for an integrated day care center in the same community and have regular contact with public health and private speech pathologists who see children with autism.

STRUCTURED TEACHING AND
BEHAVIOR MANAGEMENT

As discussed before, structured teaching provides the primary basis for educational continuity in the TEACCH Program since it can be adjusted to individual levels of communication and on a continuum applicable from the developmentally impaired to the nondisabled. Such structuring provides environmental accommodation to some of the primary learning deficits seen in children with autism. These deficits include problems with organization, memory of things other than special interests, difficulty with auditory processing, and making transitions from one topic to another. Conversely, children with autism tend to be relatively strong in visual processing, and special interests can be used for motivating learning.

By accommodating the learning environment to the deficits associated with autism, independent functioning of each student is gradually increased and many frustrations and behavior problems are avoided. Mild negative consequences (e.g., having a child sit in a chair in the corner for 30 seconds, removing a favorite object from the table for a minute) are employed, but the emphasis is much more on positive strategies and using structure to minimize difficulties before they occur to the extent possible. The prevention of behavior problems is difficult to study and, to date, we have not done so systematically. Nevertheless, clinical estimates suggest that appropriate structured teaching at home and at school can prevent many typical behavior problems associated with autism.

A combination of cognitive and behavioral interventions are also employed. This strategy of multiple approaches can be illustrated for one of the frequent preschool sources of behavior problems, the area of toilet training. Figure 6.3 presents an illustration using an iceberg metaphor. Above the water line are specific behavior problems such as soiling or wetting. Below the water line are listed explanatory deficits. By careful observation and parent interviews, an informed assessment is made of antecedent circumstances and behaviors. If, for example, a child soils himself, it may be that he or she does not understand the sequence of undressing, sitting on the toilet, wiping, and dressing. If this assessment is correct, the sequence can be taught separately. If the soiling discontinues, the assessment and intervention were correct. If soiling continues, alternative intervention efforts must be used.

PARENTAL AND FAMILY INVOLVEMENT

Parents are seen as the first "generalists" in the treatment of their child and as absolutely central to their child's progress. A unique em-

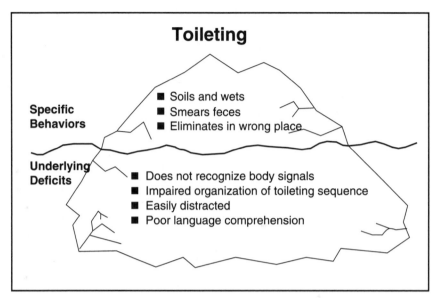

Figure 6.3.   Metaphor illustrating the relationship between behaviors and deficits.

phasis of TEACCH is to provide services to parents who have varying amounts of time and degree of commitment to working directly with their children. Home visits and joint school visits are an important part of the work with parents, as well as working with the Autism Society of North Carolina to provide advocacy and support. Every attempt is made to work around a family's particular needs and to work with the family to accomplish goals that are important to it, as well as working on goals identified by the TEACCH staff. For example, we feel strongly that most families with newly diagnosed children benefit from a period of time in which caregivers carry out structured programming (e.g., sitting at a table doing tasks such as matching, sorting, imitating, or working on receptive language) with their child in combination with regular contact with professionals who are concerned not only with the child's progress, but the desires and concerns of the whole family. The prototype of this process at TEACCH are "extended diagnostic" sessions in which each parent works with the child on a set number of specific activities for about 15 minutes a day. These activities would generally involve sitting at a table doing tasks such as matching, sorting, imitating, or working on receptive language. The parent-consultant / child-therapist team helps the family develop the home program, encourages them to modify it to best suit their needs and the child's interests and abilities, and is available to discuss any other issues that arise.

While this model is very successful with some families, others do not have the time, interest, or ability to carry out this kind of activity. In addition, while the process of learning to do structured programming may provide caregivers with invaluable general skills, often parents' greatest concerns have to do with managing specific behaviors (e.g., tantrums, spitting) or developing skills such as toilet-training. Thus, in addition to extended diagnostic sessions, the child-therapist may visit the home and school and help design and monitor a toileting program. For parents with limited transportation, therapists may arrange a series of home visits or have the parent ride into school on the school bus and meet there. As an alternative to extended diagnostic sessions, a therapist may accompany a parent on visits to possible preschool program or respite centers or arrange a coffee hour for three mothers with similar concerns who are not yet interested in the larger parents' groups. Home programs may be developed for a grandmother or a babysitter or be carried out with siblings taking turns and playing together for families that have other children close in age to the child with autism.

OUTCOME MEASURES

In general, outcome for TEACCH has been measured in terms of a very low rate of institutionalization of older children and adults (less than 8%). Recently, as a "spin-off" of a project on early diagnosis of autism of children referred to TEACCH, we have been able to document positive changes during the first few years after referral of a substantial number of very young children with autism and communication disabilities (Lord, 1991). Another follow-up study that included many subjects from TEACCH showed greater academic achievement in high-functioning adolescents and adults than expected from earlier research (Venter, Lord, & Schopler, 1992). While these studies are not systematic tests of a particular intervention, they provide follow-up data of young children who received TEACCH services. A number of other follow-up studies have allowed us to trace the course of autism for young children first seen at TEACCH in the preschool years (Lord & Schopler, 1989b). These studies have indicated that substantial increases in IQ scores are quite common in children first assessed at ages 3 or 4, regardless of the intensity of treatment. For example, nonverbal 3-year-olds who received initial IQs between 30 and 50 showed a mean increase in IQ by age 7 years of 22 to 24 points; nonverbal 4-year-olds reassessed at age 9 gained an average of 15 to 19 points, though both groups remained in the range of mild mental disability. Gains in the preschool years were greatest for very young, nonverbal children and for children who acquired language between the first and second assessment. The role of particular tests and the demands those tests place on children at different ages and developmental levels has also been documented (Lord & Schopler, 1989a).

Psychoeducational therapists keep records of each session and teachers keep detailed notes concerning the outcome of educational programs for each child. School visits are also documented and a system of self-evaluation for teachers has been developed.

MAJOR ISSUES FOR FUTURE EFFORT

There are a number of philosophical and clinical issues that confront the preschool services at TEACCH. First is the appropriateness of diagnosis of very young children, particularly nonverbal children age 3 years and younger. While recent studies suggest that clinical diagnoses of these very young children may be quite stable (Gillberg et al., 1990), other studies suggest that there may be large differences in criteria and methods for diagnosis across samples and clinicians, and that this stability cannot be taken for granted (Knobloch & Pasamanick, 1975). It is also not clear, even if clinicians can judge if a child will be autistic a year later, that they are necessarily using the same criteria by which autism is diagnosed in older children (Lord, 1991). Work is underway to define criteria and methods (and their limits) appropriate for the diagnosis of autism in very young children.

A question of intense interest is how to provide services to the increasing number of children and teachers serving young children with autism in integrated settings. In the past, TEACCH has been able to provide intensive training and support for teachers by centralizing resources for staff and children in self-contained classrooms for children with autism/communication disability. However, this is no longer feasible nor appropriate in all cases since many children are clearly benefitting from less restricted environments. The question remains how to train and provide support for teachers who have only one child with autism in their classrooms. While the teacher of a "TEACCH" self-contained classroom is expected to have attended 1 week of summer training before he/she begins and 4 to 6 days of inservice training per year, the needs of a regular preschool teacher with one child with autism in his/her class or a teacher of a noncategorical preschool class are somewhat different. A TEACCH therapist typically visits a new teacher of a self-contained class for six children with autism once a week; if these six children all have different "new" teachers, weekly visits are not possible. How to maintain standards of training, support, and staff selection while providing each child an opportunity for education in the setting most appropriate for him/her is a question currently receiving much attention.

A related question is how best to structure programs for very young children, particularly children with autism with mental ages under 2 years of age. What does the concept of "structure," a conceptualization that underlies much of TEACCH training and consultation for older children, mean for children who are intellectually functioning as infants? How much of an emphasis should be placed on independence versus interactive learning? To what extent and how can peers (i.e., autistic classmates, nondisabled models, or children with other disabilities), be used as a resource for children at this age and how may this be done best?

Another question concerns how services can be provided for all families of children with autism, not just families with extraordinary financial resources and energy. TEACCH is a state-funded agency mandated to work with all of the families of North Carolina and does not have the luxury of choosing only families who are willing and able to participate in highly intensive extra treatments. One question is whether such intensive treatments have results that are truly unique and, if so, how can families who are not able carry them out be supported to do so? If such intensive treatments do not have unique results, what other factors determine positive outcome? In this same context, what demands are appropriate to make of school systems and state agencies providing early intervention? What is the critical mass of treatment, skill, and support that can be demanded of such agencies in order to ensure that the children with autism of North Carolina reach their highest potential?

The early 1990s have been an exciting time for the field of autism with the advent of many new and creative approaches to treatment. A number of research achievements help us better understand the nature and course of autism (Lord & Rutter, in press). However, it is not clear how much these exciting changes affect the daily lives of the preschool age children with autism for whom TEACCH is responsible. The TEACCH program originated as a service to help educate children with autism and provide their families with support. An essential component of the TEACCH model is to recognize that children with autism are individuals who are part of unique families and unique communities. Our goal is to use the resources available at each of these three levels (e.g., child, family, community) to facilitate the greatest independence and happiness for each child with autism in our state.

REFERENCES

American Psychiatric Association. (1987). *Diagnostic and statistical manual of mental disorders*, (3rd ed.–revised). Washington, DC: Author.

Bayley, N. (1969). *Manual for the Bayley Scales of Infant Development*. New York: The Psychological Corporation.

DiLavore, P., Lord, C., & Rutter, M. (1993). *Prelinguistic Autism Diagnostic Observation Schedule (PL–ADOS)*. Unpublished manuscript, Division TEACCH, University of North Carolina, Chapel Hill, NC.

Dunn, L. M., & Dunn, L. M. (1981). *Peabody Picture Vocabulary Test–Revised: Manual for forms L and M*. Circle Pines, MN: American Guidance Service.

Elliott, C. D. (1990). *Differential Ability Scales (DAS)*. San Antonio, TX: The Psychological Corporation.

Gillberg, C., Ehlers, S., Schaumann, H., Jakobsson, G., Dahlgren, S. O., Lindblom, R., Bagenholm, A., Tjuus, T., & Blidner, E. (1990). Autism under age 3 years: A clinical study of 28 cases referred for autistic symptoms in infancy. *Journal of Child Psychology and Psychiatry, 21*, 921–934.

Hedrick, D. L., Prather, E. M., & Tobin, A. R. (1975). *Sequenced inventory of communication development*. Seattle, WA: University of Washington Press.

Knobloch, H., & Pasamanick, B. (1975). Some etiologic and prognostic factors in early infantile autism and psychosis. *Pediatrics, 55*, 182–191.

Lord, C. (1991, April). *Follow-up of two-year-olds referred for possible autism*. Paper presented at the biennial meeting of the Society for Research in Child Development, Seattle, WA.

Lord, C. (1993). The complexity of social behavior in autism. In S. Baron-Cohen, H. Tager-Flusberg, & D. Cohen (Eds.), *Understanding other minds: Perspectives from autism*. Oxford, England: Oxford University Press.

Lord, C., & Rutter, M. (in press). Autism and pervasive developmental disorders. In M. Rutter, L. Hersov, and E. Taylor (Eds.), *Child and adolescent psychiatry* (3rd ed.). Oxford, England: Blackwell Scientific Publications.

Lord, C., & Schopler, E. (1989a). The role of age at assessment, developmental level, and test in the stability of intelligence scores in young autistic children. *Journal of Autism and Developmental Disorders, 19*, 483–499.

Lord, C., & Schopler, E. (1989b). Stability of assessment results of autistic and nonautistic language-impaired children from preschool years to early school age. *Journal of Child Psychology and Psychiatry, 30*, 575–590.

Mullen, E. (1989). *Mullen Scales of Early Learning.* Cranston, RI: TOTAL. Child, Inc.

Rutter, M., Lord, C., & Le Couteur, A. (in press). *Brief report: Autism Diagnostic Interview–Revised. Journal of Autism and Developmental Disorders.*

Schopler, E., Brehm, S. S., Kinsbourne, M., & Reichler, R. J. (1971). Effect of treatment structure in autistic children. *Archives of General Psychiatry, 24*, 415–421.

Schopler, E., Lansing, M., & Waters, L. (1983). *Individualized assessment and treatment for autistic and developmentally disabled children: Vol. 3. Teaching activities for autistic children.* Baltimore, MD: University Park Press.

Schopler, E., Mesibou, G. B., & Hersey, K. (in press). Structured teaching. In E. Schopler & G. B. Mesibou (Eds.), *Assessment and management of behavior problems in autism.* NY: Plenum.

Schopler, E., Reichler, R. J., Bashford, A., Lansing, M. D., & Marcus, L. M. (1990). *Psychoeducational Profile–Revised.* Austin, TX: PRO-ED.

Schopler, E., Reichler, R., & Lansing, M. (1980). *Individualized assessment and treatment for autistic and developmentally disabled children: Vol. 2. Teaching strategies for parents and professionals.* Baltimore, MD: University Park Press.

Schopler, E., Reichler, R., & Renner, B. R. (1986). *The Childhood Autism Rating Scale (CARS) for diagnostic screening and classification of autism.* New York: Irvington Publishers.

Sparrow, S., Balla, D., & Cicchetti, D. (1984). *Vineland Adaptive Behavior Scales.* Circle Pines, MN: American Guidance Service.

Stutsman, R. (1931). Guide for administering the Merrill-Palmer Scale of Mental Tests. In L. M. Terman (Ed.), *Mental measurement of preschool children* (pp. 139–262). New York: Harcourt, Brace & World.

Venter, A., Lord, C., & Schopler, E. (1992). A follow-up study of high-functioning autistic children. *Journal of Child Psychology and Psychiatry, 33*, 489–507.

Watson, L., Lord, C., Schaffer, B., & Schopler, E. (1988). *Teaching spontaneous communication to autistic and developmentally handicapped children.* New York: Irvington Press.

Wechsler, D. (1989). *Manual for the Wechsler Preschool and Primary Scale of Intelligence-Revised.* San Antonio, TX: The Psychological Corporation.

World Health Organization. (1987). *ICD-10 1986 draft of chapter 5 categories F00–F99, Mental, behavioural and developmental disorders.* Geneva: Author.

Chapter 7

The Princeton Child Development Institute

LYNN E. McCLANNAHAN and PATRICIA J. KRANTZ

Founded in 1970 as a private nonprofit agency, the Princeton Child Development Institute initially offered a special education program for children with autism. Today, the Institute's programs include a preschool and school; services to families; two community-based, family-style group homes; and career development and supported employment programs for adults. These programs are characterized by an applied behavior analysis approach and an emphasis on research as well as service.

In 1992–93, tuition for the 10-month school year was $29,212 and tuition for the 5-week summer session was $4,219—a total of $33,431 per child. Tuitions, paid by children's local school districts, covered approximately 80% of costs; the remainder came from grants from public agencies and private foundations and from the fund-raising endeavors of an active and committed governing board.

The Institute is not departmentalized; instead, all managers and supervisors participate in program administration, staff training, staff performance evaluation, and ongoing analysis and evaluation of people's progress. Thus, the community living programs coordinator may conduct performance evaluations of Adult Life-Skills Program personnel; the head teacher may assume responsibility for all staff members' consumer evaluations of program administration; the education program coordinator may review data on group home residents' progress; and all supervisors offer workshop training, provide instruction to novice home programmers, participate in ongoing review and revision of program evaluation procedures, and collectively determine training schedules and evaluation assignments. This fluid organizational structure, supported by regular, ongoing exchange of data across all branches of the program, prevents disjunctions between policies and/or practices (e.g., discrepancies between staff training goals and staff training procedures, between staff training and staff evaluation procedures, or between programs implemented in the school or preschool and in the group homes or children's own homes). The absence of administrative, training, and evaluation "departments" also prevents inequitable distribution of program resources and facilitates optimal deployment of training and evaluation services.

PRESCHOOLERS

The first preschoolers were enrolled in 1975. Since then, 32 preschool children have received services and of these, six are presently enrolled in the preschool, 12 have transitioned or are in transition to public school classrooms, 12 are enrolled in the Institute's school program, and two withdrew from the Institute. Of the 32 children, four are girls; two are African-American, two are Asian and the remainder are Caucasian. Their mean age at intake was 43 months (range = 30 to 58 months).

Because of board members' and administrators' belief in the efficacy of small versus large settings, the combined population of the preschool and school programs is limited to approximately 25 children at any given time. As an alternative to an ever-expanding child population, the Princeton Child Development Institute offers technical assistance to other agencies in order to promote the development of additional services for youngsters with autism.

Research on age at intervention and treatment outcome (Fenske, Zalenski, Krantz, & McClannahan, 1985) underlined the importance of early intervention and lead to changes in intake policy. Thus, preschool vacancies are created when: (a) a preschool or school-age child transitions to public school, (b) a youth completes his/her schooling, or (c) a child withdraws from the preschool or school program. In short, virtually all vacancies in the preschool and school programs are filled by preschoolers.

A child is eligible for services if: (a) a diagnosis of autism has been conferred by one or more persons or agencies beyond the Institute, (b) the child meets the DSM-III-R (American Psychiatric Association, 1987) criteria for autism, and (c) direct observation based on the Institute's own assessment instrument supports a diagnosis of autism. IQ scores, skills or skill deficits, and challenging behavior (e.g., self injury) are unrelated to eligibility.

Currently enrolled preschoolers' initial scores on the *Stanford–Binet IV* (Thorndike, Hagen, & Sattler, 1986) ranged from <36 to 83 (mean = 57). At program entry, most children have little or no receptive or expressive language, are not toilet trained, do not visually attend to others at relevant times, do not imitate others, and engage in a broad range of stereotypies.

ASSESSMENT PROCEDURES

At intake and annually thereafter, the following formal assessments are administered: *Preschool Language Scale* (Zimmerman, Steiner, & Pond, 1979), *Stanford–Binet IV* (Thorndike et al., 1986), *Peabody Picture Vocabulary Test–Revised* (Dunn & Dunn, 1981), and the *Vineland Adaptive Behavior Scales* (Sparrow, Balla, & Cicchetti, 1984). On first administration, most children do not achieve basal scores on the PPVT: of the six currently enrolled preschoolers, none achieved a basal score on this instrument.

STAFF, STAFFING PATTERNS, AND STAFF TRAINING

Most staff members have bachelor's or master's degrees in psychology or education; the number with education certifications meets or exceeds the standards specified by the New Jersey Department of Education. Doctoral students from Queens College of the City University of New York and from the University of Kansas occupy paid positions while completing their degree requirements. In addition, undergraduate interns from local and foreign colleges and universities earn academic credits by serving as data collectors and intervention aides. In the preschool, the staff-child ratio varies between 1 1:5 and 1 1:2.

At the time of employment, few staff members have any prior experience in providing intervention to people with developmental disabilities, and few are acquainted with applied behavior analysis. Preservice and inservice workshops are conducted in order to develop shared vocabularies and to build good relationships between trainers and trainees. However, data on trainees' pre- and post-workshop performances indicate that, although didactic training typically results in improved paper-and-pencil test scores, it does not enable trainees to display relevant intervention skills at criterion levels. Thus, most training is "hands on." Trainers accompany trainees to classrooms, playgrounds, or children's own homes, model the target skills, create supervised practice opportunities, and provide immediate positive and corrective feedback (McClannahan & Krantz, 1985). Typically, more hands-on training is delivered in a staff member's first 2 years than in subsequent years, but all teachers and therapists continue to receive such ongoing training throughout their employment at the Institute.

Much of the content of *in vivo* training is specified by a training protocol that includes observation and measurement of the trainee's use of behavior-specific (and contingent) praise, delivery of opportunities for children to respond, distribution of interactions across children, and number of incidental teaching episodes completed during designated time periods. Observational data are also collected on the engagement or "on-task" levels of children for whom the staff member is responsible. In addition, the protocol includes a series of behavioral checklists that assess skill areas such as shaping; prompting and fading prompts; teaching language and social competence; decreasing inappropriate behavior; using functional environmental design and classroom arrangements; maintaining the quality of the intervention environment; and building and maintaining positive relationships with children, colleagues, and trainers. Each of these content areas results in performance feedback to the trainee.

After 6 to 8 months of hands-on training, new staff members' intervention skills are evaluated. The evaluation protocol is identical to the training protocol, ensuring that precisely those skills that are trained are the skills evaluated; however, the evaluator is a supervisor or trainer who has not been the staff member's primary trainer. On the day of an evaluation, the evaluator observes 4 to 5 hours of the trainee's work with children, collects observational data, and scores the behavioral checklists. Verbal feedback, delivered at the end of the observation period, is followed, within 30 days, by extensive written performance feedback. Occasionally, a pair of evaluators assesses a teacher's or therapist's performance; this practice is used to train new evaluators, as well as to check interobserver agreement between experienced evaluators.

Training and evaluation procedures are designed to maximize staff members' successes. Hands-on training continues throughout employment—the training protocol *is* the evaluation protocol—and evaluators' written recommendations are included in subsequent training plans. Further, trainer and trainee outcomes are yoked; that is, a trainer's skills are recognized and appreciated when the majority of his/her trainees passes the evaluation. All staff members are evaluated at least annually, and a successful evaluation is a prerequisite for reappointment in the following school year.

CURRICULUM

The curriculum began in 1975 as a series of individualized programs that were developed to address the skill deficits and behavior problems of the children then enrolled. With the arrival of each new child, more programs have been written and implemented. This ideographic approach to curriculum development has resulted in a continuously expanding data base that presently contains more than 600 programs relevant to preschool and school, home, and community settings. Some illustrative content areas are: activity schedules, community participation, expressive language, handwriting, keyboard skills, leisure skills, motor imitation, peer interaction, physical education, reading, receptive language, self-care, social skills, and toileting. The curriculum reflects almost two decades of experience in programming for children with autism, and although some programs are suitable for many youngsters, most programs stored on disk are revised to reflect the learning characteristics and stimulus preferences of specific children.

Some instructional programs are based on commercially available curricula—for example, the *Edmark Reading Program* (1977), *The Sensible Pencil: A Handwriting Program* (1985), and *Functional Speech and Language Training for the Severely Handicapped* (Guess, Sailor, & Baer, 1976). Others are written with reference to our own, or others' published research—for example, using prepositions (McGee, Krantz,

& McClannahan, 1985), using pronouns (Lovaas, 1977), verbally initiating to teachers (Halle, Baer, & Spradlin, 1981) and peers (Krantz & McClannahan, 1993), and reporting temporally remote past events (Krantz, Zalenski, Hall, Fenske, & McClannahan, 1981). And many programs such as riding a tricycle, remaining in a designated play area, and interacting with a new sibling, are straightforward applications of behavioral technology.

As computer-based instructional programs have become available, selected software has been included in the curriculum [e.g., *First Words* (Wilson & Fox, 1982), *Touch 'N' Write* (1989), and *IBM SpeechViewer Application Software* (1988)] that targets voice volume, vowel accuracy, sustained vocalization, and inflection. Because a large proportion of the commercially available software does not include the detailed task analyses, branch programs, or measurement systems that are important in intervention for children with autism, other computer-based instructional programs have been developed at the Institute; for example, alphabet letter recognition, counting, and spelling programs.

Children enrolled in the Institute's preschool do not occupy self-contained classrooms; instead, their daily schedules call for many transitions across rooms and activity areas and across staff members. This strategy is used to promote the transfer of new skills. For example, an expressive-language skill acquired during a verbal-imitation session may be requested by a different teacher during outdoor play; lunch time may be an opportunity to probe peer imitations taught during the morning; counting responses that are the topic of a pre-math class may be targeted for incidental teaching during toy play; or a response that is incompatible with stereotypies may be measured and rewarded in the bathroom as well as the hallway. Stokes and Baer (1977) noted that "discriminated behavior changes may well be the rule if generalization is not specifically programmed" (p. 365); this observation is unquestionably relevant to children with autism. Scheduling children to enter multiple settings and to encounter multiple instructors creates many opportunities to assess and promote generalization across settings, persons, responses, and time.

Children do not have the same schedules of activities—instructional targets are selected with reference to each child's skills and skill deficits (Dunlap & Robbins, 1991) as well as with consideration for families' interests and concerns. Table 7.1 displays representative schedules for three preschoolers.

Although individuality is emphasized, most youngsters' initial instructional programs share common features. Learning to follow simple

TABLE 7.1. Sample Daily Schedules for Three Preschoolers

Time	Heather	Duncan	Justin
		Child	
8:50	Photographic activity schedule	Handwriting	Answering questions
9:10	Expressive language (nouns)	Verbal imitation of words	Expressive language (nouns)
9:30	Following complex directions	Conversation skills	Number-object correspondence
9:45	Receptive language (nouns)	Verbal imitation of words	Counting to a number
10:00	Edmark Reading	Following complex directions	Using playground equipment
10:15	Undressing	Using construction toys	Riding a tricycle
10:30	Using playground equipment	Using playground equipment	Edmark Prereading
10:45	Social initiations	Social initiations	Edmark Prereading
11:00	Providing personal information	Reading (computer software)	Photographic activity schedule
11:15	Following complex directions	Following complex directions	
11:30	Lunch	Lunch	Lunch
12:00	Verbal imitation of words	Verbal imitation of words	
12:15	Story (Expressive language)	Story (Expressive language)	Motor imitation
12:40	Receptive language (nouns)	Receptive language (nouns)	Expressive language (nouns)
1:00	Receptive language (verbs)	Receptive language (verbs)	Pre-handwriting
1:25	Alphabet letter identification	Expressive language (nouns)	Using construction toys
1:45	Pre-handwriting	Dressing	Matching skills (computer software)
2:00			Pre-handwriting (computer software)

directions (e.g., "come here," "look at me," "stand up," "sit down," and "hands down") is a necessary prerequisite to most other learning tasks. Acquiring motor and verbal imitation skills promotes repertoires that are incompatible with stereotypies and contributes to the development of expressive language; in addition, establishing generalized imitation within and across motor and verbal response classes may facilitate later acquisition in many skill areas (Young, Krantz, McClannahan, & Poulson, 1992).

Typically, initial programming also focuses on matching tasks and then on picture-object correspondence skills. When these goals are achieved, children learn to follow photographic activity schedules that enable them to work and play independently, to change activities, and to move across settings without verbal prompts from adults. Schedule-following skills are taught using *only* manual prompts, delivered from behind the child; use of a most-to-least prompt sequence results in a relatively errorless teaching procedure, and prompts are faded as quickly as possible.

After a child learns to open his/her picture schedule book, point to a photograph, obtain the depicted materials, complete the scheduled activity, put materials away, and turn to the next photograph, pictures are resequenced to ensure that the child is not merely following a now-familiar routine but is "reading" the pictorial cues. After a youngster achieves a high level of accuracy in following the frequently resequenced schedule, new photographs (of previously taught activities) are introduced (cf. MacDuff, Krantz, & McClannahan, 1993). An initial photographic schedule for a preschooler might include photographs of a frame-tray puzzle, nesting cups, a picture-matching task, a stacking toy, and a snack; upon completion of the five depicted activities, the teacher provides praise and access to preferred stimuli. The length of the schedule is gradually extended, and the teacher's presence is gradually faded.

Photographic activity schedules (and written schedules, if children acquire reading skills) provide an excellent format for teaching youngsters to make choices among different activities, to manage changes in daily routines, and to initiate interactions with others. In addition, such schedules promote generalization of new skills from the preschool to home and community settings (Krantz, MacDuff, & McClannahan, 1993).

Preschool programs place a strong emphasis on language development. The Institute does not employ specialists (e.g., occupational therapists, recreational therapists, speech therapists); instead, all intervention personnel are trained to implement children's individualized programs and to teach receptive and expressive language skills in *every* activity of the school day. Thus, not only classroom activities but also toilet training sessions, transitions from one activity to another, outdoor play, and lunch times are occasions for expanding children's receptive and expressive language repertoires. Language instruction encompasses discrete trial, incidental teaching, time delay, and video modeling procedures (Charlop & Milstein, 1989; Krantz, MacDuff, Wadstrom, & McClannahan, 1991).

Of 32 children served by the preschool, 27 had no functional expressive language at program entry; presently, their levels of performance range from the use of labels as mands to age-appropriate verbal repertoires. Because of these outcomes, the Institute does not teach manual signs, which address specialized audiences; however, some children use communication boards, computerized communication boards (e.g., AllTalk), Canon Communicators, or Apple computer keyboards while expressive language skills are being acquired.

Research on children's uses of standard communication boards and communication boards that feature electronic "voices" showed that when both devices displayed identical pictures of the participants' preferred stimuli, the not-yet-verbal children used a standard communication board and an electronic communication board (TouchTalker) with equal frequency. But when given a choice, the two participants in the study more often used the device with the voice synthesizer (McClannahan, Zalenski, Franzoni, & Krantz, 1987). It may also be noted that, although most children at the Institute use computer keyboards for a variety of learning activities, and although keyboard use is typically taught via manual prompts that are gradually faded, we have never observed the phenomena described by proponents of "facilitated communication."

Preschoolers who acquire necessary receptive and expressive language skills are quickly advanced to preacademic and academic programs. Reading receives special emphasis; development of textual behavior (Skinner, 1957) is viewed as an important part of a comprehensive program to promote verbal behavior. Art (e.g., coloring, cutting, and pasting), arithmetic, handwriting, and social play skills are addressed as soon as children have achieved the prerequisite skills in preparation for public school enrollment.

During the 1991–92 school year, a total of 152 intervention programs were delivered to six preschoolers during their school day; this represents a mean of 25 programs per child. Not all programs were implemented simultaneously—some were discontinued after children mastered the target skills and were supplanted by different curriculum.

Of the 152 programs, 148 were skill acquisition programs and four were designed to decrease inappropriate behavior such as tantrums and stereotypies. Initially, all behavior problems are addressed via rich schedules of reinforcement. Children who engage in finger play or hand flapping are taught to carry toys and book bags, to put their hands in their pockets when not manipulating learning materials, or to hold and lower the toilet seat after flushing the toilet. Children who display toe walking are rewarded for "heels down," and children who aggress or self-injure are rewarded for "hands down," "good sitting," and many other alternate responses. Most dysfunctional responses decrease as a function of the systematic reinforcement of appropriate behavior. But when serious behavior problems do not respond to positive reinforcement procedures, other procedures (e.g., response cost, chair time out, facial screening) are evaluated.

ASSESSING PROGRESS

A written protocol (McClannahan & Krantz, 1992) defines an individualized program as a document in a child's record that includes at minimum: (a) a written response definition that provides an objective description of a target behavior, (b) a written description of a measurement procedure, (c) a written description of an instruction or intervention procedure, and (d) a graph or other form of data summary that displays levels of behavior over time. The protocol also defines four categories that are used to evaluate the effects of individualized programs: (a) behavior change in a desired direction, (b) no behavior change, (c) behavior change in an undesired direction, or (d) behavior change cannot be ascertained.

Institute staff members and their trainers regularly use this instrument, and the results are reported and discussed at weekly staff meetings. In addition, at the time of each staff member's performance evaluation, the evaluator uses the protocol to score all of the intervention programs for which that staff member is responsible, and the results are summarized as part of the trainee's post-evaluation feedback. Finally, at the end of each program year, a recognized expert who is not affiliated with the Institute is invited to use the protocol to evaluate intervention programs.

In the 1991–92 program year, an independent evaluator reviewed 38% of all instructional programs (a sample drawn by the evaluator) and 100% of all behavior-reduction programs. Of the preschool programs reviewed, 100% were scored as meeting the criteria used to define an individualized program, and 86% were scored as displaying behavior change in a desired direction. Pairs of professionals, using this assessment procedure, have typically achieved appropriate levels of interobserver agreement. And repeated measures, representing successive years of assessment, now serve as bench marks against which to compare the current year's data. On the basis of more than a decade of experience with this evaluation process, we expect that on each annual assessment, 80% to 90% of intervention programs will be scored as achieving behavior change in a desired direction.

INTEGRATION: A COMPLEX ISSUE

All of the preschoolers served by the Institute have lived with one or both parents in apartments, condominiums, or single-family dwellings typical of the residences of other families in our state. A large majority of the children have nondisabled siblings, and virtually all of them are members of families who (like other families) enjoy visiting parks; local restaurants; community events; or the homes of friends, grandparents, or other relatives. But at the outset of intervention, none of the 32 preschoolers displayed systematic visual attending to other children; none interacted appropriately with parents, grandparents, or other relatives; none shared toys or engaged in cooperative play with siblings; none imitated peers; and none participated in community outings without displaying behavior problems. Prior to intake, many of them attended local programs for typical children or children with special needs but were disenrolled because either they did not progress or program personnel were unable to manage their atypical performances. In effect, repertoires associated with autism segregated them from others, including their own parents, brothers, and sisters. Under these circumstances, the Institute's preschool program for children with autism focuses on building skills that enable children to become participants in family life and to transition to public school classrooms as soon as possible.

Specific behavioral characteristics are identified as prerequisites for transition to public school settings. These include: exhibiting sustained engagement with learning and leisure materials, systematically following adults' instruction, responding favorably to delayed reinforcement procedures (e.g., behavioral contracts, home-school notes, allowances), displaying responses not specifically taught (e.g., generative speech or imitation of peers' play behavior), and generalization of new skills to another setting. In addition, very low or zero levels of inappropriate behavior (e.g., tantrums, self-injury, aggression, stereotypies) are viewed as a precondition for transition.

Early in the process of preparing for transition, "safe" preliminary settings are identified. Summer day camps, church schools, neighborhood play groups, after-school recreation programs, gymnastics or dance classes, and similar activities offer opportunities to assess children's group participation and to design remedial programs without risking unsuccessful experiences in children's local school systems.

When children achieve readiness for transition, parents, representatives of the local school district, and Institute personnel meet to discuss placement options. Subsequently, visits are made to potential kindergarten, elementary, or special education classrooms. Whenever children's skills permit, they are placed in regular, rather than special education classes, and whenever possible, classroom teachers are not informed of the diagnosis of autism (cf. Lovaas, 1987).

Efforts are made to select classrooms in children's own school districts on the bases of class size, teachers' skills, and teachers' willingness to participate in the transition process. It should be noted, however, that placement decisions ultimately rest with public schools; Institute personnel make recommendations and offer assistance but have no formal authority to determine placement arrangements.

After a public school classroom is identified, visits are made to observe the teacher's instructions and the children's activities and daily routines. Then, skills that will be called for in the target classroom are prioritized and taught before the transition begins. Typically, the curriculum used in the public school classroom is introduced to the child at the Institute, before he or she enters the new setting. In addition, the youngster is taught many specific responses that will be expected—how to request a bathroom pass; how to open a locker or use a cubby; how to correctly articulate the teacher's name; how to manipulate a book bag, pencil case, or gym bag; how to use classroom materials with which he or she may not be familiar; and how to put materials away. Concurrently, the child gains further experience with a home-school note or behavioral contract that mediates increasingly delayed rewards for appropriate performance.

When the transition begins, the child usually attends the target class for a few hours each day and returns to the Institute for the remainder of the day to rehearse new responses that are called for in the public school. Initially, the youngster is continuously accompanied by an Institute staff member who collects observational data that are used to structure teaching activities at the Institute and consults with the classroom teacher about the child's academic work and use of the home-school note; this person's presence is faded as quickly as possible, first to the periphery of the classroom and then to the hall. As the child's time in attendance increases, the observation schedule gradually decreases to an aperiodic schedule of unobtrusive monitoring and ultimately to a schedule of telephone contacts with parents and the classroom teacher. Of course, the emergence of performance problems results in immediate adjustments in the classroom visit schedule and, in some cases, supplemental instructional sessions at the Institute.

Depending upon children's acquisition rates and characteristics of public school classrooms, transitions may extend over weeks or months. When children's full-time attendance in target classrooms is uneventful, follow-up contacts initiated by the Institute gradually decline to an annual schedule; follow-up services remain available at the request of parents or school personnel. In some cases, no follow-up services are requested after transitions are successfully completed; in other cases, youngsters receive follow-up services over a period of several years. Although there is no mandatory funding mechanism to support these services, some school districts pay for transition and follow-up programs.

FAMILY SUPPORT

Occasional parent meetings are designed as social occasions that enable parents to meet other parents and to interact with Institute staff members. But due to the diversity of children's repertoires, services to families are entirely individualized (McClannahan, Krantz, & McGee, 1982). Each family is assigned a home programmer (a teacher or therapist) who regularly visits their home; during the 1991–92 school year, home programmers serving preschoolers averaged 28 visits per family.

In discussions with their home programmer, parents identify and prioritize their goals for their child. Subsequently, the home programmer and his/her trainer develop individualized programs to help the child acquire the target skills; these programs are initially implemented in the preschool. When observational data indicate that the child is displaying the desired behavior in the treatment setting, the program is introduced at home. The home programmer describes and models the intervention procedures and teaches the parents to use them.

Because children's programs are implemented in the treatment setting before they are implemented at home, and because generalization of new skills from the preschool to home is specifically programmed, parents achieve a high success rate. During the 1991–92 school year, parents of preschoolers implemented 37 home intervention programs. An outside expert reviewed 21 of the 37 programs (a 57% sample drawn by the evaluator) using the evaluation protocol described earlier (McClannahan & Krantz, 1992). All programs reviewed conformed to the definition of an individualized program, and 86% were scored as achieving favorable behavior change for children. These programs addressed toilet training, receptive and expressive language, play skills, direction following, dressing skills, interaction with family members, tantrums, stereotypies, and learning to follow photographic activity schedules that included a variety of social, self-help, and home-living activities.

Some families devote more time to home treatment than others; some are interested in data collection, and others are not; some acquire intervention skills more rapidly than others. But because services to families are individualized, all participate at some level. If both parents are employed and hire a sitter, the parents and the surrogate may be taught to implement the child's home treatment programs. If parents enjoy participating in treatment but are uninterested in performance measurement, the home programmer may assume responsibility for data collection and/or may use a daily phone call to invite parents' reports on the presence or absence of critical responses. Some families concurrently implement a dozen intervention programs, and others choose to address one issue at a time.

The individualized services that facilitate parents' participation in treatment require a cadre of skilled home programmers. Thus, teachers and therapists receive specific training in how to provide family support. For example, they are taught how to build relationships with families and how to develop agendas for home visits. Novice home programmers are accompanied by trainers until they have acquired the relevant skills.

Subsequently, trainers review home programming agendas before each home visit, participate in revisions if necessary, and help home programmers rehearse requisite skills.

TREATMENT OUTCOMES

Of 32 preschoolers served by the Institute, 6 are presently enrolled in the preschool, 12 have transistioned to public schools or are in transition (1), 12 are enrolled in the Institute's school program, and 2 withdrew from the program. Because of the small N, the percentage of preschoolers successfully transitioned to public school classrooms has varied considerably from year to year—from 46% to 67%. Calculation of the percentage of successfully transitioned children does not include children who were withdrawn from the program before an outcome had been achieved, and does not include children who are presently enrolled in the preschool.

Time in treatment for the 11 children who entered the program before 60 months of age and who completed transitions to public schools ranges from 9 to 141 months (mean = 39 months). Five of the 11 families requested and received follow-up services from the Institute after their children's transitions were complete, and two continued to receive follow-up services in the 1991–92 school year. Two of the children are lost to follow-up contacts because their families relocated and their current addresses are unknown.

The eight males and one female still available for follow up presently range in age from 6 to 20 years; the youngest recently completed kindergarten, and the two oldest are in college. Six are in regular education, and three are in special education classes; of the regular education students, two received special services in the form of individual or group counseling after their transitions to public school. All school-aged children continue to live at home with their own families; the two college students now live away from home. One college student has a part-time job; none of the other young people is yet employed.

Follow-up data have sometimes been gathered via mailed questionnaire and sometimes by telephone interview. During the 1991–92 school year, telephone interviews were preceded by letters to parents informing them that a phone call would soon be made and providing a 7-point rating scale that they were asked to use during telephone interviews (see Table 7.2).

Eight mothers and one father participated in the structured interviews. After inquiring about the child's place of residence, school placement and grade level, employment status, and use of special services, the interviewer asked the parent to use the rating scale to respond to the following questions: (a) How satisfied are you with your child's current participation in your family and in family activities? (b) How satisfied are you that your child has been able to make friends and to participate in social activities with his/her peers? (c) How satisfied are you with your child's academic performance, that is, that s/he is doing as well as you feel s/he should? (d) How satisfied are you with your child's recreational activities, that is, that s/he participates in sports or hobbies, or finds other appropriate ways to use leisure time? (e) How satisfied are you with your child's self-care skills, that his/her personal appearance is as good as other young people's of his/her age? and (f) How satisfied are you with your child's present quality of life—that s/he is happy, well adjusted, and appreciated by others? Responses to these questions are shown in Table 7.2.

Parents were most satisfied with their children's participation in family life, their academic performances, and their present quality of life, and least satisfied with their abilities to make friends and participate in social activities with peers—deficits characteristic of autism.

It would be interesting to know how these parents' ratings would compare with ratings by parents whose children never received the diagnosis of autism. Perhaps parents of children who have no history of developmental disability are not completely satisfied with their offsprings' personal appearance or use of leisure time. It would be useful to gather competitive data in conjunction with future follow-up contacts.

FUTURE RESEARCH AND PRACTICE

Several investigators (e.g., Freeman, Rahbar, Ritvo, Bice, Yokota, & Ritvo, 1991; Gillberg, 1991; Lovaas, Koegel, Simmons, & Long, 1973) have identified IQ score as a predictor of outcome for children with autism, but outcomes for children who are initially unable to obtain basal scores on standardized assessment instruments are rarely discussed. Our experience suggests that preschoolers' preliminary failure to obtain basal

TABLE 7.2. Parents' Satisfaction with Treatment Outcomes

Item	Number of Parents Assigning a Satisfaction Rating of							
	1	2	3	4	5	6	7	Mean
1 Participation in family					4	1	4	6.0
2 Making friends		1	2		1	4	1	4.9
3 Academic performance					1	6	2	6.1
4 Recreation activities			2	1		5	1	5.2
5 Personal appearance	1	1			1	3	3	5.4
6 Quality of life					3	3	3	6.0

Note. On this 7-point, Likert-type scale, 1 = completely dissatisfied, 2 = dissatisfied, 3 = slightly dissatisfied, 4 = neither satisfied nor dissatisfied, 5 = slightly satisfied, 6 = satisfied, and 7 = completely satisfied.

scores on instruments such as the *Stanford–Binet* and the *Peabody Picture Vocabulary Test* may be a weak predictor; on subsequent assessments, some children's scores move from severe to moderate to mild retardation, and some youngsters ultimately score in the normal range. It is likely that the diminution of stereotypies as well as the acquisition of functional language (Schreibman, 1988) mediate these results. Data on treatment outcomes for children who do not attain basal scores on initial tests would be of interest.

In addition, more data are needed on the relationships between known etiologies and treatment outcomes. Among the 12 children who enrolled in the preschool when they were less than 60 months of age and remain in treatment, there is one case in which autism is associated with tuberous sclerosis, one in which autism is associated with fragile X syndrome, and two others in which epilepsy appeared during childhood (cf. Gillberg, 1991). None of these syndromes has been noted among children who successfully transitioned to public school classrooms.

In practice, continuity of treatment appears to be important. Some children who were unable to participate in public school classrooms at the end of their preschool years continued to receive systematic intervention in the Institute's school and later made the transition to their local school districts at the ages of 6, 7, or even (in one case) 15. Disjunctions in programming might have impeded these positive outcomes.

It has been noted that contingent reinforcement (e.g., providing praise, edibles, and preferred activities) is the single procedure most frequently addressed in staff training for teachers of severely developmentally disabled students (Reid, McCarn, & Green, 1988). But an expanding behavioral literature on antecedent variables—time delay, child-initiated instruction, stimulus shaping, video modelling, environmental modification, and use of pictorial prompts—suggests that improvements in treatment efficacy may be achieved if we pursue these lines of research and if research results are included in staff training programs.

ACKNOWLEDGMENTS

The authors thank Edward C. Fenske, Education Program Coordinator, and Stanley Zalenski, Head Teacher. They have made key contributions to the progress of preschoolers with autism.

REFERENCES

American Psychiatric Association. (1987). *Diagnostic and statistical manual of mental disorders.* (3rd ed., revised). Washington, DC: American Psychiatric Association.

Charlop, M. H., & Milstein, J. P. (1989). Teaching autistic children conversational speech using video modelling. *Journal of Applied Behavior Analysis, 22,* 275–285.

Dunlap, G. D., & Robbins, F. R. (1991). Current perspectives in service delivery for young children with autism. *Comprehensive Mental Health Care, 1,* 177–194.

Dunn, L. M., & Dunn, L. M. (1981). *Peabody Picture Vocabulary Test–Revised: Manual for Forms L and M.* Circle Pines, MN: American Guidance Service.

Edmark reading program. (1977). Bellevue, WA: Edmark Corporation.

Fenske, E. C., Zalenski, S., Krantz, P. J., & McClannahan, L. E. (1985). Age at intervention and treatment outcome for autistic children in a comprehensive intervention program. *Analysis and Intervention in Developmental Disabilities, 5,* 49–58.

Freeman, B. J., Rahbar, B., Ritvo, E. R., Bice, T. L., Yokota, A., & Ritvo, R.

(1991). The stability of cognitive and behavioral parameters in autism: A twelve-year prospective study. *Journal of the American Academy of Child and Adolescent Psychiatry, 30,* 479–482.

Gillberg, C. (1991). Outcome in autism and autistic-like conditions. *Journal of the American Academy of Child and Adolescent Psychiatry, 30,* 375–382.

Guess, D., Sailor, W., & Baer, D. M. (1976). *Functional speech and language training for the severely handicapped.* Lawrence, KS: H & H Enterprises, Inc.

Halle, J. W., Baer, D. M., & Spradlin, J. E. (1981). Teachers' generalized use of delay as a stimulus control procedure to increase language use in handicapped children. *Journal of Applied Behavior Analysis, 14,* 389–409.

IBM Personal System/2 Independence Series SpeechViewer Application Software (1988). Atlanta, GA: IBM National Support Center for Persons with Disabilities.

Krantz, P. J., MacDuff, G. S., Wadstrom, O., & McClannahan, L. E. (1991). Using video with developmentally disabled learners. In P. W. Dowrick (Ed.), *Practical guide to using video in the behavioral sciences* (pp. 256–266). New York: John Wiley & Sons, Inc.

Krantz, P. J., & McClannahan, L. E. (1993). Teaching children with autism to initiate to peers: Effects of a script-fading procedure. *Journal of Applied Behavior Analysis, 26,* 121–132.

Krantz, P. J., MacDuff, M. T., & McClannahan, L. E. (1993). Programming participation in family activities for children with autism: Parents' use of photographic activity schedules. *Journal of Applied Behavior Analysis, 26,* 137–138.

Krantz, P. J., Zalenski, S., Hall, L. J., Fenske, E. C., & McClannahan, L. E. (1981). Teaching complex language to autistic children. *Analysis and Intervention in Developmental Disabilities, 1,* 259–297.

Lovaas, O. I. (1977). *The autistic child: Language development through behavior modification.* New York: John Wiley & Sons, Inc.

Lovaas, O. I. (1987). Behavioral treatment and normal educational and intellectual functioning in young autistic children. *Journal of Consulting and Clinical Psychology, 55,* 3–9.

Lovaas, O. I., Koegel, R., Simmons, J. Q., & Long, J. S. (1973). Some generalization and follow-up measures on autistic children in behavior therapy. *Journal of Applied Behavior Analysis, 6,* 131–165.

MacDuff, G. S., Krantz, P. J., & McClannahan, L. E. (1993). Teaching children with autism to use photographic activity schedules: Maintenance and generalization of complex response chains. *Journal of Applied Behavior Analysis, 26,* 89–97.

McClannahan, L. E., & Krantz, P. J. (1985). Some next steps in rights protection for the developmental disabled. *School Psychology Review, 14,* 143–149.

McClannahan, L. E., & Krantz, P. J. (1992). *Evaluating intervention for persons with severe developmental disabilities.* Unpublished manuscript.

McClannahan, L. E., Krantz, P. J., & McGee, G. G. (1982). Parents as therapists for autistic children: A model for effective parent training. *Analysis and Intervention in Developmental Disabilities, 2,* 223–252.

McClannahan, L. E., Zalenski, S., Franzoni, N., & Krantz, P. J. (1987). *Teaching autistic children to communicate without adult prompts: Voice synthesizer versus communication board.* Unpublished manuscript.

McGee, G. G., Krantz, P. J., & McClannahan, L. E. (1985). The facilitative effects of incidental teaching on preposition use by autistic children. *Journal of Applied Behavior Analysis, 18,* 17–31.

Reid, D. H., McCarn, J. E., & Green, C. W. (1988). Staff training and management in school programs for severely developmentally disabled students. In M. D. Powers (Ed.), *Expanding systems of service delivery for persons with developmental disabilities* (pp. 199–215). Baltimore: Paul H. Brookes.

Schreibman, L. (1988). *Autism.* Newbury Park, CA: Sage Publications, Inc.

Sensible pencil: A handwriting program (1985). Birmingham, AL: Ebsco Curriculum Materials.

Skinner, B. F. (1957). *Verbal behavior.* New York: Appleton-Century-Crofts.

Sparrow, S. S., Balla, D. A., & Cicchetti, D. V. (1984). *Vineland Adaptive Behavior Scales, Interview Edition, Survey form Manual.* Circle Pines, MN: American Guidance Service.

Stokes, T. F., & Baer, D. M. (1977). An implicit technology of generalization. *Journal of Applied Behavior Analysis, 10,* 349–367.

Thorndike, R. L., Hagen, E. R., & Sattler, J. M. (1986). *The Stanford-Binet Intelligence Scale* (4th ed.). Chicago, IL: Riverside Publishing Co.

Touch 'N' Write (1989). Pleasantville, NY: Sunburst Communications, Inc.

Wilson, M. S., & Fox, B. J. (1982). *First words.* Winooski, VT: Laureate Learning Systems, Inc.

Young, J. M., Krantz, P. J., McClannahan, L. E., & Poulson, C. L. (1992). *Generalized imitation and response class formation in children with autism.* Unpublished manuscript.

Zimmerman, I. L., Steiner, V. G., & Pond, R. E. (1979). *Preschool Language Scale Manual.* Columbus, OH: Charles E. Merrill.

Chapter 8

The Walden Preschool

GAIL G. McGEE, TERESA DALY, and HEIDI A. JACOBS

Walden, a laboratory preschool, offers early education, social integration, and incidental teaching to children with autism and typical children. The name "Walden" reflects a blend of Skinner's (1948) utopian education with a natural developmental approach symbolized by Thoreau (1847). The curriculum is grounded in the assumption that preschool education for all young children should appropriately concentrate on language and social development and that incidental teaching procedures offer an ideal medium for accomplishing the goals of integration. A distinctive approach to behavior management emphasizes the promotion of engagement by highlighting children's preferred materials and activities. Finally, active family collaboration is achieved by offering meaningful parental choices.

The full-day, full-year preschool program is provided in the context of a university-based lab school, which makes it possible to address questions of what is possible under nearly ideal conditions. The program was originally established in 1985 as the Walden Learning Center, and was affiliated with the Department of Psychology at the University of Massachusetts at Amherst (effective August of 1991, the May Institute contracted with the University of Massachusetts to assume clinical responsibility for the Amherst classroom). In the Fall of 1991, the Walden project relocated to the Department of Psychiatry and Behavioral Sciences at the Emory University School of Medicine, where it is a component of a comprehensive Emory Autism Resource Center. The new preschool classroom, the Walden Preschool at Emory, opened in February 1992.

The program originated as a systematic replication of the Toddler Center Model for typical children's day care (O'Brien, Porterfield, Herbert-Jackson, & Risley, 1979). Of key importance was the model's organization of staff and setting to maximize naturally-occurring teaching opportunities (Allen & Hart, 1984; Doke & Risley, 1972; Twardosz, Cataldo, & Risley, 1974). Hallmarks of the model are an overlapping activity schedule and designated teaching zones (LeLaurin & Risley, 1972; Risley & Favell, 1979). However, substantial adaptations have been needed to meet the needs of children with autism, to serve an integrated group spanning a broad age range, and to incorporate new findings on incidental teaching and peer interactions.

From the outset, overlapping grant funding has been available to foster research and development activities. Laboratory resources have made it feasible to obtain empirical answers to questions that arise in the preschool, and the preschool has provided for practical field tests of research findings. An additional benefit of accompanying research support has been the capability for securing expert input on preschool issues, and colleagues have responded with interest and substance across the years.

Vigorous start-up efforts were also invested in obtaining community input, both in the original (Sulzer-Azaroff, Jones, & McGee, 1986) and new program sites. Community Advisory Boards have played key roles in ensuring program responsiveness to both rural (Western Massachusetts) and urban (Atlanta) concerns. Relocation also required adaptation to vastly different political and philosophical orientations in the Northeast and the South. For example, the original decision to integrate the program was in response to community input that integration of children with disabilities was desirable, although at that time children with autism were not yet being integrated into the areas' public school preschool programs. Six years later, social integration continues to be an uncommon practice in most of the South. In Georgia, however, there is rigorous attention to educational outcomes, whereas in Western Massachusetts a more laissez-faire developmental approach was the community norm. The program is responding by elaborating the academic preparation of typical children as well as of children with special needs.

The cost per child with autism for the Walden preschool approached $24,000 in the most recent program year, although the funding mechanisms have varied considerably across program locations. In Massachusetts, state law and funding reimbursements made it possible for local school districts to support full tuition and travel costs for children with autism. In Georgia, parents pay an annual tuition of $10,920, plus the cost of a fee-for-service family program, and the Emory Autism Resource Center subsidizes additional costs (via funds raised by parents and private donors). In both locations, parents of typical children pay rates comparable to other area preschools, with some scholarship arrangements. Regional differences in funding mechanisms have also yielded a program impact. While accessibility is an obvious problem where private tuitions are required, accountability is especially strong when paying parents regularly come to observe the preschool as they deliver and pick up their children.

Healthy to the goals of integration, the primary regulatory standards in both states have been monitored by the day care licensing agencies. The program is classified as a private preschool, and day care regulations for typical children have been applied to all children. Although quality programs for children with special needs require that such standards be exceeded in many areas (e.g., adult-to-child ratios), environmental normalization has been encouraged, and accepted special education practices have been challenged (e.g., staff is prohibited from using a "disapproving tone" to correct toileting accidents). When the program was established in Massachusetts, there was a regulatory limit of 15 children per classroom, so the program opted for seven children with autism and eight typical children. Expansion of the limit to 18 children in Georgia permits the inclusion of a larger majority of typical children.

PARTICIPATING CHILDREN

To date, Walden has enrolled a total of 83 children. A breakdown of population characteristics is presented in Table 8.1. Of these children, 28% were from low-income families, and 39% represented minority groups (predominately African-American and Asian).

TABLE 8.1.   Characteristics of Population Served

	Children with Autism	Typical Children
Sex	21 male	30 male
	6 female	26 female
Average Age at Entry (range)	3 years, 8 months (2–6 to 5–6)	3 years, 8 months (2–8 to 5–2)
Average IQ at Entry (range)	57 (plus 7 untestable) (<29–91)	112 (90–134)

INITIAL SCREENING AND ASSESSMENT

Children with autism have received at least one (and preferably two) diagnoses of autism by independent physicians or psychologists who are experienced diagnosticians. The Program Director and Preschool Coordinator complete a screening process that consists of a review of records, a semi-structured interview with the parents, and direct observation of the child that is accompanied by administration of the *Childhood Autism Rating Scale* (CARS, Schopler, Reichler, De Vellis, & Daly, 1988). Cumulative information is then compiled and reviewed for documentation of the presence of the behavioral characteristics of autism, based on DSM-III-R criteria (American Psychiatric Association, 1987) and based on evidence of generalization deficits, overselectivity, and developmental scatter across skill areas. No child with autism has been rejected based on IQ, perceived severity, or the presence of documented neurological findings. There is a preadmission understanding that children may not be maintained on psychotropic or other behavior control medications while enrolled in the preschool.

There had been no screening of typical children until the relocation to Georgia, where the Advisory Board suggested that the integration would attract parents of children with a variety of mild disabilities. At this time, an informal classroom visit by prospective typical children is used to screen for age-appropriate language and social skills, so that the children can readily serve as peer models for children with disabilities. However, children with English as a second language have been accepted throughout the program's history, with experience indicating that these young typical children rapidly become English-fluent. It may also be noted that in university-based settings, participation by gifted "typical" students is common.

For purposes of describing participants in collateral research projects, all children are tested within 6 months of admission with the following standardized instruments: *Stanford-Binet,* 4th edition (Thorndike, Hagen, & Sattler, 1986) (previously, the Stanford-Binet, form L-M, or the Kaufman Assessment Battery for Children), the *Peabody Picture Vocabulary Test–Revised* (Dunn & Dunn, 1981), and the *Expressive One-Word Picture Vocabulary Test* (Gardner, 1990). To expedite educational planning, all children are also assessed on the *Brigance Inventory of Early Development* (Brigance, 1978), and children with autism are evaluated on the *Vineland Adaptive Behavior Scales* (Sparrow, Balla, & Cicchetti, (1984) (parents as respondents). Comprehensive reinforcer assessments (Mason, McGee, Farmer-Dougan, & Risley, 1988) are administered to children with autism at entry and monthly thereafter.

Most important for progress assessment are objective behavioral measures taken from an ongoing videotaped database, which is a luxury afforded by lab-school status. Each child is videotaped daily for 5 minutes, according to a systematic sampling procedure arranged to track children across different activities, times of day, and days of the week. The unique feature of the video database is that there are no contrived observational conditions; children are videotaped at preset times wherever they happen to be, doing whatever they happen to be doing. Videotapes are scored by a highly trained research team, which obtains objective, reliable measures of more than three dozen language, social, and engagement variables.

PRESCHOOL PERSONNEL

The Director and an outstanding team of graduate and undergraduate students developed the program in Massachusetts. Eight psychology graduates (most of whom had been with the project throughout much of their college preparation) relocated with the Director to Atlanta, where they have been joined by additional talent.

The Program Director is a Licensed Clinical Psychologist with a background in behavior analysis and 12 years experience in treatment of children with autism. Among the most crucial roles served by the

Director are direct clinical planning of treatment for children with autism and primary responsibility for the quality of education for all enrolled students.

The preschool staff comprises a Preschool Coordinator (who serves on-line as Lead Teacher for part of each day), backup Lead Teachers, and teachers. The Preschool Coordinator is responsible for day-to-day management of the program. The position requires astute clinical judgment, effective training skills, efficient administration abilities, and a superb sense of parent and public relations. The Preschool Coordinator must be experienced in both behavior analysis and the Walden approach, and Lead Teachers must be proficient in all teaching and training routines.

A 1:3 adult-to-child ratio is maintained throughout the day, so that at any given time, a Lead Teacher and four to five teachers are working with the children. Due to the intensity of the teaching demands, "on the floor" time is limited to 4 hours per day for each staff member.

Backgrounds of the preschool staff have varied across program years, which has afforded interdisciplinary enrichment. Staff have presented undergraduate to post-doctoral training in Psychology (Clinical, Developmental, Educational, Experimental, and School), Early Childhood Education, Special Education, Communication Disorders, Occupational Therapy, Theater, etc. Selection is based on "Peace Corps" levels of enthusiasm, energy, patience, and professional motivation; these qualities are easier to select for than to train. Specific credentials and experience are less important due to the availability of a rigorous program of training and supervision. In fact, the training opportunities have yielded a largely overqualified staff over the years.

Significant support staff from collateral projects include family program and research personnel. The Family Coordinator and Research Coordinator must be experienced in the classroom, and they contribute directly to clinical planning, staff training, and child instruction. Collateral projects permit full-time employment for part-time teachers, as well as provide varied training opportunities for personnel. At Emory, the program has backup expertise from the Emory Autism Resource Center, including the Medical Director who is a Psychiatrist and Pediatrician, and the Community Consultation Director, who is a Social Worker and doctoral-level Special Educator.

The Walden curriculum was developed with the assistance of an array of interdisciplinary consultants, including ongoing input from several nationally recognized experts. Consultation is usually secured in the form of program development advice, based on the premise that children with autism need specialty input blended into their daily activities. However, speech and language expertise has been arranged on a continuous basis to ensure regular monitoring of implementation of the language curriculum.

STAFF PREPARATION AND SUPERVISION

The acquisition and maintenance of new skills is accomplished via intensive "hands-on" training and feedback, with consistency of performance ensured through ongoing performance appraisal (Morrier & Daly, 1991). Preschool staff are trained to mastery in every routine they will be assigned. For example, all teachers are trained in zone-based routines such as managing free-play, conducting small group activities, and serving snack or lunch. Based on assignments, some are trained for specialized zones such as dramatic play, peer incidental teaching, or social games. All teachers are also prepared in procedural proficiency, such as teaching independence, preventing behavior problems, safety/emergency procedures, and of course, in incidental teaching. Lead teachers are trained and supervised similarly, through use of a checklist that assesses both their training and classroom management skills.

Initial staff training takes place over a period of 2 to 3 weeks. An apprenticeship training system includes opportunities to observe and model an experienced teacher (while reviewing the designated zone checklist), along with opportunities for direct practice with immediate feedback. As the trainee gains familiarity with the routines, providing opportunities for positive feedback, their performance begins to be evaluated with a zone-based checklist. An example of the performance checklist for the Free-Play Manager routine is shown in Figure 8.1. The specificity of the checklist components prompts the trainers (the Lead Teacher or experienced teachers) to comment on relevant aspects of the trainee's performance, immediately after observing for a 5-minute period. Training continues on zone-based checklists until the trainee reaches a mastery criterion of two consecutive perfect checklists for each routine.

Procedural checklists are introduced over the next several weeks, using a similar training format. Based on research and experience in the preschool setting, training of incidental teaching has been broken into

Walden Preschool at Emory **Free Play Manager** Criterion: +, 0, or NA				
Observer				
Date				
1. Tell the previous FP Manager that s/he is taking over, wear FP arm band?				
2. Move around entire play area, contacting each child frequently (13–15 contacts in 5-minute observation)? Tally:				
3. Talk to each child at his or her eye level?				
4. Present incidental teaching interactions appropriate to child's skill level (model higher level, expand on language)?				
5. Teach to at least 5 children? Tally:				
6. Get responses from at least 3 children? Tally:				
7. Follow up child responses with praise and confirming response and expand on them?				
8. Make 3 or fewer contacts with unengaged children (except as specified in special procedures)?				
9. Follow behavior management plan correctly?				
10. Use Sharing Program correctly?				
11. Keep back to wall and remain visually alert?				
12. Use hobby boxes correctly?				
13. Helps pick up when able?				
14. Focus on zone goal (engagement, vocabulary, social)?				
15. Stay in FP zone until another teacher takes over?				
Feedback received?				

Figure 8.1. Free-play manager's training checklist.

two phases. First, teachers are given checklist-based training in the easiest-case scenario, a one-to-one session with preselected materials and clearly designated written instructions for teaching a specific skill (Izeman, Mann, & McGee, 1987). Training in more sophisticated incidental teaching skills follows (Izeman & McGee, 1988) in which teachers are prepared to adjust the timing of their prompts to children's differing initiation skills (e.g., the teacher learns to approach and wait for a child's initiation, then to comment on the child's activity, and, if necessary, to gently control access to the child's preferred materials or activities).

Maintenance of proficiency is ensured by at least monthly performance appraisals using a more general classroom checklist. If there is slippage on the general checklist or if there are any concerns regarding teacher performance, there is a return to training-to-mastery on specific zone- or procedure-based checklists. The checklists serve as a mechanism for providing frequent, specific praise to teachers, which keeps staff morale and performance quality at high levels.

Didactic training and written materials are also provided, although the assumption is that skills are acquired *in vivo,* and that workshops and readings provide knowledge and rationales for the procedures teachers have learned. During orientation, weekly staff meetings, and periodic curriculum days, training presentations are offered in areas such as incidental teaching research, promoting peer interactions, or positive behavior management. All management-level staff, including the Preschool Coordinator and Lead Teachers, also participate in weekly clinical meetings, which have a goal of training clinical problem-solving skills. Finally, preschool staff have access to visiting consultants, and the program covers expenses of management personnel to make presentations at regional and national conferences.

AN INCIDENTAL TEACHING CURRICULUM THAT PROMOTES SOCIAL INTEGRATION

An interface of skillful teachers and an environment rich with children's choices permits children to enjoy their early childhood years while receiving intensive instruction. Effective participation in society is the overriding goal. Incidental teaching and social integration offer a powerful mix of early educational technologies. However, the complexities of this approach have required development of a curriculum that specifies what children need to learn, what teachers need to do to individualize for children at wide-ranging developmental levels, and what classroom organization will foster children's and teachers' best performances.

Benefits and Challenges of Social Integration

Typical children are wonderful intervention agents for children with autism—they are active and interesting and they provide invaluable social learning opportunities. Walden makes an assumption that learning how to learn from peers is best accomplished when children are as young as possible. An advantage of integration for preschool programs is that daily observation of typical children assists in the selection and pursuit of functional, normalized intervention goals for children with autism.

Socially integrated programs afford typical children the benefits of enriched classrooms (i.e., high teacher-child ratios, well-prepared and closely supervised teachers, individualized instruction), possibilities of improved self-esteem (Devin-Sheehan, Feldman, & Allen, 1976), and advanced skills in how to get along with others (Daly, 1991). Although more difficult to validate, it is hoped that early social integration gives children a lasting appreciation of differences among people.

However, mere exposure to typical peers is not sufficient for remediation of the severe developmental delays associated with autism. True social integration does not occur without directly teaching both typical children and children with autism how to interact with one another. Careful planning and scheduling of activities that promote integration are essential to prevent clumps of segregated interactions in different areas of a so-called integrated classroom. In a free-choice classroom, teachers must "market" various activities to keep all areas constantly integrated. Most crucially, socially integrated preschools must incorporate the intensive and systematic treatment needed by children with autism into an environment that is stimulating and fun for typical children.

Incidental Teaching in an Integrated Preschool

Teaching in the course of children's ongoing play activities is a traditional early childhood strategy for ensuring that children enjoy and cooperate with instruction. However, teaching in the course of ongoing activities in typical environmental settings is a marked departure from traditional methods of educating children with autism. Rather, traditional education for children with autism has usually consisted of highly structured, sit-down activities that are offered in distraction-free settings. Incidental teaching procedures provide an alternative, which meets the needs of both typical children and children with autism and blends well with normalized preschool activities.

Incidental teaching procedures were first developed to facilitate normal (and disadvantaged) children's use of complex language forms (Hart & Risley, 1968; 1974; 1975; 1982); this background is of relevance because the ultimate success of social integration requires concurrent attention to the needs of typical children as well as those of children with special needs. The most significant findings from incidental teaching research are reports of enhanced generalization for both typical children (Hart & Risley, 1980) and children with autism (McGee, Krantz, Mason, & McClannahan, 1983; McGee, Krantz, & McClannahan, 1985, 1986). In sum, research suggests that incidental teaching procedures will maximize learning by all children.

Despite some recent popularity of incidental teaching that has broadened the term to encompass friendly, pleasant, "chit-chat," Walden maintains a classical definition of incidental teaching as a systematic protocol of teaching interactions. Components include: (a) *a natural environment is arranged to attract* children to desired materials and activities (e.g., preferred toys are displayed in activity areas and teachers circulate continuously among children to promote high levels of engagement); (b) *the child "initiates" the teaching process* by indicating an interest in an item or topic, either gesturally or verbally (e.g., the child points to a block or says "I want the block"); (c) *the teacher uses the child's initiation as an opportunity to prompt an elaboration* related to the child's topic of interest (the teacher asks "What shape block?"); and (d) *the child's correct response to the teacher's prompt results in a confirming response, then contingent access* to the item/topic of interest (e.g., the child says "I want a square block" and the teacher immediately provides it, saying "Terrific, here's a square block, let's build a tower with it").

Incidental teaching in a socially integrated preschool requires teachers to maintain high levels of enthusiasm as they make a rapid series of complex teaching judgments. Thus, in addition to performing the normally demanding duties of providing child care and enriching preschool activities, incidental teachers must constantly track children's interests to identify the perfect timing of the "teachable moment." Because children with autism have deficits in initiation abilities, the process of using children's preferences requires extra attention to the selection and display of reinforcing materials. Additionally, the purposeful inclusion of normally available distractions highlights the importance of methods of maintaining high levels of child engagement.

Curriculum Topics for an Integrated Preschool

A comprehensive incidental teaching curriculum was developed to ensure that each child receives intensive, individualized instruction in the course of his/her preferred play activities. In an incidental teaching environment, the child determines *when* instruction will occur (by initiating about a topic of interest); the teacher responds by engaging the child in a teaching interaction. An incidental teaching curriculum must specify the teachers's agenda or the extent of the elaboration that will be requested. A comprehensive curriculum must ensure that *what* is taught is a systematic representation of the competencies children need to learn.

Because normalization is the goal for children with autism, it is necessary to attempt fundamental change in the core language and social disabilities associated with autism. When most successful, an incidental teaching approach yields broad, generalized improvements beyond those that have been specifically programmed into the curriculum. Children learn to respond in moderately high arousal conditions that represent the multiple cues and distractions inherent in everyday environments. The Walden emphasis on language and social development is compatible with goals of integration because language and social growth are the primary agenda for all young children.

Progression of Curriculum Goals

Consideration of normal developmental sequencing has yielded the following progression of curriculum targets, although specific objectives and the relative distribution of time across areas varies with individual needs. Social responsivity to teachers and engagement with classroom materials and activities is the initial focus. In an incidental teaching environment, children with autism must be prepared to tolerate and enjoy teachers' approaches (Burns, 1991). Concurrently, early, and, if necessary, continuing emphasis on maintaining high levels of engagement is essential to setting the stage for "teachable moments."

Verbal objectives, expressive language or learning how to talk, are the major priority for children with autism in their first year of program enrollment. An incidental teaching environment provides frequent opportunities to make choices and to experience the natural consequences of language. Elaboration of conversational skills continues throughout the second year for all children, with a shift in emphasis to peer interactions.

For children with autism, the second year highlights the skills requisite for learning from other children. Thus, while it is necessary to directly teach age-appropriate skills in responding to and initiating interactions, taking turns, tolerating touch, making eye contact, etc., the broader goal is to prepare children to learn how to learn from peers so that the content of their interactions will shift appropriately with advancing years. Specifically, successful children have learned "when in doubt, do what other children are doing," a strategy that highlights the importance of continuing integration. It may be noted that the difficulty of building durable peer interactions skills has led to a gradual shift toward addressing social goals from the outset, although the major emphasis on language first continues because natural peer interactions require good verbal skills.

Secondary goals in the first year include play and daily living skills, with an emphasis on independence. Kindergarten readiness, including academic advancement, receives increased priority in the second year. Examples of specific objectives for children with autism are presented in Table 8.2.

Classroom Organization That Supports Teachers' Use of the Curriculum

The environment and staff are arranged into teaching zones. Zones are designated by teaching activity rather than by space, per se. Clearly defined zones help teachers identify the children and teaching agendas they are responsible for at a given moment. Teaching occurs continuously throughout traditional preschool activities, during play (free-play,

TABLE 8.2.   Examples of Walden Objectives According to Circular Area

Goals	Objectives
Language	• Will distribute verbalizations across 12% of the preschool day
	• At snack, will request food using sentences with descriptors ("I want grape juice")
Social	• Will be engaged over 80% of the school day, across activities, maintaining focus of attention on adults at least 10% of time when a teacher is in proximity
	• During a peer-incidental teaching session, will initiate peer interactions by commenting about preferred toys presented by a typical peer, at least five times per session
Daily Living Skills	• Will put on and remove shoes and outerwear, wash hands, and brush teeth, with teacher prompts faded to partial verbal inquiries ("What do you need to do?")
Kindergarten Readiness	• Will participate in Pre-kindergarten group, learning to identify and write letters

playground, games), during instructional sessions (morning circle, kindergarten readiness groups, art and science activities, story, one-on-one), and during care routines (snack, lunch, toileting, naps). Children move through teaching zones as their interests draw them, increasing their receptivity to teaching because they select the materials and activities that are used for instruction.

A schedule (as shown in Table 8.3) of multiple and concurrent zones overlaps up to four activity options at any given time. Overlapping activities minimize group transitions, eliminate wasted waiting times, and permit children to begin and end activities at their preferred pace. By providing children with choices as to how to spend their time, occasions for incidental teaching are plentiful.

The Lead Teacher assists children with transitions across zones, capitalizing on children's desires to change activities as prime language instruction opportunities. If a teacher needs extra scissors at an art activity, rather than disrupt teaching, the Lead Teacher is available to cover

TABLE 8.3. Daily Schedule (and Teaching Goals)

Time	Zone 1	Zone 2	Zone 3	Zone 4
9:00	Health Check (Body Part Labels)	Free Play (Engagement, Play Skills)	Arrivals (Toileting, Dressing)	Arrivals (Greetings, Independence)
9:15	Health Check (Body Part Labels)	Free Play (Engagement, Play Skills)	Special Activity (Language, Fine Motor, Art, Science)	One-to-One (Prepositions)
9:30	One-to-One (Conversation)	Free Play (Engagement, Play Skills)	Special Activity (Language, Fine Motor, Art, Science)	One-to-One (Non-echoic Verbalizations)
9:45	Snack (Verbal Requests)	Free Play (Engagement, Play Skills)	Independence (Hand washing, Clean Up)	One-to-One (Vocalizations)
10:00	Snack (Verbal Requests)	Free Play (Engagement, Play Skills)	Table Activity (Language, Fine Motor, Art, Science)	Toothbrushing (Independence)
10:15	Morning Meeting (Group Attending/Music)	Free Play (Engagement, Play Skills)	One-to-One (Kindergarten Readiness)	
10:30	Transition to Outside (Independence in Dressing)	Toileting (Independence)	Ready Table (Independent Play)	Outdoor Free Play (Language, Gross Motor)

(continued)

TABLE 8.3. *Continued*

Time	Zone 1	Zone 2	Zone 3	Zone 4
10:45	Slide (Language, Gross Motor)	Swings (Language, Gross Motor)	Outdoor Free Play (Social Interaction, Gross Motor)	One-to-One (In Context Verbal Imitation)
11:00	Cooperative Games (Social Interaction)	Outdoor Free Play (Safety)	One-to-One (Participation in Games)	Exercises (Imitation, Gross Motor)
11:15	Swings (Language, Gross Motor)	Slide (Language, Gross Motor)	Outdoor Free Play (Social Interaction)	One-to-One (Sentences)
11:30	Transition Inside (Independence)	Free Play (Vocabulary)	Jobs (Language, Independence)	Workjobs (Kindergarten Readiness, Math)
11:45	Dramatic Play (Peer Interaction)	Free Play (Vocabulary)	Lunch (Peer Conversation, Eating Independence)	Peer Teaching (Peer Interaction)
12:00	Peer Teaching (Peer Interaction)	Free Play (Vocabulary)	Lunch (Peer Conversation, Eating Independence)	One-to-One (Action Words)
12:15	Peer Teaching (Peer Interaction)	Free Play (Vocabulary)	Lunch (Peer Conversation, Eating Independence)	One-to-One (Play Skills)

(continued)

TABLE 8.3. *Continued*

Time	Zone 1	Zone 2	Zone 3	Zone 4
12:30	Dramatic Play (Peer Interaction)	Free Play (Vocabulary)	Lunch (Peer Conversation, Eating Independence)	Toothbrushing (Independence)
12:45	Pre-Kindergarten Group (Kindergarten Readiness)	Free Play (Vocabulary)	Jobs (Language, Independence)	
1:00	Story (Group Attending)	Free Play (Vocabulary)	Table top game (Turn Taking)	One-to-One (Turn Taking)
1:15	Nap (Rest)	Quiet Activity (Independent Play)	Computer (Reading)	
2:00	Social Games (Social Interaction)	Free Play (Peer Interaction)	One-to-One ("Yes," "No")	One-to-One (Attending Social Games)
2:15	Snack (Verbal Requests)	Free Play (Social Interaction)	Social Games (Peer Interaction)	One-to-One ("Yes," "No")
2:30	Snack (Verbal Requests)	Free Play (Social Interaction)	Independence (Hand washing, Clean up)	One-to-One (Pronouns)
2:45	Social Games (Peer Interaction)	Free Play (Social Interaction)	Departures (Dressing, Toileting)	Departures (Farewells, Independence)

logistics so that the zone manager's focus remains constantly on the children. Physical and functional separation of teachers across zones also contributes to child focus.

Each zone is overlaid with teaching goals. Designation of which goal(s) will be the teaching focus in each zone has permitted preplanning of environmental arrangements, preferred instructional materials, activities, and teaching procedures. In many zones, the curriculum is presented in levels to help teachers adjust to children's wide-ranging abilities, so that all children can be kept happily challenged. Cue cards posted in the classroom remind teachers what the desired elaborations are for children at differing levels, and ongoing performance appraisals promote teachers' use of classroom prompts.

For example, requests are targeted at two daily snacks. When a child with no language reaches for his snack, he may be prompted to vocalize a sound. A child with new language will be prompted for requests of one-word, then two-word phrases, and gradually for complete sentences. At the highest level, children are encouraged to request more abstract information from one another ("Where does milk come from?").

Similarly, new vocabulary is taught in a midday free-play zone. Words targeted each week correspond to play materials in the classroom, with words rotating weekly. Words are leveled so that there are some for all to learn (receptively and/or expressively), with some for more advanced children. Body parts are taught within a morning health check activity and child-culture conversational language (e.g., "Wow," "Awesome") is promoted during lunch (Daly, 1988).

A series of activities interspersed throughout the day offers direct instruction and practice in peer interactions. During peer incidental teaching, a typical child learns to use preferred toys and something to say to get a response from a peer with autism (McGee, Almeida, Sulzer-Azaroff, & Feldman, 1992). Dramatic play sessions alternate daily activities such as McDonald's or beauty parlor, and interactions are directly prompted among two typical children and one child with autism (Odom & Strain, 1986; Strain, Hoyson, & Jamieson, 1985; Strain & Odom, 1986). Cooperative, noncompetitive games are played by all children at recess, followed by an outdoor exercise session to promote gross motor imitation of peers. Each afternoon, three social games are selected from a rotating pool designed to attract children with autism via a salient sensory component (e.g., taking turns spinning in a chair, or painting to opera music; Daly, Hendler, & McGee, 1990). Afternoon free-play also targets a leveled social skill each week (e.g., one week, nonverbal children may be prompted to wave to their peers, while higher-level children are encouraged to use each other's names).

Some individualized incidental teaching sessions are provided daily to each child with autism, usually in areas that require massed teaching opportunities (e.g., social orienting; Mann, 1988). However, sessions that preclude the availability of typical peers are kept at a minimum (i.e., no more than five 15-minute sessions per child per day). Where possible, 1:1 instruction is scheduled to occur within other group activities.

Academics are targeted at various tabletop activities and through the use of commercially available computerized instruction. Prereading and reading materials are available on request in children's individual hobby boxes (McGee, Daly, Izeman, Mann, & Risley, 1991), and work jobs adapted from the *Mathematics Their Way* curriculum (Baratta-Lorton, 1976) are also marketed on an individualized basis. Daily living skills are taught as opportunities arise naturally in the classroom routine (e.g., brushing teeth after lunch), and some teaching opportunities are subtly contrived (e.g., Walden children do not wear shoes in the classroom, providing practice in independently getting shoes on and off at arrivals, recess, and departures).

Assessment of Child and Curriculum Progress

In an incidental teaching environment, teachers cannot be burdened with routine data collection responsibilities. The solution has been to construct a series of assessment probes that vary in frequency and format depending on the goal. Two-week blocks of daily videotapes are scored at quarterly intervals to assess goals pertaining to generalized improvements across the day. Language curriculum components are monitored at least biweekly by a speech-language consultant to determine whether children are assigned to appropriately challenging levels and to ensure precise curriculum implementation. Some practical teacher-collected probes have been built into daily routines (e.g., in vocabulary free-play, teachers record each child's first response of the day, and probes comprise responses across five consecutive days). More traditional trial-by-trial assessment can be conducted during 1:1 sessions.

Child and program assessment data comprise a comprehensive program evaluation system. Adapted from the Toddler Center Model (O'Brien et al., 1979; Schweitzer & Izeman, 1986), the system monitors areas such as teacher performance appraisals, safety, behavior difficulties, and children's participation in activities. A Program Evaluator conducts systematic observations, which are combined with probe and classroom monitoring data into a weekly report. The report and accompanying data are presented to the Director, who in turn reviews the results with the Program Coordinator in an individual supervisory meeting. The edited report then serves as the agenda for weekly teacher staff meetings.

POSITIVE BEHAVIOR MANAGEMENT

The typical children in integrated settings provide constant reminders that perfect behavior is not a normal goal for young children. Moreover, traditionally acceptable strategies for management of behavior problems in autism treatment programs are often unacceptable to parents of typical children. On the other hand, integration does impose some requirements that disruptive or bizarre behaviors are minimized. Future success in kindergarten requires that all children learn to control their environment through positive means.

The overriding behavior management philosophy at Walden is that increasing fun decreases problem behaviors. More precisely, prevention of behavior problems buys time to teach long-term replacements for problem behaviors. The curriculum vigorously targets skills such as verbal expression of displeasure, needs, and desires; sharing and turn taking; and, following conventional classroom rules. Effective teaching of appropriate behavior requires powerful fuel in the form of children's most highly preferred play materials and activities, the presence of which helps to reduce or crowd out problem behaviors.

The classroom curriculum yields numerous side effects of improved behavior. Research (Carr & Kologinsky, 1983) and practice indicate that incidental teaching yields decreased behavior problems because incidental teaching requires that children make choices of where they want to be and what they want to be doing. Zone-based classrooms with multiple, overlapping activity schedules minimize waiting or "down time," which are prime opportunities for problem behaviors. Ongoing procedures for assessing reinforcer preferences ensure that highly preferred materials are constantly available, which yields virtually automatic decreases in levels of problem behavior (Mason, McGee,

Farmer-Dougan, & Risley, 1989). Additional research has shown that levels of autistic behavior are lower when children with autism are in close physical proximity to typical peers (McGee, Paradis, & Feldman, 1993).

The promotion of engagement is the primary strategy for prevention of behavior problems at Walden, and research and development has been invested in procedures for securing and maintaining consistently high levels of engagement. For example, a plan for biweekly rotation of classroom toys has been shown to reduce problem behaviors such as name calling, tattling, and fighting, while increasing positive social behaviors such as peer cooperation (Daly, McGee, Izeman, & Mann, 1990).

Procedures for arranging access to individualized materials have also proven effective in promoting high levels of engagement (McGee et al., 1991). Thus, color-coded hobby boxes are available around the classroom on teacher-height shelves. Each child with engagement difficulties has a white hobby box that contains preferred items that sustain engagement in the absence of constant teacher attention. When the child is unengaged, the teacher markets available classroom toys once, and if necessary twice; if redirection is unsuccessful, a more sure-bet item is readily available in the child's hobby box. Children without engagement problems also wanted hobby boxes, so blue boxes were prepared with individualized academic work and a special toy the child could "buy" at the classroom store. Hobby boxes provide occasions for children to initiate interactions with teachers to obtain their materials, and they learn elaborate requests. In fact, the words "hobby" and "box" are often among first words for children with autism at Walden.

The program is designed to avoid power struggles between children and teachers. This is accomplished by limiting the number of classroom rules and by preparing teachers in planned ignoring of insignificant problem behaviors (e.g., whining). Frequent praise, tickles, hugs, and access to preferred activities are abundantly available for appropriate engagement. A sharing program is also in place, in which a timer is set for 2 minutes to help children negotiate the transition of a disputed toy (i.e., the toy must be relinquished after 2 minutes if an appropriate request to share has been offered).

When behavior problems do occur, analysis and teaching of natural consequences are the rule. Initial analysis focuses on whether preventive environmental arrangements are feasible (e.g., can toy shelves be relocated to break up a classroom racetrack?). If several children are displaying problems in an activity, it may be that the activity is boring or requires preparation (e.g., videos were added to nap time, and the school year begins with a very brief circle activity that gradually increases in duration as children learn the songs and other skills needed for participation).

A series of natural consequences is associated with classroom rules. For example, baskets of blocks knocked off the shelves must be picked up, with gentle physical assistance if necessary. When a child is disruptive at an activity (e.g., splashing others at the water table), there is immediate yet matter-of-fact redirection to another zone. Aggression toward teachers is consistently ignored, but peer aggression is regarded as a "felony." Peer aggression results in immediate removal from other children, with redirection to a sit-down play activity for two minutes.

Individualized behavior management programs are necessary on rare occasions, but the number of such programs is kept as low as possible in the interest of ensuring precise teacher implementation. A functional analysis precedes the design of any behavior reduction program, and there is a firm prohibition on presentation of aversive stimuli. For example, a child with limited language who tantrums to leave an activity may be taught to point, and later to say "go" in order to exit. In sum, behavior reduction programs must be instructional in the interest of building skills that contribute to future prevention.

There are tradeoffs in implementing positive-only procedures for behavior management. Given an incidental teaching approach, it is crucial to avoid the undesired side effects of punishment. Social avoidance of approaching teachers precludes teaching opportunities. Traditional compliance training is not used because it may reduce the spontaneity of initiations. Although redirection strategies are not without risk of providing attention for misbehavior, careful monitoring and staff training have proven effective in preventing inadvertent reinforcement of undesired behaviors. Experience over the years in gradually relinquishing even mild behavior reduction procedures (e.g., overcorrection for toileting accidents, contingent observation for classroom rule violations) has indicated that proactive behavior management requires incredibly hard work, planning, and careful teacher supervision. However, it is possible to accomplish fundamental changes in language and social behaviors that will yield normalized behavior control in children's futures.

AN INCIDENTAL TEACHING
FAMILY PROGRAM

The Walden Family Program (Jacobs, Regnier, & McGee, 1992) is designed to further intensify preschool intervention for the children with autism and to expedite early enablement for their parents. The program also seeks to enhance communication among the preschool and parents of all the children.

The family program bridges the gap between parents of children with autism and professionals by providing meaningful options for parents to collaborate in their child's treatment. Consistent with an incidental teaching approach, participating families are given a broad array of program choices from which they determine the focus of their individualized program. There is an assumption that parents will be most effective in providing and advocating for children's treatments that are compatible with their self-identified needs (Dunst, Leet, & Trivette, 1988). Although parent choice regarding hours of treatment investment is respected, parents are informed of prior evaluation results. In sum, more hours of parental participation translates to more child improvement at home.

Parents are provided with a series of opportunities to learn the skills and knowledge that prepare them to teach and advocate for their child. The emphasis is on blending teaching naturally into family life. Format options for parents include: (a) a 6-month intensive (weekly) individualized program; (b) ongoing consultation; (c) a biweekly parent information seminar; (d) an integrated family component, and (e) school communication.

Intensive Program

The 6-month intensive program offers home, school, or clinic-based contacts with the Family Coordinator. The parents design their individualized family plan by selecting topics from a menu of 47 prepackaged modules. Accompanying each module are written materials, which have been edited by parents to be "parent-friendly." Reference materials and videotaped vignettes are available as appropriate. Modules are grouped into five categories: Incidental Teaching, Advocacy, General Information, Family Issues, and Other Instructional Packages.

The Incidental Teaching modules are designed to enable parents to teach language and social skills in the course of their daily routines at home. Some examples of the daily routines that parents have chosen to use for teaching are: mealtimes, bathtime, outside play, dressing, meal preparation, chores, car trips, and having neighborhood children over to play.

The Advocacy modules provide parents with the information, knowledge, and skills that enable them to be effective advocates for their children. Advocacy modules on the menu include: integration; knowing the laws; professional jargon; negotiating individualized educational plans; available community programs and activities; state-of-the-art intervention technology; and evaluation of future classrooms.

General Information modules are focused on helping parents to understand their child's disability and to help them plan improvements in the quality of their family life. Thus, there is information available on autism, balancing personal and parenting time, and issues pertaining to inclusion of extended family members. For example, infants have been involved in simple interactive games such as tickling, preschool-aged and older siblings have been prepared for incidental teaching during playtime (Harris, Sulzer-Azaroff, & McGee, 1992), and grandparents have learned incidental teaching of cute talk. Grandparent information groups have also been well received. These modules are aimed at enabling parents to build support systems and capitalize on the resources available within their own family.

Other Instructional packages are empirically validated procedures created by colleagues. Thus, popular options include assistance in developing home schedules (MacDuff, Krantz, & McClannahan, 1993) and remote reporting skills (Krantz, Zalenski, Hall, Fenske, & McClannahan, 1981), a package to improve behavior on grocery-store shopping trips (Clark, Greene, Macrae, McNees, Davis, & Risley, 1977), and the classic (albeit modified) methods for toilet-training (Azrin & Foxx, 1974). Special requests and circumstances are also accommodated so that we have helped parents learn to train respite workers, therapeutic nannies, and Sunday school teachers. Thus, the emphasis is on effective management of their child's life at home and in the community.

Ongoing Consultation

Less frequent contact is desired by some parents, who prefer regular updates and information on their child's progress at school. Parents who have participated in the intensive program usually opt for monthly consultation at follow-up. They have learned the skills to develop their own home programs but appreciate advice on fine-tuning their procedures or on arranging school-home coordination. When children are in preparation for transition, the Family Coordinator may accompany parents on school-selection visits or assist with training of a classroom aide.

Parent Information Seminar

Parents choose the topics and scheduling of group meetings, which include didactic presentations, written materials, and videotaped examples. Currently, parents prefer biweekly meetings, which they supplement with a parent-organized support group and informal brunches. A schedule of topics is selected every 3 months, on topics such as autism, selecting toys, or promoting good behavior in public places. Guest speakers are also invited to present (e.g., an attorney on disability law, a speech-language pathologist on language milestones, etc.).

Integrated Family Events

Group meetings and social events are also arranged to provide all parents with an opportunity to get to know each other and their children's teachers. Learning about the trials and tribulations that parents of typical children experience helps parents of children with autism put their child's development in perspective. Thus, parents are often reassured to learn that few young children behave well on long mall trips, or that restaurants can be an ordeal for all. It is also important for the parents of typical children to gain an understanding of the benefits of integration for their own children. Friendships formed between parents of typical children and parents of children with autism lay a foundation for community integration (e.g., birthday parties, weekend outings), and more importantly, for integration beyond their children's preschool years (Hall, 1987).

School Communication

The classroom maintains an "open-door" visitation policy, which is facilitated by the presence of a one-way observational mirror. All children take home daily notes to inform parents of eating, napping, and instructional events, and these set the occasion for conversation about the child's day at school. Monthly classroom newsletters offer more detail on classroom activities (e.g., new vocabulary words, songs).

Synopsis of the Family Program

The structure of the program enables parents to maximize their child's overall progress and to advocate for education and lifelong community integration. The program's flexibility also provides a means for parents who have less time and resources to have an important and useful impact on their child's life. In sum, program goals have been accomplished when incidental teaching is incorporated into home routines in such a way that parents can play a crucial role in their child's treatment while enjoying normal family and community living.

CHILDREN'S OUTCOMES

Verbalizations

Incidental teaching is a powerful method for promoting the development of functional, generalized language skills. All but 1 of 14 Walden graduates left the program with meaningful verbal language, many at age-appropriate levels. Successful verbal language outcomes were achieved by children at all levels of functioning.

Language gains were supported by objective scoring of videotapes to assess the distribution of language across the day. This measure provides a conservative, and predominately generalized measure of how much children are talking throughout preschool activities. As shown in Figure 8.2, the average level of verbalizations by children with autism at entry was 4% (range 0% to 14%). At the time of exit, the average level of verbalizations was 13% (range 1% to 37%). In sum, language use by children with autism tripled across time in the program, nearing (and in

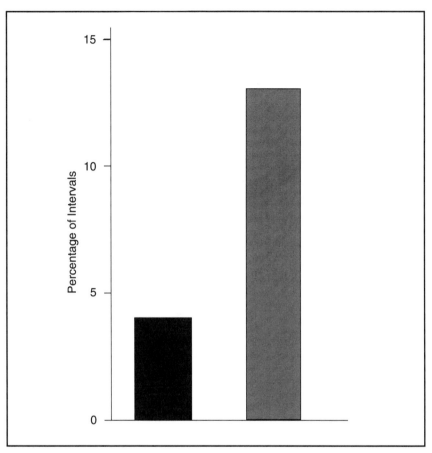

Figure 8.2.   Mean percentage of intervals scored for verbalizations by 14 children with autism, at entry (black bar) and exit (grey bar).

some cases overlapping) the 27% levels of the typical children. Improvements tended to show up during children's first year of enrollment, corresponding to curriculum goals.

Peer Interactions

A similarly conservative marker reveals more difficulty in the area of peer interactions. Specifically, an indirect assessment of each child's social proficiency is obtained by measuring the distribution of children's receipt of social bids from other children. Comparing entry and exit data on this measure, 6 of 14 (43%) graduates with autism showed improvements. It should be noted that all children had shown more substantial gains as a function of direct peer interventions, but generalized and durable improvements remained problematic for most (cf. McGee, Alwaida, Sulzey-Azaroff, & Feldman, 1992).

The initial hope had been that early, dramatic language gains would automatically lead to improvements in peer-related social behavior, but the data have consistently indicated that language and peer interactions are separate response classes. The program has responded to these data by adjusting both curriculum and research efforts. Thus, more time each day is now invested in peer interaction activities under an assumption that "practice makes perfect." Social interventions are also started at a younger age. As a result, in the current classroom a majority (57%) of children have shown substantive peer interaction increases within 3 months of program entry.

Moreover, the predominant research focus has shifted from incidental teaching to social behavior. Present research is examining the social development of the typical children in comparison to children with autism in an effort to identify naturally occurring events that support and maintain children's social interactions.

Future Placements

Early in the program's development, a team of experts was asked to review research measures to determine their suitability for future outcome studies. The team's conclusion was that the measures were solid but that the ultimate outcome boils down to where do the children end up. We argued that future placements were politically contaminated; virtually no children with autism were then being mainstreamed in the area. Yet their bottom-line position was difficult to dispute.

On this count, the program has achieved striking success. Twelve of 14 graduated children with autism have been fully mainstreamed into regular classes at their local public schools. It must be qualified that the children exited with low, medium, and high treatment outcomes. Varying levels of support have been provided to more than a dozen school districts. Transition assistance (Regnier, 1991) has ranged from intensive preparation of classroom aides to occasional follow-up consultation (which was gradually withdrawn).

Informal follow-up has been accomplished via phone interviews with parents and biannual reunion parties, which have been well attended by children with autism and typical children. Given concern over exiting social interaction data, reports of continuing social advancement by all integrated children have been remarkable. Thus, they have friends in their classrooms and neighborhoods, and they'participate in extracurricular activities (such as judo classes, gymnastics, and gospel groups). To their parents' delight, there are many reports of invitations to birthday parties and visits to friends' homes.

Walden's relocation is requiring the establishment of new community liaisons, and committed parents have initiated this process early in their children's treatment. The program's high visibility in an area where the concept of early inclusion is new adds to the challenge to provide superb preparation to all participating children.

FUTURE DIRECTIONS

There are two major areas in which more information is needed to fully realize the potential of early treatment for children with autism. The core social deficits that are characteristic of autism have proven quite difficult to remediate in lasting and meaningful ways, and the literature on social development provides far fewer guidelines than were available in the quest to develop language.

Secondly, although there is growing recognition that age of entry into treatment may well be the most crucial factor influencing treatment outcomes, numerous heuristic limitations and logistical problems impede early treatment of autism.

Social Behavior

Although intervention research has yielded significant advances in teaching children with autism to behave in socially appropriate ways, social interventions have largely been developed with a minimum of empirical information on the nature of appropriate social behavior. There has been little research to date focused on the environmental stimuli present that evoke or consequate social behavior in naturalistic settings.

To improve development of positive social behavior in children with autism, it becomes necessary to better understand the environmental conditions under which social behavior normally develops. Then it may be possible to construct interventions that will better generalize and maintain.

To be specific, interventions designed to remediate social deficits most often consist of procedural manipulations that represent best guesses as to how to achieve the desired behavior change. Although such procedures have become increasingly effective in yielding immediate changes, generalization and maintenance of treatment effects have been problematic because the intervention conditions are not naturally available in normal everyday environments. The ability to produce more significant and lasting developmental change in children with social disabilities requires that we learn more about the basic configurations of normal social development, and that we apply this knowledge to advance the field of social interventions for children with autism.

Earliest Intervention

A major limitation on efforts to fully evaluate early intervention for children with autism has been difficulty in getting children into treatment at the earliest possible age. Because autism is such a low incidence disorder, many medical and early intervention professionals have had little or no personal experience with children with autism, and they are unprepared to recognize the characteristics. Complicating the matter, the younger the child, the more ambiguous the diagnostic picture can be. The result is that professionals are understandably reluctant to label a child with such a severe diagnosis, especially in the absence of referral options.

Researchers have only recently taken an interest in obtaining information on the early characteristics of autism. Additional contributions to a database on the early presentation and course of autism would expedite both research and practice. Professional training programs must incorporate quickly new information in order to prevent the loss of valuable treatment time for future children with autism.

Moreover, despite widespread recognition that in treatment of autism, early is essential and more is better, the current state-of-the-art treatment in early intervention for autism is good preschool education. When children with autism enter treatment before preschool ages, they are usually provided with a diluted preschool curriculum. There is a void of information on *what* is most crucial to teach toddlers with (or at risk for) a diagnosis of autism, or *how* to best teach them. This is a critical problem, given the relatively short time frame in which early intervention must occur. In sum, it is important to know how to best lay a foundation for the growing number of effective preschool interventions.

CONCLUSIONS

We have found a comprehensive incidental teaching approach to be both socially palatable and empirically effective, for both children with autism and typical children. Unfortunately, combining incidental teaching and social integration technologies to produce a maximally powerful program is not easy. High-quality education of any variety does not come naturally. Yet we believe that the venture has been worth the effort, given the mission of accomplishing fundamental, sweeping changes in outcomes for children with autism.

Regarding integration, it is clear that children with autism can be prepared for integration while they are integrated. In fact, it is difficult to imagine how to build normalized peer interactions in the absence of normal peers. Integration has, in short, provided innumerable benefits to program development. Typical children have enjoyed the enriched education afforded by a lab school, and children with autism have learned how to have friends in their classrooms and communities.

Finally, it seems worthwhile to note that this has been joyous work. Early intervention for autism is an exciting and rapidly progressing field. From the beginning, we have found our early intervention colleagues to be generous in the exchange of their ideas, materials, and findings. This substantial cooperation makes sense in an area where normalization of a severe disability is the goal, and approximations are not successes.

AUTHOR NOTES

Research and development activities were supported in part by grants #G008535122, #G008019001, and #H133G10162 from the National Institute on Disability and Rehabilitation Research, and in part by grant #G00873002888 from the Division of Personnel Preparation, OSERS, U.S. Department of Education. The opinions expressed herein do not necessarily reflect the policy of the U.S. Department of Education, and no official endorsement should be inferred.

Special credit is due to Beth Sulzer-Azaroff and Robert S. Feldman, who co-founded the initial project; and to Todd R. Risley, who has mentored the project throughout. Provost Glen Gordon (UMass) and Child Psychiatry Division Chief Mina Dulcan (Emory) also deserve recognition for administrative vision. Virtually all Walden staff, most especially the first and current Walden teams, have contributed substantially.

Correspondence may be addressed to Gail G. McGee at the Emory Autism Resource Center, 718 Gatewood Road, Department of Psychiatry and Behavioral Sciences, Emory University School of Medicine, Atlanta, Georgia 30322.

REFERENCES

Allen, K. E., & Hart, B. M. (1984). *The early years: Arrangements for learning*. Englewood Cliffs, NJ: Prentice-Hall.

American Psychiatric Association (1987). *Diagnostic and statistical manual* (3rd ed.). Washington, DC: Author.

Azrin, N. H., & Foxx, R. M. (1974). *Toilet training in less than a day*. New York: Pocket Books.

Baratta-Lorton, M. (1976). *Mathematics their way*. Menlo Park, CA: Addison Wesley.

Brigance, A. H. (1978). *Brigance Inventory of Early Development*. Waburn, MA: Curriculum Associates.

Burns, J. J. (1991, May). Using normative data and descriptive analyses to guide and interpret social interventions. In G. G. McGee (Chair), *Empirical support for an incidental teaching approach to early social intervention for children with autism*. Symposium presented at the annual meeting of the Association for Behavior Analysis, Atlanta.

Carr, E. G., & Kologinsky, E. (1983). Acquisition of sign language by autistic children: II Spontaneity and generalization effects. *Journal of Applied Behavior Analysis, 16*, 297–314.

Clark, H. B., Greene, B. F., Macrae, J. W., McNees, M. P., Davis, J. L., & Risley, T. R. (1977). A parent advice package for family shopping trips. *Journal of Applied Behavior Analysis, 10*, 605–624.

Daly, T. (1988, May). "In-context" teaching of social talk. In G. G. McGee (Chair), *Normalizing the socialization of autistic children*. Symposium presented at the annual meeting of the Association for Applied Behavior Analysis, Philadelphia.

Daly, T. (1991). *Social behavior and social understanding of mainstreamed and non-mainstreamed typical preschoolers*. Unpublished doctoral dissertation, University of Massachusetts, Amherst.

Daly, T., Hendler, J., & McGee, G. G. (1990, May). *Rocking the boat: Sensory stimulation and social interaction*. Paper presented at the annual meeting of the Association for Behavior Analysis, Nashville.

Daly, T., McGee, G. G., Izeman, S. G., & Mann, L. H. (1990, May). *Evaluation of systematic toy management of children's engagement in an integrated classroom*. Paper presented at the annual meeting of the Association for Behavior Analysis, Nashville.

Devin-Sheehan, L., Feldman, R. S., & Allen, V. L. (1976). Theory and research on cross-age and peer interaction: A review of the literature. *Review of Educational Research, 46,* 355–385.

Doke, L. A., & Risley, T. R. (1972). The organization of day-care environments: Required versus optional activities. *Journal of Applied Behavior Analysis 5,* 405–420.

Dunn, L. M., & Dunn, L. M. (1981). *Peabody Picture Vocabulary Test–Revised*. Circle Pines, MN: American Guidance Service.

Dunst, C. J., Leet, H. E., & Trivette, C. M. (1988). Family resources, personal well-being, and early intervention. *Journal of Special Education, 22,* 108–116.

Gardner, M. F. (1990). *Expressive One-Word Picture Vocabulary Test–Revised*. Austin, TX: PRO-ED.

Hall, L. J. (1987, May). An evaluation of parents' requests for assistance in an integrated preschool program. In G. G. McGee (Chair), *Advances in early social integration*. Symposium presented at the annual meeting of the Association for Behavior Analysis, Nashville.

Harris, T. A., Sulzer-Azaroff, B., & McGee, G. G. (1992, May). *Promoting reciprocal interactions between children with developmental delays and their typical siblings through instruction in incidental teaching*. Paper presented at the annual meeting of the Association for Behavior Analysis, San Francisco.

Hart, B. M., & Risley, T. R. (1968). Establishing the use of descriptive adjectives in the spontaneous speech of disadvantaged children. *Journal of Applied Behavior Analysis, 1,* 109–120.

Hart, B. M., & Risley, T. R. (1974). Using preschool materials to modify the language of disadvantaged children. *Journal of Applied Behavior Analysis, 7,* 243–256.

Hart, B. M., & Risley, T. R. (1975). Incidental teaching of language in the preschool. *Journal of Applied Behavior Analysis, 8,* 411–420.

Hart, B. M., & Risley, T. R. (1980). In vivo language intervention: Unanticipated general effects. *Journal of Applied Behavior Analysis, 13,* 407–432.

Hart, B. M., & Risley, T. R. (1982). *How to use incidental teaching for elaborating language*. Lawrence, KS: H & H Enterprises.

Izeman, S. G., Mann. L. H., & McGee, G. G. (1987, May). *Verbal interactions in a natural learning environment.* Paper presented at the annual meeting of the Association for the Advancement of Behavior Therapy, Chicago.

Izeman, S. G., & McGee, G. G. (1988, May). A teaching technology that accommodates social integration. In G. G. McGee (Chair), *Normalizing the socialization of autistic children.* Symposium presented at the annual meeting of the Association for Behavior Analysis, Philadelphia.

Jacobs, H. A., Regnier, M. C., & McGee, G. G. (1992, May). *An incidental teaching family program.* Paper presented at the annual meeting of the Association for Behavior Analysis, San Francisco.

Krantz, P. J., Zalenski, S., Hall, L. J., Fenske, E. C., & McClannahan, L. E. (1981). Teaching complex language to autistic children. *Analysis and Intervention in Developmental Disabilities, 1,* 259–297.

LeLaurin, K., & Risley, T. R. (1972). The organization of daycare environments: "Zone" versus "man-to-man" staff assignments. *Journal of Applied Behavior Analysis, 5,* 225–232.

MacDuff, G. S., Krantz, P. J. & McClannahan, L.E. (1993). Teaching children with autism to use photographic activity schedules: Maintenance and generalization of complex response chains. *Journal of Applied Behavior Analysis, 26,* 89–97.

Mann, L. H. (1988, May). Trends in the development of non-verbal behavior. In G. G. McGee (Chair), *Normalizing the socialization of autistic children.* Symposium presented at the annual meeting of the Association for Behavior Analysis, Philadelphia.

Mason, S. A., McGee, G. G., Farmer-Dougan, V., & Risley, T. R. (1989). A practical strategy for reinforcer assessment. *Journal of Applied Behavior Analysis, 22,* 171–179.

McGee, G. G., Almeida, M. C., Sulzer-Azaroff, B., & Feldman, R. S. (1992). Promoting reciprocal interactions via peer incidental teaching. *Journal of Applied Behavior Analysis, 25,* 117–126.

McGee, G. G., Daly, T., Izeman, S. G., Mann, L. H., & Risley, T. R. (1991). Use of classroom materials to promote preschool engagement. *Teaching Exceptional Children, 23*(4), 43–47.

McGee, G. G., Krantz, P. J., Mason, D., & McClannahan, L. E. (1983). A modified incidental teaching procedure for autistic youth: Acquisition and generalization of receptive object labels. *Journal of Applied Behavior Analysis, 16,* 329–338.

McGee, G. G., Krantz, P. J., & McClannahan, L. E. (1985). The facilitative effects of incidental teaching on preposition use by autistic children. *Journal of Applied Behavior Analysis, 18,* 17–31.

McGee, G. G., Krantz, P. J., & McClannahan, L. E. (1986). An extension of incidental teaching procedures to reading instruction for autistic children. *Journal of Applied Behavior Analysis, 19,* 147–157.

McGee, G. G., Paradis, T., & Feldman, R. S. (1993). Free effects of integration on levels of autistic behavior. *Topics in Early Childhood Special Education, 13,* 57–67.

Morrier, M., & Daly, T. (1991, May). Data-based preschool design to accommodate incidental teaching activities. In G. G. McGee (Chair), *Empirical support for an incidental teaching approach to early social intervention for children with autism.* Symposium presented at the annual meeting of the Association for Behavior Analysis, Atlanta.

O'Brien, M., Porterfield, P. J., Herbert-Jackson, E. & Risley, T. R. (1979). *The toddler center manual: A practical guide to day care for one- and two-year olds.* Baltimore: University Park Press.

Odom, S. L., & Strain, P. S. (1986). A comparison of peer-initiation and teacher-antecedent interventions for promoting reciprocal social interaction of autistic preschoolers. *Journal of Applied Behavior Analysis, 19,* 59–71.

Regnier, M. C. (1991, May). Preschool to elementary school: Transition, follow-up and outcomes. In G. G. McGee (Chair), *Empirical support for an incidental teaching approach to early social intervention for children with autism.* Symposium presented at the annual meeting of the Association for Behavior Analysis, Atlanta.

Risley, T. R., & Favell, J. E. (1979). Constructing a living environment in an institution. In L. Hamerlynch (Ed.), *Behavioral systems for the developmentally disabled, II* (pp. 3–24). New York: Brunnel-Mazel.

Schopler, E., Reichler, R. J., De Vellis, R. F., & Daly, K. (1988). *The Childhood Autism Rating Scale.* Los Angeles: Western Psychological Services.

Schweitzer, J., & Izeman, S. G. (1986, May). *Development and implementation of a staff supervision program.* Paper presented at the annual meeting of the Association for Behavior Analysis, Milwaukee.

Skinner, B. F. (1948). *Walden Two.* New York: Macmillan.

Strain, P. S., Hoyson, M. H., & Jamieson, B. J. (1985). Normally developing preschoolers as intervention agents for autistic-like children: Effects on class deportment and social interactions. *Journal of the Division for Early Childhood, 9,* 105–115.

Strain P. S., & Odom, S. L. (1986). Peer social interactions: Effective intervention for social skills development of exceptional children. *Exceptional Children, 52,* 543–551.

Sulzer-Azaroff, B., Jones, E., & McGee, G. G., (1986, May). *The making of an integrated laboratory preschool.* Invited address presented at the annual meeting of the Association for Behavior Analysis, Milwaukee.

Thoreau, H. D. (1847). *Walden, or, Life in the Woods.* New York: C. N. Potter/Crown Publishers.

Thorndike, R. L., Hagen, E. R., & Sattler, J. M. (1986) *The Stanford-Binet Intelligence Scale,* 4th ed. Chicago: The Riverside Publishing Co.

Twardosz, S., Cataldo, M. F., & Risley, T. R. (1974). Open environment design for infant and toddler day care. *Journal of Applied Behavior Analysis, 7,* 529–549.

Sparrow, S. S., Balla, D. A., & Cicchetti, D. V. (1984). *Vineland Adaptive Behavior Scales: Interview Edition.* Circle Pines, MN: American Guidance Service.

Chapter 9

The Berkshire Hills Learning Center

MICHAEL D. POWERS

The Berkshire Hills Learning Center (BHLC) was created in 1991 by the Berkshire Hills Regional School District, a regional public school system in Western Massachusetts serving the communities of Stockbridge, Great Barrington, and West Stockbridge. While children with varying disabilities have been served by the school system in preschool through secondary programs throughout the years, it was not until the identification of several preschoolers with autism that the district elected to create a specialized program specifically for these youngsters.

Western Massachusetts is a largely rural, geographically diverse region of the state, made up of many small towns and two small cities (Springfield and Pittsfield). In contrast to the more densely populated eastern portion of the state, the number of children with autism under age 5 in Berkshire County (where the district is located) is low, approximately 17 based on the 1990 Census figures. Given the mostly rural nature of the county, it comes as no surprise that few public school programs had sufficient numbers of eligible students to justify creation of a comprehensive, specialized program to serve the needs of these children and their families.

The decision to establish such a program was prompted by historical, public policy, and economic considerations. The Berkshire Hills Regional School District has enjoyed a reputation for innovation and educational excellence for many years. It is also a system that strives to respond to the needs of children, families, and the communities served individually and collectively. The identification of several children with autism in late 1990, presented the administration and the school committee with both a challenge and an opportunity. The district had available for placement consideration a private, integrated preschool for children with autism located approximately 90 minutes away. In addition, the district maintained its own integrated prekindergarten program for children with special needs. Advocacy by parents and professionals in the district successfully highlighted the risk of dislocation from the community, excessive travel requirements, and the lack of school system awareness and preparation for the children during their elementary years inherent in the private school option. The learning and behavioral needs of the three identified children, including the need for a more intensive teacher-student ratio, suggested that the district's own excellent integrated prekindergarten classroom would be a better "next, least restrictive" placement rather than the initial placement option.

Recognizing the need to provide educational services for these children throughout their elementary and secondary school careers, the district decided to create an integrated preschool program of its own as the first step in developing a continuum of educational programs for these children and others who might be identified in the future.

The BHLC integrates up to six children with autism and up to seven typically developing peers in a program providing a combination of individual, small-group, and large-group instruction. Children attend the program from 9 a.m. to 3 p.m. Tuesday through Friday, and 9 a.m. to noon Mondays (allowing time for weekly program staff meetings from 12:30 to 3:30 p.m.), for a total of 27 hours each week of in-class instruction. The program operates for approximately 220 instructional days per year, following the regular school calendar for vacations from September through June. The BHLC incorporates instructional and curriculum practices that have received empirical support with preschoolers with autism over the past 15 years. These include the use of systematic instruction, generalization, and behavior management technologies; integration and parent training procedures; and developmental/behavioral curricula emphasizing skills needed in the "next, least restrictive environment." These components are described in detail by Powers (1992).

Because the BHLC is located in a comprehensive K–5 elementary school with a private day care program—the aforementioned pre-kindergarten special needs program and a full-day kindergarten also in the building—a broad range of structured and informal integration opportunities are utilized for instructional purposes. Thus, there are upwards of 40 typically developing peers available daily for structured and incidental (e.g., playground) teaching activities, across several instructional environments (i.e., the two integrated classrooms, the kindergarten, and the playground). While the children with autism spend the majority of their instructional time in the BHLC classroom, the pre-K, day care, and kindergarten programs are used on an individualized basis to expand their learning experiences and to teach tasks in instructional environments requiring larger numbers of students.

Any preschool age child with autism who resides within the district is eligible for placement in the BHLC. When openings are available, children with autism from other communities are admitted on a tuition, space-available basis, up to a total of six students with autism. Typically developing peers are recruited from communities throughout the county and must spend a minimum of 3 days per week in the program.

The BHLC is located in the Plain School in Stockbridge, Massachusetts. Financial support comes in the form of state and federal funds for children with special needs provided the district and from tuition paid by outside districts enrolling their children in the program. In 1992–93 the cost-per-pupil estimate is approximately $19,000. This figure includes the cost of transportation for the three in-district children.

Special education in Massachusetts is mandated by Chapter 766 of the Department of Education regulations. This law is noteworthy for its inclusion of the requirement that special education interventions must provide for the "maximum feasible benefit" to recipients of those interventions. This represents a significant improvement over the requirement in the federal law that interventions be "appropriate" (but need not be exemplary).

Thus, Chapter 766 provides for a far more stringent application of special educational safeguards for children with disabilities. The passage of the Individuals with Disabilities Education Act in 1991 and the inclusion of autism as a separate educational classification, coupled with the extensive empirical base for teaching children with autism available in the professional literature, provides parents and professionals with a substantive basis for requiring that educational interventions for preschoolers with autism be effective.

POPULATION SERVED BY THE BHLC

Since its inception, a total of seven preschoolers with autism have been enrolled in the BHLC. For the 1992–93 school year there are six students with autism and an average of 4.5 peers each day (range: 3–5). Of these six, three reside within the district and three attend on a tuition basis from neighboring towns. Peers accepted into the program have no known learning or behavioral special needs, and range in age from 46–60 months.

All children with special needs referred to the program were independently diagnosed with Autistic Disorder or Pervasive Developmental Disorder, Not Otherwise Specified according to *DSM-III-R* criteria (American Psychiatric Association, 1987). On referral each child's diagnosis is confirmed (or established) by the program team (i.e., consulting psychologist, school psychologist, classroom teacher, speech pathologist) during a psychoeducational assessment using the *Childhood Autism Rating Scale* (CARS; Schopler, Reichler, DeVellis, & Daly, 1988) and the criteria for Autistic Disorder from the *DSM-III-R*. Children who do not meet the criteria for autism established by the *CARS* are not enrolled in the program. The mean score on the *CARS* for children enrolled in the program is 41 (range: 33–46). The distribution of males-to-females of the children with autism is 5:1 respectively, and is roughly consistent with the incidence ratios reported in the literature. Typical peers are equally distributed by gender. The mean age of children with autism at admission is 35 months (range: 33–39 months). Developmental assessments done at admission indicate that children with autism entering the program are performing at approximately one-third of their expected chronological age-scores. Formal IQ testing is not undertaken at intake due to the absence / low rates of instructional control, basic attending skills, and general compliance to task demands of the children.

ASSESSMENT PROCEDURES

Assessment procedures used at the BHLC follow the model described by Powers and Handleman (1984). Both nomothetic and idiographic assessment data are obtained on enrollment and at regular intervals thereafter. In addition to providing objective indexes of current levels of developmental functioning, nomothetic measures such as the *Brigance Inventory of Early Development* (Brigance, 1978) and the *Peabody Picture Vocabulary Test–Revised* (Dunn & Dunn, 1981) permit comparisons of functioning during and after intervention. Moreover, to the extent that independent variables such as developmental level and severity of autism at intake are more objectively defined, comparisons across programs serving similar children are possible (Powers & Egel, 1988).

Once current levels of functioning are established at intake, instructional objectives are proposed and incorporated into each child's Individualized Educational Plan (IEP). The assessment of each instructional objective is idiographic; that is, the behavioral assessment process identifies the rate, topography, frequency or duration, and magnitude of the behavior/skill at baseline as well as criterion performance parameters expected. Behavioral assessment using objective and reliable direct observation procedures provide formative and summative outcome evaluation data, informing decision-making while treatment is in progress as well as summarizing the effectiveness of the intervention once completed. In this way a child's instructional program for any given IEP objective is highly individualized and can be evaluated against the response criterion established in the operational definition of the objective.

In addition to developmental assessments and measurement of initial levels of functioning, program staff assess each child's learning style and stimulus preferences at intake and then regularly throughout placement. The assessment of stimulus preferences permits a more precise description of sensory properties of various materials that may be preferred (i.e., reinforcing) to a child. The assessment process begins with observation and identification of preferred materials and activities for each child, followed by functional analysis of presumed preferences (Dyer, 1987). Information obtained from the stimulus preference assessment is then used to identify learning characteristics particular to a given child and to help determine materials that are most likely to provide highly reinforcing sensory feedback. For example, a child with visual and kinesthetic stimulus preferences who also demonstrates strengths in visual perceptual processing and visual sequencing will be offered a range of reinforcing materials and activities that provide visual or kinesthetic feedback. Visual cues will be incorporated into learning and activity routines, and a schedule board might be used to order these routines sequentially if the child has difficulty transitioning from one activity to another.

Medical evaluations required for admission into the program do not differ from those required for children enrolling in any other educational program in the district. Typically, children with autism referred to the BHLC have had comprehensive pediatric neurological workups. Some have had full interdisciplinary team evaluations completed by outside facilities. In all cases, data from these evaluations add to the assessment and treatment planning process.

TEACHING AND ADMINISTRATIVE STAFF

Provision of highly specialized services to children with autism requires a core group of professionals and paraprofessionals with a basic understanding of autism and minimum competencies in systematic instruction procedures, behavior management strategies, and working with families. Development of a new program within an existing system, as this school district did, often entails utilizing some existing staff as well as hiring new staff.

Development of the program model for the BHLC involved identifying existing human resources as well as those to be added. It was determined that an outside consultant was needed to guide the initial development of the program and to provide ongoing technical assistance and staff training. Teaching staff specializing in autism were not available within the district; these were additional hiring needs. In addition, because the administration was interested in the long-term integration of the preschoolers with autism into the regular education mainstream and their communities, the need for an "in-house" expert on autism who would be able to respond to clinical, administrative, and community concerns raised by the children was identified. It was determined that this role would be filled by one of the school psychologists already employed by the district, working over several years' time with the outside program consultant.

Program staff consist of direct service providers (teachers and instructional assistants), related service professionals (speech/language pathologist, school psychologist, occupational and physical therapists), administrative staff (building principal, director of pupil personnel services), community support staff (community liaison specialist), and technical support staff (program consultant). The teacher, instructional assistants, speech/language pathologist, school psychologist, and program consultant are considered members of the "core team" and meet weekly for a 3-hour clinical staffing to review child progress and make program recommendations and changes. Each is described below.

The classroom teacher holds certification in special education as well as in early childhood special education. He or she is responsible for the day-to-day operation and planning of the class, implementation of IEP objectives, and supervision of home-based parent training. There are four instructional assistants assigned to the program who in addition to classroom teaching responsibilities conduct the home-based parent training at least twice monthly with each family. Speech and language services are provided by a member of that department in the district who is assigned to the program for both consultative and direct services to children, per their IEP. The school psychologist on the team serves several functions in addition to activities traditionally identified with that role. This individual has been identified as the "in-house expert" to be trained by the program consultant as part of the long-term team building process. As such he or she co-chairs all staffings, attends all trainings, and participates in clinical and administrative decision-making. From the earliest phases of program development and implementation this individual worked closely with the program consultant to ensure that, when appropriate, the consultant's role could shift from clinical and administrative decision-making to that of periodic technical consultation to the core team. Because the program is within the public school system, administrative supervision and support is provided by the building principal (a former teacher of preschoolers with special needs) and the director of pupil personnel services. Additional support services are provided by the building and special education department secretaries.

From the beginning, the district envisioned the BHLC as the first part of a continuum of services for children with autism. Given the dual objectives of providing a program to deliver "maximum feasible benefit" to these children and of integrating the children and their families into the fabric of the community, the district created a unique position for a Community Liaison Specialist to assist and support families, regular educators, and community members in the integration of children with autism into the schools and community. The school psychologist on the core team fills this role in addition to his or her other responsibilities. As the "systems level consultant" between the community and the school, the Community Liaison Specialist facilitates the needs of families beyond the direct parent training services provided by the teaching staff. Developing a support group for parents, identifying respite services, or facilitating a relationship between the local public health clinic and families in the BHLC are examples of tasks the Community Liaison Specialist might address. In concert with the parent educators, this individual works to make the children and their families part of the communities where they reside by providing training and identifying natural sources of support within the community for the family.

The technical support during program development and implementation has been provided by an outside consultant with experience in the education and treatment of preschoolers with autism and their families. The program model called for the consultant to provide intensive training, supervision, and administrative support during the first year of operations, gradually fading back in years two and three to technical assistance for specific treatment issues as core staff competencies are demonstrated. As the program enters its second full year of operation, the anticipated timeline for consultative services has been maintained.

As noted earlier, staff training and clinical supervision are provided by the program consultant in conjunction with the classroom teacher. All core staff attend the weekly clinical staffing, as well as inservice training specific to the needs of children with autism. Finally, staff are encouraged to attend relevant regional conferences on autism, behavior analysis, and developmental disabilities.

CURRICULUM

The BHLC curriculum is based on the assumption that the heterogeneity of strengths and needs of preschoolers with autism and the multiplicity of settings used to educate them argues against a traditional approach to curriculum development. In addition to its intensive focus on the development of language and reciprocal social interactions, the curriculum emphasizes several components: (1) the characteristics of the current typical and next, least restrictive environments and the competencies necessary to succeed in each setting; (2) instructional domains which include play, social routines, transitions, school-readiness skills and "survival skills"; (3) the integration of developmental and behavioral approaches to curriculum development; and (4) the particular behavioral and academic strengths, needs, and excesses in the preschooler's repertoire. It is beyond the scope of this chapter to describe each component in detail; for this the reader is referred to Powers (1992).

Articulation of a coherent curriculum scope and sequence can be a challenging task for a program attempting to address the wide range of skills and deficits presented by preschoolers with autism. To supplement the components noted above, the BHLC uses the *Individual Goal Setting Curriculum* (IGS, Romanczyk & Lockshin, 1982) as a guide for instructional objective selection. The IGS provides several hundred possible instructional objectives across 16 different goal areas for use with children with autism. When used in conjunction with the curriculum development considerations noted above, the IGS provides staff with a cohesive scope and sequence of objectives for teaching language, social, self-help, cognitive, gross and fine motor skills. Sample objectives are provided in Table 9.1 (see page 173).

Student progress on each instructional objective is facilitated by the development of a formal, written teaching program for each objective. In addition to specifying the instructional objective and operational definition of the target behavior, the program details instructional methodology, error correction strategies, data collection method, and strategies to promote generalization and maintenance to be used. Beyond promoting consistency in teaching, the written program provides a measure of accountability for parents as well as a valuable tool for use in supervision of instructional activities.

At any given time, a student is actively engaged in approximately 7 to 10 IEP objectives from across the range of curriculum domains. While objectives typically are presented in a developmental sequence, functional considerations may dictate that objectives on the IEP be addressed out of sequence. Data on each objective are obtained according to the written program, not less than with twice-weekly probes (consisting of at least 10 teaching trials or behavioral opportunities for each probe day). Programs requiring more intensive one-to-one or small-group instruction using discrete trial teaching are evaluated daily. Programs using task analytic teaching procedures typically are probed twice weekly during a naturally-occuring opportunity. All data are graphed by instructional staff, each of whom has case management responsibilities for one or two children. These data are presented by each child's case manager at weekly staff meetings for team review and discussion.

Implementation of the curriculum across the day is facilitated by daily schedules in the context of monthly themes. Instructional time in one-to-one, small-group, and large-group settings is scheduled for each child with autism depending on his or her needs. Activity centers, lunch and snack times, integration into activities in other less restrictive classrooms (e.g., music or library with the kindergarteners), and playground provide the opportunities for incidental teaching throughout the day. Table 9.2 provides an example of a typical daily schedule.

INTEGRATION VERSUS SEGREGATION

The BHLC is an integrated preschool and is committed to the value of inclusive education. In addition to vastly expanded opportunities for peer modeling and teaching, we believe that typically developing children benefit from their experience with children with autism and from the excellent teaching provided by staff who individualize instruction for all children. This value notwithstanding, we also believe that children with autism have the right to the most effective teaching possible. As such, the BHLC approaches the issue of inclusion as a continuum of instructional settings ranging from least to most included. Placing a given child on the continuum is a relative process requiring attention to his or her instructional needs for the particular task, the task's demands, and the instructional needs of the other learners in the setting. Thus, it is conceivable that a child will initially receive more instruction in one-to-one settings than in groups if basic instructional control is absent or in the presence of severe aggressive or disruptive behaviors. However, as these instructional targets come under control, the child will move through the inclusion hierarchy to the least restrictive setting, culminating in full integration within the classroom for all activities.

We believe that the individualization of instructional objectives demands careful consideration of learner characteristics as well as characteristics of the instructional setting (including peers), and that children with autism should receive educationally valid interventions within an instructional context that promotes correct responding and generalization and maintenance of skills. Flexibility in balancing instructional tasks, learner characteristics, behavioral considerations, and integration with peers has allowed us to respond to each child individually and to maintain children with challenging learning and behavioral profiles in a fully integrated classroom. To allow maximum flexibility, several integration options are available. In addition to the peers enrolled in the BHLC program, staff access children enrolled in the private day care program, in the other integrated pre-kindergarten program, and those in the full-day kindergarten.

TABLE 9.1.   Examples of Instructional Objectives

Attending Skills
> Sits appropriately in large group (e.g., circle)
> Physically and visually attends to speaker

Gross Motor Skills
> Rides a tricycle 25 feet
> Rolls a ball 15 feet toward plastic bowling pins

Fine Motor Skills
> Cuts with a scissors
> Traces shapes within the lines of a template

Language Skills
> Points to 6 body parts
> Identifies self by name
> Follows 1-step commands
> Identifies preferred activities/reinforcers by name

Socialization
> Engages in reciprocal turn-taking
> Greets classmates and staff by name
> Demonstrates appropriate use of 3 toys

Cognitive
> Discriminates circles, squares, triangles
> Matches common objects to sample

Self-Care Skills
> Demonstrates independence in toileting
> Demonstrates independence in handwashing

BEHAVIOR MANAGEMENT

The behavioral challenges of children with autism have been the source of considerable debate within the profession over the past 10 years. The BHLC strives to implement two complementary principles in this regard: the use of empirically validated procedures and the use of community-referenced behavioral interventions. The location of the BHLC in a comprehensive elementary school demands attention to behavior management strategies that are at once functional (i.e., effective) and

TABLE 9.2.   Sample Daily Schedule

9:00–9:30	Arrival; put away coats, lunchboxes, toileting, deliver attendance, structured activities in Centers
9:30–9:45	Circle
9:45–10:20	Snack
10:20–11:45	Individual, small group instruction; structured activities in Centers or play area
11:45–12:20	Lunch
12:20–1:00	Quiet time
1:00–2:15	Individual, small group instruction; structured activities in Centers or play area
2:15–2:45	Playscape
2:45–3:00	Circle and dismissal

socially acceptable to regular educators and typical peers. Failure of the functionality principle relegates some children with autism to segregated programs because their behavior is viewed as too challenging for regular educators or students to contend with. Failure of the community-referenced intervention principle presents an even greater risk. Interventions outside the norms of the community highlight discrepancies between the intervention methods used with typical students and those with autism (possibly reinforcing the belief that the latter could never respond to more traditional methods of behavior management). In addition, extraordinary intervention practices place the student with autism at risk for the effects of inconsistency, failures in stimulus and response generalization, and lack of access to natural communities of reinforcement.

To address these issues the BHLC emphasizes the use of stimulus control strategies in behavior management, environmental manipula-

TABLE 9.3. Behavior Management Strategies

Differential reinforcement of communicative behavior

Differential reinforcement of incompatible behavior

Environmental rearrangement

Curriculum modification

Behavioral momentum

Interruption and redirection

Planned ignoring

Contingent observation

Brief time out

Brief (10 sec) manual restraint

tion, curriculum modification, and teaching functional and appropriate communicative alternatives to aberrant behavior. Consequent procedures in use emphasize access (or denial of access) to highly reinforcing materials or activities, *always* used in conjunction with differential reinforcement procedures. Table 9.3 identifies examples of behavior management procedures.

PARENTAL AND FAMILY INVOLVEMENT

Involvement of families to the extent requested by the family has been a key component of the BHLC's philosophy. Four principles guide implementation of this philosophy: (1) parents are co-teachers of their children; (2) families are the most enduring resource a child with autism will ever have; (3) services provided to families must be flexible and respond to the family's needs; (4) intervention and evaluation strategies must be "family friendly" and responsive to the other demands the family faces. Putting these principles into practice has led to the development of five separate service components available to families of children with autism in the program. Parents are free to choose any, all, or none of these options. Each is described briefly below.

Home-Based Parent Training

At least twice monthly instructional staff conduct home visits lasting 60 to 90 minutes to address teaching or behavioral issues at home and to promote generalization of skills taught or learned in school to the home (and vice versa). A home visit summary report highlights the visit's tasks and outcomes.

In-School Parent Training

Parents can sign up to come into the classroom and work with their own child on specific targeted skills with the purpose of acquiring new skills for use at home. Staff work with the parent and child during these sessions and utilize guided demonstrations and performance feedback to build parent competencies.

Volunteering

Parents may volunteer to help with or teach a particular activity (e.g., art, music) with staff assistance. In contrast to the in-class parent training, this experience is more general and not specific to the parent's own child. The general objectives are to increase familiarity and involvement.

Attendance at Weekly Staffings

On a rotating basis parents can sign up to attend the first hour of a weekly staff meeting, with such time devoted to the child's progress on IEP objectives and parent participation in the discussion and decision-making. In addition, parent reports of generalization and maintenance of skills at home, or of newly acquired skills at home, are addressed. Parent observation of and participation in the team process is an important goal of this component.

Newsletter

Staff produce a newsletter to inform families of monthly themes, classroom news, and activities, as well as upcoming events of interest in the community.

OUTCOME MEASURES

After the first year of the program's operation, one child moved from the BHLC to a less restrictive preschool setting (the integrated prekindergarten in the district). Program staff provide substantial transitional support to the receiving classroom teacher and will continue to be available as this child (and others) complete the preschool program and move into other educational settings within the school system.

Part of the outcome evaluation conducted by staff includes comparing measures of developmental functioning on the *Brigance* (1978) at intake with measures taken after 12 months of intervention. Using the *Proportional Change Index* (Wolery, 1983), these comparisons document accelerated rates of language, cognitive, and self-help skill development for the children with autism.

MAJOR ISSUES FOR FUTURE EFFORT

Development and implementation of the BHLC has been a dynamic, evolutionary process. Given the infancy of the program, we expect continuing changes over the next several years, particularly with regard to addressing the needs of a diverse group of students with autism in a single setting.

As a public school program, the BHLC has an obligation to provide services to all children with autism between the ages of 3 to 5 residing within the district. Given the small overall population base, however, it is highly unlikely that sufficient numbers of children with autism will be identified to create a second classroom. As such, we find ourselves some-times challenged by the mandate to provide individualized, responsive instruction within the context of significant behavioral challenges in an integrated classroom. Our efforts at creating "micro-teaching" environ-ments, at environmental modification, and in the use of data from stim-ulus preference assessments to develop instructional and behavioral con-trol suggest to us that we are on the right track. Given our commitment to applying the best instructional and behavioral technology available in a public school program with the attendant restrictions on clinical and administrative control, we look forward to creative solutions necessitated and informed by the setting, the community, and the children.

One of the critical tasks for the future involves creation of a broad "continuum of placement options" for graduates of the BHLC, including development and validation of entrance criteria for each option. Ideally, these options should be as responsive and integrated as the BHLC. We have already begun this process with the transition of one child into the developmental pre-kindergarten program in the district. We anticipate program options for the future to include placement in a noncategorical resource room (currently staffed by a teacher who spent a year as an instructional assistant in the BHLC); placement in a typical kindergarten without or with an instructional aide; and placement in a categorical resource room with mainstreaming as appropriate into chronologically age-appropriate activities.

The process of developing an integrated preschool for children with autism within a public school system has demonstrated for us the value of such an undertaking from social, educational, economic, and tech-nological perspectives. The question remaining for future clinicians, ed-ucators, and parents is not whether such programs *are* viable, but rather how to allow programs to *remain* viable and at the forefront of service delivery.

ACKNOWLEDGMENTS

Dr. George Lane, Superintendent of Schools, and the families and staff of the BHLC have provided the vision and commitment to making the program succeed. Their efforts are gratefully acknowledged.

REFERENCES

American Psychiatric Association. (1987). *Diagnostic and statistical manual of mental disorders* (3rd ed.–revised). Washington, DC: Author.

Brigance, A. H. (1978). *Brigance Inventory of Early Development.* Woburn, MA: Curriculum Associates.

Dunn, L., & Dunn, L. (1981). *Peabody Picture Vocabulary Test–Revised.* Circle Pines, MN: American Guidance Service.

Dyer, K. (1987). The competition of autistic stereotyped behavior with usual and specifically-assessed reinforcers. *Research in Developmental Disabilities, 8,* 607–626.

Powers, M. D. (1992). Early intervention for children with autism. In D. Berkell (Ed.), *Autism: Diagnosis, assessment and treatment* (pp. 225–252). Hillside, NJ: Lawrence Erlbaum.

Powers, M. D., & Egel, A. L. (1988, May). *Child and family factors in preschoolers with autism.* Paper presented at the 14th annual convention of the Association for Behavior Analysis, Philadelphia, PA

Powers, M. D., & Handleman, J. S. (1984). *Behavioral Assessment of Severe Developmental Disabilities.* Austin, TX: PRO-ED.

Romanczyk, R. G., & Lockshin, S. (1982). *The I.G.S. Curriculum.* Vestal, NY: CBTA.

Schopler, E., Reichler, R. J., DeVellis, R. F., & Daly, K. (1988). *The Childhood Autism Rating Scale (CARS).* Los Angeles: Western Psychological Services.

Wolery, M. (1983). The proportional change index: An alternative for comparing child change data. *Exceptional Children, 50,* 167–170.

Chapter 10

The Children's Unit for Treatment and Evaluation

RAYMOND G. ROMANCZYK, LINDA MATEY,
and STEPHANIE B. LOCKSHIN

SETTING

The Children's Unit for Treatment and Evaluation serves children 12 months through 12 years of age. It is located on the Binghamton University campus which is part of the State University of New York system. It is one of the two direct service components of the Institute for Child Development. The Children's Unit was established in 1975 and granted special status in 1977 through an act of the New York State Legislature (Senate Bill 5911-A) which allowed the Unit to exist with a dual status as a fully certified New York State Education Department private school and at the same time organizationally as part of Binghamton University. The bill permits school districts and other state agencies to contract directly with the Children's Unit.

This chapter will focus on the preschool component of the Children's Unit, but it is important to note that the preschool and school-age programs differ only on the basis of the age of the children served rather than through structure or specific activity. The preschool program is conducted between 9:00 a.m. and 2:30 p.m., 5 days per week, 12 months per year. Children may be admitted and discharged at any time throughout the calendar year. Referrals originate from a wide range of sources including school districts, physicians, social services, family court, mental health professionals, and parental self-referral.

Funding for student placement comes from two sources dependent upon child age. For those children below 3 years of age, placement decision is approved by family court and administratively processed by the Department of Health. The tuition is paid for by the county in which the child resides. For children between the ages of 3 to 5, each school district's Committee for Preschool Special Education approves placement with a member of the County Health Department sitting in as an ad hoc member of the committee. Once again, tuition is paid by the county in which the child resides. The 1992–93 tuition for a child who attends our 12-month program was $18,250.

As a New York State Education Department certified private school, the Children's Unit must comply with regulations of the State Education Department with respect to child/staff ratios; age distribution, and programmatic as well as operational regulations including such items as periodic on-site evaluations and external fiscal auditing. The program is also implicitly evaluated by the University with respect to the substantial physical plant that it occupies and other resources allocated to it.

PHILOSOPHY

The philosophy behind the creation of the Children's Unit was to serve as an adjunctive component to services offered in the surrounding communities. That is, it was designed as a short-term program and not to be a parallel program in which children would enter and remain for many years. Its focus was to achieve an approximately 3-year duration of placement that would result in sufficient change to permit the child to function within the context of the services available within their local community. Because of this philosophy the emphasis is upon a focused rather than balanced curriculum (Romanczyk & Lockshin, 1984). However, this focused approach, which may also be termed a deficit-oriented approach, seeks to identify the factors that are most crucial in preventing the child from benefiting fully from the continuum of services in the local community. By focusing upon these deficits and problem areas, rather than attempting to provide a balanced curriculum, it is possible to provide in a brief span of time the necessary intensity of services that permit the relatively speedy transition to community-based services. This model is of particular importance with respect to preschool children, as early identification, in many cases several years before placement within the school system would typically take place, permits intensive services to come to bear at a particularly opportune point in the child's development. Because of this focus upon child participation in services within their local community and the focus upon individual child characteristics that are impeding such placement, the criteria for discharge for the program reflects a specific child / local community interaction. That is, because the Children's Unit serves children from dozens of different communities, from urban to suburban to rural, and the resources available in these different communities vary to an extreme degree, an absolute level of progress is not utilized for discharge decisions, but rather progress relative to what is required within the child's local community becomes the criteria. This approach allows maximum flexibility for families and their local school district.

DEMOGRAPHICS

Since its inception in January of 1975, the Children's Unit has served 70 preschool children. The first preschool child served entered the program in July of 1976, and in 1992, 12 preschool children were served. This equals 36% of the total Children's Unit enrollment for the year. It is important to note that in New York State an educational classification is used to determine if the child is eligible for specific special educational services. The classification is determined by the Committee for Preschool Special Education, based on recommendations from committee members. Within New York State, each child who receives special education services must be classified as having one of the following 11 disabling conditions: autism, emotional disturbance, learning disability, mental retardation, deaf, hard of hearing, speech impaired, visually impaired, orthopedically impaired, other health impaired, or multiply disabled. The Children's Unit is approved to serve preschool youngsters with the classifications of autism, emotional disturbance, and multiple disabilities. To date, 38 children with autism and 32 children classified as having emotional disturbance have been enrolled in our preschool program. It should be noted that educational classifications are not synonymous with a psychiatric diagnosis. However, in New York, a child's educational classification solely determines eligibility for special education services.

The gender distribution of the preschool population of children with autism is 73% males and 27% females. The demographic characteristics of the preschool children in attendance from 1976 to 1992 at the Children's Unit are summarized in Table 10.1.

In summary, children with an educational classification of autism enter our program at a younger age and the length of stay is greater than those children classified as having severe emotional disturbance. However, there is also a significant difference between the two classifications with respect to mental age level at admission. As can be seen, children with severe emotional disturbance typically enter the Children's Unit with a mental age that is 2 years higher than those children with the classification of autism.

When comparing the family structures, proportionately more intact families were present at admission in homes with children with autism and more foster placements were provided for children with severe emotional disturbance. Social services involvement was greatest in single-parent households in both cases, with more families of children with severe emotional disturbances overall receiving social services. Finally, the families receiving public assistance in this sample were entirely from single-parent families and here too more families of children with severe emotional disturbance received such aid.

ASSESSMENT PROCEDURES

In New York State, procedures enabling a preschool aged child to receive special education services follow a specific sequence of events. First, any professional or parent who feels that a preschool child is not developing appropriately or has special or specific needs, may make a request to the Committee for Preschool Special Education (CPSE) to have an evaluation performed to assess the child's current developmental, behavioral, and social levels. The committee chair is then required to provide the referring party with a list of approved preschool evaluators from which to select an agency to conduct an evaluation. The evaluating agency's role is to assess the child's development for the purpose of

TABLE 10.1.   Child Demographics at the Time of Admission to the Program

	Age	Age Range	Duration	Mental Age
Autism	3.6 years	1.4–4.8 years	3.1 years	2.1 years
ED	4.2 years	3.3–4.8 years	2.2 years	4.3 years

	Two parents	Single parent	Foster parents
Autism	74%	16%	10%
ED	50%	19%	31%

		Social Services	Public Assistance
Autism	two parent	8%	0%
	single parent	67%	50%
ED	two parent	0%	0%
	single parent	83%	83%

determining whether or not special education services are warranted. The evaluating agency is *not* to make a specific placement referral but merely to assess whether or not special education services are indicated. The CPSE then makes a decision regarding classification and whether or not the child requires special education services. If so, a placement is determined and the child begins services at the designated agency.

If the Children's Unit is the chosen preschool evaluation site, a number of assessment procedures are utilized. The *Denver Developmental Screening* (Frankenburg, Dodd & Fandall, 1973) and *Slosson Intelligence Test* (Armstrong & Jensen, 1981) are frequently utilized. Speech and language is evaluated using the *Peabody Picture Vocabulary Test* (Dunn & Dunn, 1981), and the *Carrow Test of Elicited Language* (Carrow, 1973), and the *Goldman-Fristoe Articulation Test* (Goldman & Fristoe, 1969). Videotaped formal and informal language samples are obtained which are then evaluated by the speech pathologist to determine age appropriateness of communication. In the area of social development, a *Vineland Adaptive Behavior Scale* (Harrison, 1985) score is obtained via interviews with the parent, guardian, or referring party. In addition, videotapes are taken of the child in a one-to-one work and play session with an adult, one-to-one play session with a single peer, and small-group play session. Upon reviewing such videotapes, characteristics such as child's ability to attend, his/her level of play skills, social behavior and social interactions, as well as overall behavior are assessed. Additional records from consulting physicians, specialists, occupational or physical therapists, and social service records are reviewed. A complete social history is obtained from the referring party which includes not only parental, birth, and infant development issues, but also current interaction styles with various significant others in the child's environment and a review of social, habilitative, and maladaptive behaviors in the child's repertoire.

This evaluation is conducted by a licensed psychologist, special education teachers, speech pathologist, and psychology interns. Consultants who are also available to provide input on specific cases include occupational and physical therapy, adaptive physical education, a nurse, and a medical professional. Although such consultants are not used for every evaluation, such professionals are consulted if there are questions that might be important in determining the child's need for special education services.

Assessments Upon Admission

When a child is enrolled at the Children's Unit, a battery of formal and informal assessments are conducted by various members of the Children's Unit staff. Included are instruments listed in our preschool evaluation section that have not yet been administered. In addition, assessments utilizing the Individualized Goal Selection (IGS) curriculum are conducted throughout a 30-day period to assess the child's specific level of functioning in all developmentally appropriate areas. These assessments are conducted periodically over the 30-day period to ensure that the performance obtained is representative and not based on atypical emotional, behavioral, or social responses at any given time. In addition, baseline data are taken on identified problematic behaviors as well as adaptive skills to determine their presence, intensity, frequency, and duration. Several parent interviews are typically conducted during this 30-day assessment period as well.

Also during this time, the child is exposed to and encouraged to participate in various classroom activities where group size, constitution, subject area, setting, and lesson duration are systematically monitored to evaluate the child's reaction and ability to benefit from each. From this, an Individual Education Plan (IEP) can be developed to meet each individual child's needs with these parameters in mind. A number of settings, group sizes, etc. may be required in a single period of time depending on the lesson and skills being addressed, and thus the IEP is developed to allow for such individualization. For example, if a child requires a one-to-one setting for speech and language but is able to benefit from peer observational learning in a concept formation group, his or her schedule will reflect group sizes of both types.

TEACHING AND ADMINISTRATIVE STAFF

As mentioned previously, our preschool and school-age programs have identical components. The staffing pattern listed below is for the entire program. Staff are not assigned to one or the other programs but participate fully in both.

Teachers

The Children's Unit currently employs seven special education teachers; this includes five classroom teachers, one head teacher and one coordinating teacher. Special education teachers, all certified by the State Education Department, are directly responsible for the formulation and implementation of IEPs, the creation of the specific educational programs needed to execute the IEPs, the provision of direct educational services, and supervision of paraprofessional staff involved in the program implementation. Further, they are responsible for the systematic and detailed evaluation of child progress. Teachers provide information regarding children's programs and progress to the parent coordinator to ensure systematic and complete feedback to the child's parents.

The head teacher is also responsible for serving as a role model in assessing, implementing, and developing child programs. Providing feedback to teachers, aides, and undergraduates on their classroom performance is an additional role assumed by the head teacher.

The coordinating teacher's primary responsibility is to ensure the quality of the children's programs; this is accomplished through direct contact with children to perform assessment and exploratory educational and behavioral programs. This is also accomplished by consulting with professional staff in the development and implementation of programs; reviewing child progress; coordinating and reviewing the IEP process and all computer assisted analyses; monitoring the daily activities of the Children's Unit; and the scheduling of child instructional groups, the professional, and paraprofessional staff. In addition, this individual serves as a liaison between the director and the direct care staff as well as the Children's Unit representative to school districts, parents, community groups, and professionals.

Speech Therapists

The Children's Unit employs one full-time and one part-time speech pathologist who are responsible for assessment and implementation of speech and language programs. These individuals consult with all professional staff in performing their duties so as to create unified language programs that are conducted by the entire staff consistent with the Children's Unit philosophy of integration of services. The speech pathologist provides direct services as well as supervising paraprofessional staff.

Other Therapists

The Children's Unit population does not typically require individualized occupational therapist or physical therapist services and so the Children's Unit does not employ such individuals on a full- or part-time basis. Instead, consultants are used and visit the Children's Unit on a monthly basis to review videotapes and work with specific children on goals that are required in the various areas of their discipline. The emphasis is on training all staff to implement programs so that such objectives will be integrated into the child's daily activities. By training staff to implement such programs and procedures, the child is able to benefit from continual assistance on specific skills as opposed to isolating practice in these areas to two or three half-hour periods per week with a specific individual.

There are, however, cases in which individual occupational or physical therapy is recommended for a given child and in those instances the required professionals deliver the services at the Children's Unit.

Psychologists

The Children's Unit employs two levels of psychological services. The director of the program, a New York State licensed psychologist, provides psychological services and supervision, as well as chairs the weekly full staff meeting. This individual assists the staff in the creation, implementation, and evaluation of intervention programs.

A second level of psychological services are those of the clinical psychology graduate interns. Typically there are two graduate interns who assist in the daily activities of the Children's Unit including standardized assessment, behavioral assessment, and data management and analysis. The primary role of the clinician is to serve as a consultant to the teachers, assist in the behavioral development of the children, and conduct child therapy groups that focus on social skills and emotional expressions. Clinical interns are also an integral part of the parent program to be discussed later on in this chapter.

Administrators

The director and a full-time administrative assistant comprise the administrative staff. The responsibilities of these individuals include development, coordination, monitoring, and updating of Children's Unit policies, procedures, staff training, and organization as is necessary to provide appropriate and effective services to the children. This includes complying with New York State regulations for monitoring and record-keeping service provisions.

Teaching Assistants

The Children's Unit currently employs eight teacher aides, all certified by the State Education Department. Many of the teacher aides currently have or are pursuing bachelor's and master's degrees. An explicit career ladder has enabled many aides to be promoted to teacher through taking necessary advanced coursework (tuition is subsidized by the Children's Unit) and by demonstrating superior competence in the role of aide.

All aides attend and are considered participating members of the weekly staff meeting and are also encouraged to attend professional conferences. Their role extends beyond that of traditional teacher aide and includes: (1) assisting the special education teachers with the preparation and implementation of individual education plans, (2) general organization of classroom records, (3) maintenance of instructional materials, (4) attending home visits with the teacher, (5) collecting and collating performance and behavior data, and (6) implementing highly specialized educational and treatment programs. In addition, they are responsible for general organization of classroom records and materials as well as various additional Children's Unit functions necessary to enhance child progress.

Undergraduates and Volunteers

To date over 1,000 undergraduates have participated in the Children's Unit as paraprofessionals. Participation earns the student course credit. The course syllabus, in addition to an extensive sequence of skill training prior to interaction with children, also includes reading current literature in the field and collecting, analyzing, and presenting data in a convention poster format. There are two levels of undergraduates—the first is program trainees. These paraprofessionals are the least experienced of the Children's Unit staff and are under supervision by professional staff members at all times. In the initial stages of training, the paraprofessional is given the opportunity to assist staff with a particular child or group of children. Professional staff provide oral and written feedback to these individuals until proficiency and program implementation and knowledge of Children's Unit procedures are acquired. The length of this phase of training varies as a function of the pace at which the individual paraprofessionals acquire skills. However, a minimum time period of 4 to 6 weeks is required before any person at this level is allowed to assume aspects of program implementation for a given child.

The second level is program assistant. These individuals are responsible for serving as primary assistants to the professional staff members. These individuals, having had a minimum of 1 year experience working at the Children's Unit, use advanced instructional skills and focus the activities in an area such as language, academics, or social development.

For the last 6 years, the Children's Unit also has had volunteer foster grandparents participating in the program. Currently there are three such individuals at the Children's Unit whose role is to provide one-to-one interaction. Interactions tend to be of a social or play nature and are often utilized as a reinforcer for a given child. The grandparents in the program are required to adhere to specific guidelines, but their interactions with the children are designed to be relatively unstructured and spontaneous.

Behavior Analyst

The Children's Unit employs one individual who is specifically trained in data collection, analysis, and evaluation methodology. It is this person's responsibility to monitor, organize, catalog, graph, and retrieve child data in a manner which facilitates in-depth progress analysis and evaluation. A primary component of this position is to conduct observation of child behavior in addition to that conducted by the staff in order to provide additional information for the purpose of critical analysis of specific child behavior. This individual is responsible for approximately 1,700 IEP goals and over 250 individual behavior programs throughout the school year, as well as monitoring staff to ensure that data collection, summary, and submission are completed accurately and within stated timelines.

Program Consultants

The Children's Unit staff also includes consultants whose background abilities and expertise have been solicited to assist the Children's Unit staff on various issues of program development, implementation, and evaluation. Periodically, such individuals visit the Children's Unit, both to familiarize themselves or refamiliarize themselves with the Children's Unit function, progress, and current status and also to provide direct feedback on specific issues.

PROFESSIONAL STAFF TRAINING AND SUPERVISION

Initial Training

Beginning teachers and teacher aides at the Children's Unit are supported in numerous ways including implementing a mentor philosophy (an explicit pairing of a new teacher with an experienced one). Daily opportunities to observe different facets of Unit functioning, and discussion of these facets with the coordinating teacher prior to participation is routine. A gradual increase in child-related activities/responsibilities is provided to enable each individual to acquire skills on a given level, before assuming responsibility for more advanced activities. Videotapes are made and feedback provided on interactions with the children and are periodically continued throughout the course of the child's involvement at the Children's Unit. Specific introduction to and discussion of Children's Unit policy, philosophy, and functions are conducted throughout the initial training phase that spans 6 months.

Part of a staff member's introduction to the Children's Unit involves participating in an in-service program designed to acquaint new staff members with Children's Unit policies, procedures, guidelines, and philosophy. Specific topics covered under this introduction include:

- the procedures and rationales for presenting a child case study at a staff meeting
- a review of the Children's Unit communication structure, including the various types of meetings involved and information regarding when, who, and where these meetings are to be held as well as their purpose and the responsibilities for the individual staff member
- discussions concerning professional conduct, staff interactions, child interactions, the importance of confidentiality
- implementation procedures including the steps required to develop an IEP; how to conduct assessments; how to assess skill subsets, construct operational definitions and terminal successful performance definitions, collect, summarize and analyze data
- how to conduct behavior intervention programs and baseline measurement

- how to conduct parallel programs

- how to use the computer for data input and analysis

- the appropriate manner in which to correspond with parents, agencies, and other professionals.

- how to prepare, deliver, and monitor feedback to undergraduate paraprofessionals

- review of staff evaluation processes

Ongoing Supervision and Training

Ongoing teacher supervision occurs on a daily basis via direct observation and verbal feedback on classroom performance. At weekly individual supervision meetings, the coordinating teacher addresses written lessons and progress evaluation and covers a current review of individual children and educational objectives. Overall performance in terms of timeliness, skill level, quality of written reports, etc. are discussed. In addition, two written evaluations are prepared for each teacher, each year by the coordinating teacher. The first, presented in the fourth month of the school year addresses the following 10 skill areas via an extensive (typically five single-spaced pages) narrative:

1. child interaction

2. classroom staff interaction

3. parent, agency, visitor interaction

4. interpersonal sensitivity

5. lesson preparation

6. lesson implementation

7. child progress documentation

8. classroom management

9. classroom organization

10. response to feedback

The second occurs 4 months later and consists of a list of specific objectives, each of which is evaluated in two ways. The first is an evaluation of change since the initial evaluation, and the second is by absolute skill/performance level. Both of these evaluations are completed by the coordinating teacher and reviewed with the director. A meeting is held with each teacher individually to present and discuss the evaluation. The critical component is that these evaluations are a formalization of the daily and weekly feedback given to the teachers and as such are a condensation of previously discussed issues. Thus, no information contained within the evaluation comes as a "surprise" to the teacher. In addition, the second evaluation is directly tied to the first and change toward a goal is evaluated based on the initial evaluation, as well as absolute performance level.

As part of ongoing supervision, numerous meetings are held on a weekly basis to ensure effective communication and ongoing feedback to and between staff members. These meetings are held after the children have been dismissed for the day. An example of a weekly schedule follows.

Briefing.   Held two times a week and attended by all staff members. The purpose is to communicate pertinent new procedures and/or procedural changes, to discuss the means of increasing program implementation efficiency, and to review the responsibilities involved in upcoming events, deadlines, etc.

Staff meeting.   A meeting attended by all staff members and chaired by the director. The purpose is to review child progress and determine treatment strategy changes if required.

Teacher supervision meetings.   These meetings are held individually between the coordinating teacher, special education teachers, and speech pathologist. The purpose of the meeting is to review child data, discuss new program approaches and techniques, discuss staff concerns, and review overall professional performance and expectations.

Aide supervision meeting.   On a weekly basis, there is a supervision meeting conducted by each teacher with their respective aides. The purpose of these meetings is to discuss child performance and current strategies; review current aide responsibilities and timeliness; provide feedback on performance; and discuss classroom functioning and ways to enhance efficiency, effectiveness, and a positive atmosphere.

Staff work meeting.   This meeting is scheduled 1 day a week for a 1-hour period. It is attended by all staff and serves a variety of purposes depending on current needs. For example, it may be used to carry out responsibilities with specific emphasis on those that require consultation with other staff members, to complete periodic and/or unscheduled objectives (e.g., completing report cards), to work with colleagues on special team assignments, to change or maintain classroom organization and structure, or to complete any assignments due during the current week.

Professional development meetings. These meetings are scheduled every 6 weeks. They are conducted by the coordinating teacher with each staff member and the purpose is to discuss future professional goals; current issues and obstacles of a paraprofessional; and interpersonal, philosophical, organizational, and efficiency issues.

Another component of the ongoing supervision and training of the full-time staff is that of setting deadlines and monitoring completion of responsibilities. This is an explicitly scheduled process and the staff members productivity is logged on a routine basis. An initial computer generated schedule is created for the meetings for which that staff member is responsible and individual responsibilities such as child habilitative program development, report completion, and data summary and analysis. These schedules are generated individually for each staff member and time lines are assessed based on the skill level and efficiency of the individual staff member. Times lines are set to correspond with deadlines that are necessary to ensure maximum effectiveness of child treatment. Therefore at any given time, should a staff member be unable to maintain a preestablished deadline, they are required to give notice in advance of the anticipated deadline along with written notification of when the item or task will be submitted. In this way schedules reflect the flexibility that is necessary when working with a number of individuals while still maintaining close monitoring of completion and quality control.

Quality control is also monitored by an explicit schedule for submitting any edits or revisions that are based on the staff members's initial submission. During the periods of the school year where teacher responsibilities are greatest (e.g., at the end of the school year) public posting is utilized to monitor responsibility completion. Large wall charts are created for each staff member that graphically display tasks, their time line, and current degree of completion. The purpose of such posting is to allow for all staff members to be able to coordinate activities and responsibilities. For example, a speech pathologist may organize a program development schedule to mirror the sequence chosen by the special education teacher. In this way the IEP may be completed without extended time lags between when the teacher and speech pathologist complete a given child's draft IEP.

This highly structured set of checks and balances receives a wide range of reactions from the individual staff members. Some individuals clearly work more efficiently when monitored and when progress is publicly posted. Others feel such close supervision is not necessary. However, independent of staff perceptions and opinions, the outcome is clear in that experience has shown that such monitoring is highly effective and is necessary, not only to maintain appropriate time lines, but also to be able to coordinate the efforts of multiple staff members involved in each facet of service delivery.

Paraprofessional Staff Training

Staff training and supervision for paraprofessionals has the following components:

1. An introduction to policies and procedures which provides a historical development of the Children's Unit; a description of the population served; the specifications of the service, research and training objectives; and an introduction to the physical environment, organizational structure, and the decision making processes. Their role as a paraprofessional is discussed, as well as policies and procedures regarding confidentiality and safety, functions and purposes of the computer system, and data collection tools and procedures. These objectives are accomplished by intensive workshops conducted by the professional staff scheduled throughout the first weeks of the semester.

2. The second objective focuses on paraprofessional interactions. Specific skills and behaviors are discussed concerning interactions with other staff, participation in supervision, and the type of feedback from professional staff that will be delivered in both written and oral forms.

3. The third objective is to teach principles of behavior analysis and service delivery. Specifics include introduction to the philosophy and rationale of behavioral treatment with children, understanding the functional analysis of behavior, defining and measuring behavior, fundamentals of within subject design analysis, strategies for increasing deficit behavior, ethical considerations and procedures for reducing behavioral excesses,

fundamentals of discrimination learning and generalization, and evaluating program outcome.

4. The next component is *in vivo* training to demonstrate proficiency in the use of basic behavioral teaching techniques. Methods include observation of professional staff, a sequence of "hands-on" sessions under close supervision of training coordinators, conducting child programs under direct supervision, assignment to specific children to conduct programs under close supervision of training coordinators and professional staff, and review and discussions of programs in a weekly paraprofessional seminar conducted by professional staff.

Ongoing training and supervision once competency is assessed in these areas is accomplished by: (1) the provision of paraprofessional performance feedback forms completed by a training coordinator after each of the initial sessions, (2) paraprofessional performance feedback forms completed by professional staff and distributed to paraprofessionals on a weekly basis, and (3) paraprofessional global evaluations completed and reviewed by professional staff and distributed to paraprofessionals every 4 months.

CURRICULUM

Philosophy

The Children's Unit utilizes the IGS curriculum (Romanczyk & Lockshin, 1982) which was specifically designed for young children with autism and related developmental, learning, and emotional disabilities. Its intent is to provide a broad guide or "road map" to development in 16 areas felt to be important for child progress rather than a lock step sequence of exercises. While it is organized in a developmental sequence, it is not expected that a child would simply progress through each particular item in sequence. Rather, it serves as an assessment tool, a guide, and also provides a format for setting priorities.

Structurally it is composed of 16 areas of development and levels of development are specified within each area. Further, within each level, there are stages of development and in turn within each stage there are specific behaviorally referenced tasks. The tasks then serve as the focus for activities and intervention which are then logically grouped under stages and levels of development. This organizational structure represents a filter approach in which one can use the area delineation to specify broad goals. The levels serve to set priorities within areas and the stages in turn represent specific deficit components within the levels of priority. The tasks serve as the day-to-day activities to be conducted by staff in addressing the child's needs.

For example, in the area of expressive language, a level would be "labeling" or "descriptive speech." The stage is intended to represent an annual goal or a goal that is expected to be accomplished by the close of the school year. A task is equivalent to a short-term goal and is defined as the intermediary steps necessary to achieving the annual goal. Thus, short-term goals are selected such that the mastery of successive such goals in a given stage contribute to the achievement of the annual goal. Finally, it is not expected that learning in a functional context will occur merely by the acquisition of individual goals. Therefore, within the IGS curriculum, tasks and skills exist in overlapping concepts and different stages use specific skills in various ways (see Table 10.2). This "parallel programming" is intended to insure that the child generalizes and maintains acquired skills.

The curriculum is also structured such that each of the several thousand entries has a unique code number associated with it. This code serves as the organizing principle for many activities at the Children's Unit from direct institution to administrative management. Draft IEPs are created by the staff by entering code numbers into custom-written computer software that translates such codes into full prose documents that serve as a structure for discussion. Parents are asked to use a checklist that is based on an abbreviated form of the IGS to assist in setting priorities. Once the IEPs have been approved by the parents, this information is directly transferred into a sophisticated computer database. This database is then utilized on a day-to-day basis to record child progress on each of the items in the IEP. Further, the IEP information is transferred to a combination word processor/database that permits staff to create explicit written protocols for each IEP goal. That is, staff are required to produce a document that can be read by a reasonably well trained individual and then implemented. This document serves as the keystone for maintaining high levels of staff consistency and communication. Because a large number of staff are employed and also a large

TABLE 10.2.   Outline of the I.G.S. Curriculum

Area 1   Reduction of Maladaptive Behavior
Level 1. Self-injurious Behavior
Level 2. Aggressive Behavior
Level 3. Disruptive Behavior
Level 4. Property Destruction
Level 5. Self-Stimulatory Behavior
Level 6. Non-Compliance
Level 7. Perseverative Behavior
Level 8. Echolalic Speech
Level 9. Inappropriate Speech
Level 10. Eating Problems

Area 2   Attentive Skills
Level 1. Prespeech Attentive Skills
Level 2. Group Attentive Skills
Level 3. Independent Attentive Skills

Area 3   Speech
Level 1. Non-Verbal Imitation
Level 2. Vocalization
Level 3. Vocal Imitation
Level 4. Verbal Imitation
Level 5. Remediation of Articulation
         Difficulties Through Imitation
Level 6. Spontaneous Production of
         Target Sounds
Level 7. Speech Quality

Area 4   Receptive Language
Level 1. Non-Verbal Compliance with
         Requests
Level 2. Non-Verbal Identification of
         Objects and Events

Area 5   Expressive Language
Level 1. Labeling
Level 2. Descriptive Speech
Level 3. Interrogative Speech
Level 4. Story Telling Skills
Level 5. Conversational Skills
Level 6. Advanced Syntax

Area 6   Concept Formation
Level 1. Visual Tracking
Level 2. Visual Discrimination
Level 3. Auditory Discrimination
Level 4. Visual Memory
Level 5. Auditory Memory
Level 6. Spatial Relationships
Level 7. Sequencing
Level 8. Classification

Area 7   Motor Skills
Level 1. Gross Motor
Level 2. Specific Gross Motor Activities
Level 3. Fine Motor

Area 8   Self-Help Skills
Level 1. Self-Feeding
Level 2. Self-Toileting
Level 3. Self-Dressing
Level 4. Personal Hygiene
Level 5. Food Preparation
Level 6. Purchasing
Level 7. Housekeeping Skills

Area 9   Social Skills
Level 1. Non-Verbal Interaction
Level 2. Verbal Interaction
Level 3. Play Skills

Area 10   Reading
Level 1. Readiness Skills
Level 2. Sight Vocabulary and Vocabulary
         Development
Level 3. Word Attack Skills
Level 4. Comprehension
Level 5. Spelling

Area 11   Writing Skills
Level 1. Prewriting
Level 2. Copies from a Visual Cue
Level 3. Independent Writing

(continued)

TABLE 10.2. *Continued*

Area 12   Arithmetic
Level 1. Counting and Number
Identification
Level 2. Addition
Level 3. Subtraction
Level 4. Word Problems
Level 5. Telling Time
Level 6. Measurement
Level 7. Basic Concepts
Level 8. Multiplication
Level 9. Division
Level 10. Fractions

Area 13   Cultural Skills
Level 1. Arts and Crafts
Level 2. Art Activities Integrated into the
General Curriculum
Level 3. Music and Dance

Area 14   General Information
Level 1. Basic Awareness of Environment
Level 2. Geographical Awareness
Level 3. Historical Awareness
Level 4. Nature Study
Level 5. Current Events

Area 15   School-Related Skills
Level 1. Appropriate Classroom Behavior
Level 2. Respect for Others

Area 16   Life Relevant Skills
Level 1. Prevocational Skills
Level 2. Daily Living Skills

number of volunteers are utilized, it is critical that explicit instructions be provided for each IEP goal.

As performance data are entered into the database, the same database produces interim reports for parents and staff as well as greatly facilitates preparation of year-end progress reports. Perhaps most importantly, however, the database provides an extremely detailed analysis of child progress for review at each week's staff meeting. In the absence of such comprehensive computer utilization, detailed review of child progress on such a frequent basis would not be possible. Figure 10.1 illustrates the dynamic and inter-related cues of our computer system that have proven to have significant impact on child progress (Romanczyk, 1984; Romanczyk, 1986; Romanczyk, 1991).

Curriculum Progression

As described above, the IGS curriculum provides a number of different target areas for remediation, treatment, and development. Child progress is not viewed as linear. Areas of development are intertwined in a complex network of interrelationships in day-to-day life experiences.

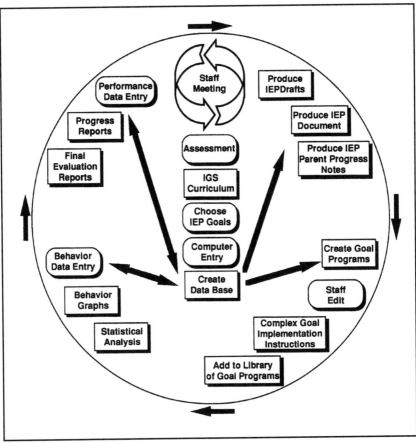

Figure 10.1.   Assessment, intervention, and evaluation represent a dynamic process that is greatly facilitated by a sophisticated computer system of information management.

Thus, progression through the curriculum is not unidirectional. Instead, in order to provide the child with a base on which to build functional use of targeted objectives, a complex linkage is required between several different curriculum areas to produce a cohesive package. This enables the child to acquire not only the specific facts or skills related to a given objective, but also to use such facts, skills, and strategies within a broader context. Thus, a goal of increasing a child's communication abilities will not only target goals in the area of expressive and receptive language but necessarily will include aspects of attentive skills, cognitive development, social skills, and content areas. In this way communication is not an isolated task or activity but is integral to day-to-day activities in a wide range of environments and activities. More concrete examples of the use of parallel or ancillary goals in the acquisition of a primary focus are illustrated. Table 10.3 is a portion of a child IEP.

Figure 10.2 illustrates the complex linkage between subject areas that is developed to ensure that the primary goal is acquired functionally in a variety of contexts. The process of developing an IEP to ensure such breadth of acquisition is a complex effort and requires the integration of input from multiple staff members as well as parents and school districts. Thus, the IEP is not developed solely by the child's teacher. Instead, given parental input and a draft IEP developed by the teacher, the next step is a consultation meeting with the coordinating teacher to ensure that components such as maintenance, generalization, and multiple approaches to building a cohesive acquisition unit are present. At this point the computer-generated draft is then distributed to parents and school districts. Further modifications and discussions are held with the Children's Unit staff. Only when consensus is obtained does the IEP become a working contract for a child.

Materials

While a large number of commercially prepared materials are available at the Children's Unit, they are typically used along with staff-created materials on a highly individualized basis. The strong emphasis at the Children's Unit is on the teaching methodology rather than materials *per se*. While certainly commercially prepared materials can be of some value, it has been our experience that focusing on the method of material presentation, prompting procedures, sequencing of tasks, and creating appropriate motivational strategies are by far the most important elements of an effective teaching environment. This approach extends even to our use of computers in instructional processes, where relatively little use is made of commercially prepared products with much of our software internally developed.

Methods of Assessing Progress

For each goal targeted in the IEP, data are collected on an ongoing, most often daily, basis. The manner in which progress is assessed varies

TABLE 10.3. An Abbreviated Example of Complex Linkages within an IEP for a Child with Low Skill Level

ATTENTIVE SKILLS

Level 1. Prespeech Attentive Skills

  Stage 1. Sitting

    Task 2. Sits independently and remains seated

  Stage 2. Eye contact

    Task 1. Establishes eye contact in response to command "Look at me"

    Task 2. Establishes eye contact in response to name only

SPEECH

Level 1. Non-Verbal Imitation

  Stage 1. Imitation of simple actions as modeled by teacher

    Task 1. Imitates single action

    Task 3. Imitates sequence of three actions

  Stage 2. Imitation of facial movements as indicated by model

    Task 3. Purses or rounds lips (kisses)

    Task 5. Moves tongue past lip line

Level 2. Vocalization

  Stage 1. Eliciting vocalizations

    Task 2. Emits sounds in presence of primary reinforcement

  Stage 2. Respondent vocalizations

    Task 1. Emits one syllable vocalizations in response to verbal stimulation

  Stage 3. Self-initiated vocalizations

    Task 3. Emits multisyllabic vocalizations in social contexts

Level 3. Vocal Imitation

  Stage 1. Single sounds

    Task 1. Imitates long vowel sounds

    Task 3. Imitates consonants

  Stage 2. Blends

    Task 1. Imitates C-V syllables with long vowels (me, foo, bo)

    Task 3. Imitates V-C syllables (om, it, up)

Level 4. Verbal Imitation

  Stage 1. Imitation of mono-syllabic words

    Task 1. Imitates C-V words (me, bye, hi)

    Task 2. Imitates C-V-C words (hat, bus, cup)

  Stage 2. Imitation of multi-syllabic words

    Task 1. Imitates two syllables of same sound (mama, papa, baba)

(continued)

TABLE 10.3.   *Continued*

RECEPTIVE LANGUAGE

Level 1. Nonverbal Compliance with Requests
    Stage 1. Simple one-part commands
        Task 2. Changes or stops activity when own name is called
        Task 3. Touches body parts on request
Level 2. Non-Verbal Identification of Objects and Events
    Stage 2. Object discrimination
        Task 1. Points to correct object upon request given a choice of two
    Stage 8. Nonverbal response to questions
        Task 1. Nods yes/no in response to questions

EXPRESSIVE LANGUAGE

Level 1. Labeling
    Stage 1. Labeling using single word
        Task 1. Produces consonant-vowel combination in response to an object
        Task 3. Labels body parts

CONCEPT FORMATION

Level 2. Visual Discrimination
    Stage 1. Matching according to a single variable
        Task 1. Matches to sample of one given one identical object
        Task 2. Matches one object in an array of two
Level 6. Spatial Relationships
    Stage 2. Identification of position in relation to environment
        Task 1. Places objects in, on, under reference objects

MOTOR SKILLS

Level 2. Specific Gross Motor Activities
    Stage 3. Group activities
        Task 4. Obstacle course
        Task 7. Plays group circle game

SELF-HELP SKILLS

Level 1. Self-Feeding
    Stage 2. Independent feeding
        Task 1. Self-feeds precut solid finger foods
    Stage 4. Appropriate use of fork
        Task 1. Scoops with fork

(continued)

TABLE 10.3. *Continued*

Level 2. Self-Toileting
   Stage 1. Specific toileting skills
      Task 1. Remains dry and unsoiled between scheduled toileting
   Stage 2. Communicating need to toilet
      Task 3. Verbalizes or signs need to toilet spontaneously
Level 3. Self-Dressing
   Stage 2. Removes upper body garments
      Task 2. Removes front opening garment with zipper

SOCIAL SKILLS

Level 1. Non-Verbal Interaction
   Stage 1. Passive tolerance of close proximity of a person
      Task 1. Looks at people
   Stage 3. Initiation of physical contact
      Task 1. Reaches for people
      Task 3. Leads adult by hand to show something or to seek help
Level 2. Verbal Interaction
   Stage 1. Verbal etiquette
      Task 1. Greets people appropriately
Level 3. Play Skills
   Stage 1. Isolate play
      Task 3. Uses simple toys independently: string toy, ball, stacking ring
   Stage 2. Parallel play
      Task 1. Plays near other children with same type of toy
   Stage 3. Cooperative play
      Task 9. Participates in play upon request

given the requirements of the specific objective. For reduction of maladaptive behavior objectives, each goal has a specific data collection schedule which is rotated from week to week to ensure that sampling occurs at all periods of the week and all parts of the day. For example, a goal that is selected to be monitored for five half-days a week will be rotated for 5 consecutive weeks to ensure that the distribution of the samples will include all parts of the child's week. With the schedule in place, the data are collected either by frequency or by percent occurrence (an interval recording system where the evaluator's score is the presence or absence of the target behavior in a 15-minute interval). In addition, each goal is individually assessed prior to collection to determine whether or not intensity ratings and elicitor ratings (i.e., the presence of a specific elicitor is assumed to be responsible for the presence

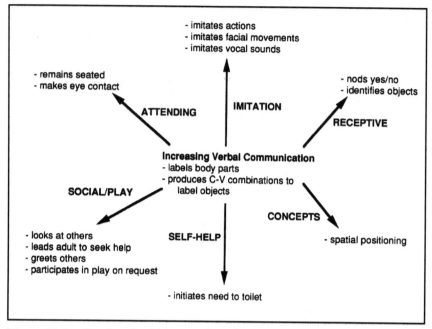

Figure 10.2. Based on the IGS curriculum, the IEP is a complex linkage of related areas and goals that are formally intertwined in order to maximize function and generalization.

of the target behavior) need to be collected. Once recorded, as mentioned above, data are entered into a computer assisted analysis and evaluation system on a daily basis. This system graphs the behavior according to frequency or percent occurrence as well as provides a temporal distribution of the occurrence of the target behavior.

Assessment of progress in habilitative areas is accomplished via continual scoring of child responses for discrete trial programs. Data are collected on the accuracy and error pattern of the responses, the child's response to prompts, emission of approximations to the correct response, and notation of failure to respond. Data are summarized on a daily basis and entered into the computer assisted analysis system on a weekly basis. Program procedure modifications may occur on a daily basis reflecting the child's performance.

There is a subset of goals for which a scale rating is used. Goals that are most appropriate for this type of data collection include appropriate use of etiquette, cooperation, and social play, and goals where quality, intensity, or degree of performance are the focus. Analysis of a child's performance on these goals occurs on a weekly basis. Performance data are compared to IEP evaluation criteria and modifications are made in the program as needed. IEP specifications are present in the classroom copy of program procedures and thus maintains the IEP document as an active part of the child's curriculum. This also enables staff members to easily compare current performance with the specified evaluation criteria.

Daily Schedule

Each child's daily schedule consists of a sequence of half-hour sessions in a variety of settings where group size, constitution, subject, instructor, and response and participation requirements vary based on the child's strengths and the requirements in each area targeted in the IEP. Table 10.4 is an example of a typical daily schedule. The first column lists child initials. Each subsequent column to the right is a half-hour lesson period. The first code number listed in each column indicates the physical location in the Children's Unit where the lesson is taught, and the second number indicates the IGS area being addressed. Thus for student AS, at 9:00 a.m. he is working in location number 16 on his area 12 (arithmetic) IEP goals.

INTEGRATION VERSUS SEGREGATION

It is interesting that individuals with severe disabilities are often inordinately caught up in various political and dogmatic issues. One of these current issues is "integration versus segregation." While at one level it is of course the case that all individuals should participate in their local community in all aspects of their daily lives, it is also the case that there is a wide range of community support and services, and there is also a wide range of needs of children with autism. Therefore, it seems apparent that it is unquestionably *incorrect* to say that all children with autism should receive services outside of local community settings, just as it is unquestionably *incorrect* to say that all children should only receive services within their community settings. Part of the difficulty may be that "education" has very different meanings. For us it does not mean attending a local school but rather means receiving the educational and

TABLE 10.4. An Example of a Typical Daily Schedule

Children's Unit for Treatment and Evaluation—Child's Schedule

	9:00	9:30	10:00	10:30	11:00	11:30	12:00	12:30	1:00	1:30	2:00
1 AS	16-12	14-14	17-8	18-9	18-13	18-7	lunch-8	16-12	4-11	15-10	15-10
2 AV	16-12	14-14	17-8	18-9	18-13	18-7	lunch-8	14-14	4-11	15-10	15-10
3 BB	4-11	17-8	1-6	18-9	18-13	18-7	lunch-8	14-14	15-10	16-12	16-12
4 BP	17-8	16-12	5-6	18-9	18-13	18-7	lunch-8	14-14	4-11	15-10	15-10
5 DA	1-6	8-3	8-3	11-2	11-2	lunch-8	1-6	8-5	18-7	18-13	18-9
6 DM	17-8	11-16	5-6	15-10	14-14	lunch-8	7-3	16-12	18-7	18-13	18-9
7 DU	4-11	7-3	1-4	14-14	15-10	lunch-8	18-9	18-13	18-7	16-12	12-8
8 JC	4-11	16-12	1-6	14-14	15-10	lunch-8	18-9	18-13	18-7	9-3	5-6
9 JG	16-12	14-14	5-6	18-9	18-13	18-7	lunch-8	7-3	15-10	8-3	4-11
10 JL	17-8	4-11	15-10	14-14	16-12	lunch-8	18-9	18-13	18-7	4-11	16-12
11 JM	12-8	4-11	15-10	16-12	5-6	lunch-8	18-9	18-13	18-7	7-3	8-5
12 JO	18-9	18-13	18-7	4-11	7-3	lunch-8	8-3	15-10	16-12	5-6	14-14

(continued)

TABLE 10.4. *Continued*

Children's Unit for Treatment and Evaluation—Child's Schedule

	9:00	9:30	10:00	10:30	11:00	11:30	12:00	12:30	1:00	1:30	2:00
13 KA	18-9	18-13	18-7	1-4	7-3	lunch-8	5-6	8-3	1-6	7-3	8-3
14 KK	4-11	15-10	16-12	17-8	5-6	lunch-8	18-9	18-13	18-7	8-3	1-6
15 LC	18-9	18-13	18-7	1-6	1-6	lunch-8	9-3	8-3	7-3	1-6	8-3
16 LD	11-16	1-6	11-16	8-3	8-3	lunch-8	12-8	1-6	18-7	18-13	18-9
17 ML	14-14	11-16	8-3	8-3	12-8	lunch-8	7-3	1-6	18-7	18-13	18-9
18 NS	1-6	15-10	14-14	4-11	7-3	lunch-8	18-9	18-13	18-7	16-12	9-3
19 SA	18-9	18-13	18-7	1-6	1-6	lunch-8	9-3	9-3	9-3	1-6	9-3
20 SB	7-3	17-8	4-11	16-12	15-10	lunch-8	18-9	18-13	18-7	14-14	1-3
21 SS	1-6	15-10	14-14	4-11	7-3	lunch-8	18-9	18-13	18-7	16-12	9-3
22 TR	18-9	18-13	18-7	7-3	11-2	lunch-8	9-3	12-8	5-6	5-6	7-3
23 TS	4-11	4-11	14-14	18-9	18-13	18-7	lunch-8	16-12	12-8	14-14	5-6
24 TW	15-10	4-11	14-14	17-8	16-12	lunch-8	18-9	18-13	18-7	7-3	5-6
25 WC	15-10	16-12	4-11	18-9	18-13	18-7	lunch-8	5-6	7-3	14-14	1-6

clinical interventions that can maximize the child's potential. Thus, for this reason, we take a moderate approach that is tied tightly to our philosophy of assessment. The choice of type and location of service is a function of the child's needs. Terms such as "least restrictive" cannot simply be applied to "bricks and mortar."

The goal of integration into the typical school setting is unquestionably correct. However, for some children a normalized setting, even with extensive support services, may not be the least restrictive setting. Central to the issue is one's definition of "least restrictive."

For some children, a strategy of a continuum of services, from an intense, focused, individualized, specialized setting to the more typical classroom with required support services, is the most appropriate. This allows for rapid acquisition of needed skills and for a choreographed approach to habilitation. Some children who are placed in the supposed "least restrictive" placement do not progress at a rate consistent with their potential. There can be an illusion of progress as they are "with their peers" and are present in various activities. This could be seen as the least restrictive placement, but from a different perspective, it is highly restrictive if one is sensitive to temporal factors. If a child is in an environment where learning takes place at some fraction of the pace that is possible in a more specialized environment, then this indeed represents a restrictive environment.

BEHAVIOR MANAGEMENT

Because of the specialized group of children that we serve, severe maladaptive behavior is often a presenting problem. Many of the behaviors displayed are extremely intense and of danger to the child and to others. However, even given this as a preface, the Children's Unit has a strong philosophy of an assessment-oriented approach rather than an intervention-oriented approach. That is, often those who claim to use behavior modification or applied behavior analysis focus too heavily on creating intervention strategies and then using the behavioral methodology to evaluate those interventions rather than using the methodology to perform detailed assessments from which interventions are derived and then appropriately used. One reason for this is the pragmatic. That is, extensive efforts at assessment involve tremendous use of resources whereas a "let's try it and see if it works" strategy can be more efficient if the intervention is indeed successful. However, such an approach, while it may, and we emphasize the word *may,* be effective for highly skilled and experienced clinicians, does not serve as a good basis for a complex organization that has many different individuals participating in the delivery of services. Under such circumstances, it is more prudent to have a series of assessment procedures that can be used to produce information to be evaluated by supervisory and more senior staff than to create intervention programs for which staff are then trained to implement. Such an approach can produce frustration for both staff and parents as the immediate request is often to "do something." It is imperative however that the focus of intervention programs be on long-term amelioration for the child rather than an immediate amelioration of adult anxiety and frustration.

With respect to assessment, certain basic strategies and tools are in place throughout the Children's Unit. As an example, all classrooms have access to videotaping facilities and camcorders are available for staff and parents to use in home settings. Further, a number of different specialized behavior recording forms are available that can be used on a consistent basis. These are also complimented by standardized global rating scales that are designed to reflect observations over extended periods of time as opposed to the more molecular recording mentioned above.

Also easily available are computer-assisted observational procedures. These take two forms. One is designed for use to analyze videotape records; the second is highly portable computers that can be taken into the classroom and various *in vivo* settings so that observations can be made in real time. All of these computer systems permit extensive and extremely rapid data analyses in various formats suitable for the different assessment questions that may be asked as well as for different levels of consumers. As an example, the programs can produce simple bar charts to indicate frequency of events but they also produce conditional probability analyses to indicate the inter-relatedness of various behaviors as well as analyze for episodic versus frequency versus duration information.

Another form of behavior analysis that is resource intensive but has tremendous payoff is the system of taking the children's daily behavior observations made by the teaching staff and entering these into a custom computer system as was mentioned previously. When the data are entered, they are entered as frequency or occurrence information within half-hour blocks of the school day. Graphs that are then computer generated are not only of the standard frequency of events per day format, but also include a separate plot of minimum, maximum, and average for each day as well as a temporal analysis, where we plot the frequency of behavior for each half hour period within those periods across days.

This latter analysis is a system first used at the Children's Unit in 1980 (Lockshin & Romanczyk, 1982; Romanczyk, Colletti, & Brutvan, 1982) and is similar to the scatter plot analysis proposed by Touchette in 1985 (Touchette, MacDonald, & Langer, 1985). However at the Children's Unit, this cluster of computer generated graphs and statistics is not a "special" analysis that is conducted when a particular problem behavior is encountered, but rather has been systematized such that all child behavior is analyzed in this format on a continuing basis. This permits analysis of trend and interaction with particular tasks or staff arrangements or even cyclical patterns while allowing for some degree of proactive intervention rather than analyzing only in the midst of severe outbursts.

While certainly it is not possible to consistently record all forms of possible behavior that a child may display, by continuously recording and analyzing a very large set of child behavior in this fashion, we are able to take advantage of naturally occurring variation as a method for assessing possible eliciting and maintaining factors. Also, having a large pool of collateral behavior is very useful in broadly evaluating various intervention strategies.

As can be seen, great emphasis is placed upon behavior analysis, and this would be a correct interpretation of many of our activities. However, we have also for many years been greatly concerned with the eliciting aspects of behavior in addition to consequent events. Eliciting factors include a wide variety of variables such as sensory modulation, social interaction, task difficulty, pacing and method of presentation of materials, and various physical internal stimuli as well as conditioned arousal-inducing stimuli. In particular, we are concerned with the role of arousal and anxiety in many complex behavior problems.

This role has been given little attention, particularly in young children, in the professional literature and in educational settings. Recently our efforts in this area have included psychophysiological monitoring, identification of social versus task escape motivated children, and the role of multiple determinants of individual topographies of various classes of behavior.

PARENTAL INVOLVEMENT

It is the philosophy of the Children's Unit that parent and family involvement is an integral part of the child's education and is critical to maximizing the students' ultimate level of functioning—habilitatively, socially, and emotionally. It is further recognized that raising a child with autism is difficult, both emotionally and physically, and that in order for parents to be effectively involved in their child's treatment, it is important to provide the parents with the skills they need to teach their children, while providing emotional and practical support in helping them achieve an appropriate balance between the efforts they must invest over time in their child with autism and other family members, careers, life pursuits, etc.

It is also recognized that ability and skill levels, as well as motivational levels of parents, vary dramatically and thus communication, participation, training, and support are offered at a variety of levels to meet the needs of the wide range of individual families. Table 10.5 lists the various components provided at the Children's Unit.

Homework serves as an illustration of the variety of approaches or requirements that are provided for the parent. Each child receives a homework assignment on a daily basis regardless of the functioning level of the child. The goal is selected by the parents in conjunction with the teacher and parent coordinator, or if the parent prefers, is selected by the Children's Unit staff. The task is selected based on the functionality of the program as well as the child's ability to perform the desired goal. Often retention of acquired skills are targeted. However, in other instances, teaching of specific skill subsets occur concurrently in the home and school settings. Once a goal has been selected, parents receive a data sheet that accompanies each assignment. The data sheet requests information of the following type: response scoring for the discrete trial programs such as $(+)$ for a correct response; $(-)$ for an incorrect response; and checklists indicating child motivation, independence level, responsivity, etc. Also required are the initials of the individual conducting the program with the child and the duration of the session. Typically, the response that is obtained from the parents varies in accord with their understanding, ability level, or motivation. However, whether the parent fills in every item required, merely initials that they have completed the assignment with their child, or completes a checklist without giving response specific data, important information on the child's

TABLE 10.5. Home/School Communication and Parent Education and Support Services

Format	Information provided	Frequency
IEP Conference	• review of assessment data • discuss priorities for instruction • outline short-term goals • discuss implementation of IEP goals	Once a year (additional follow-up meetings as necessary)
Home School Notes	• to monitor children's behavior, performance, and mood at home and at school • to serve as a means of communicating the events of the school day to parents • to provide staff with information regarding child's reactions to events and activities at home • monthly changes in category selection to address current concerns	Daily
Report Cards	• to report on child progress and school/home communication	Every 2 months
Formal Unit Reports	• to summarize child progress at the end of the school year • to provide school districts with information prior to annual CSE/ CPSE meetings	Annually In the spring of each year
Parent Notes	• to provide a mechanism for teachers to communicate with parents about special events	Weekly (additional notes when needed)
Telephone Contact	• to request information on child progress/behavior at home • to obtain data on home programs • to report child progress	As needed
Home Visits	• to observe family/child interactions • to supervise home programs	Several times a year

(continued)

TABLE 10.5. *Continued*

Format	Information provided	Frequency
Parent Teacher Meetings	• to review child progress on a regular basis • to answer questions regarding your child's progress in the school • to obtain important information about child behavior/performance in the home setting	Every 2 months
Homework	• to address maintaining and generalizing skills acquired in school setting • to address skill building • to address leisure time/daily activity skills specific to home setting • to structure appropriate, focused parent/child interactions	Daily
Parent Participation Activity	• to increase areas of parent/teacher involvement and communication • to allow parents the opportunity to participate with their child	Periodically
Parent Classroom Observation	• to provide parent opportunities to observe their child during the school day via closed circuit television	Parents are encouraged to observe any time and may arrive unannounced
Parent Consultation	• to discuss concerns which are not usually addressed in other home and school communications • to observe one's child in the classroom with a staff member so that specific questions or concerns may be addressed • to discuss topics which are too personal to raise in the group setting at the Parent Education meetings	Twice weekly

(continued)

TABLE 10.5.   *Continued*

Home Support Program	• to address specific child behaviors/skills (e.g., toilet training, appropriate behavior in public settings) • meetings are individual or in small groups depending on topic and number of families desiring participation	As appropriate (includes school and home sessions as well as specific settings, e.g., restaurants, stores
Parent Information Series	• to provide information for parents regarding the development and implementation of home programs • to teach basic behavior management skills • to teach parents effective teaching strategies • to develop home programs • to model program implementation	6-week sequence of evening meetings, each 1½ hours in length (repeated during year)
Parent Education Program	• to discuss topics relevant to the education of children with special needs	Multi-week sequence throughout the year
Parent Counseling Program	• to meet in small groups to discuss family issues, emotional stress, long-term planning, and other topics concerning the family and individual family members	12 weeks, twice a year
Respite	• specifically scheduled to provide child care services for families	Periodically
Newsletter	• to provide information on up-to-date information on research findings • to inform parents of staff involvement in professional activities	Monthly

activities and interactions in the home is provided and also serves to structure a subset of home interactions in a consistent manner.

An example of the importance the Children's Unit places on parent involvement is the policy on parent visits. Parents may visit the Children's Unit to observe the child and program unannounced, without any need to make an appointment or inform staff of their visits. On arrival they have the choice of observing the child in their classroom or through closed circuit television connected to each of the classrooms. If they choose the latter, neither staff nor children are notified of their visit and they may watch without any need to inform staff of their presence. It is felt that this complete freedom on the parents' part is clearly a parent's right and staff at the Children's Unit accept this as not being an invasion of their privacy but rather an opportunity for the parents to view what typically occurs on a given day with their child.

Parent involvement comprises many components, one of which is parent education. This aspect of the program was created to provide parents with an opportunity to learn basic techniques in working with their children, away from the distractions frequently present at home. The goals outlined for the program include the following:

1. Information on childhood disorders

2. Instruction in basic behavior management techniques

3. Direct supervision in implementing behavior management procedures (stating rules, planned ignoring, positive reinforcement)

4. Assessment of parent/child interactions

5. Targeting specific goals for home programs

6. Developing home programs

7. Method of data collection

8. Direct supervision of implementation of programs

We use several internally developed manuals which were designed to provide our parents with a good deal of the basic information and background. The inclusion of these manuals in our program enabled us to move away from a lecture format and adopt more of a seminar format during which parents and staff jointly developed programs for home implementation and reviewed child progress on specific programs. These group meetings provide parents with the opportunity to share their personal experiences and to benefit from the experiences of other parents.

A parent counseling program is offered as part of the parent services provided. The group meets on a weekly basis for 1½ hours during the evening and to assist parents in attending such meetings, free child care is provided. Child care is available not only for the specific child enrolled at the Children's Unit but also to siblings as well. The function of this group is to provide an opportunity for the parents to meet on a regular basis to discuss issues related to parenting a child with a disabling condition. Issues receiving attention include difficulties with respect to obtaining support from extended family members, time management, and coping with community reactions to child behavior. Individual counseling is also available.

OUTCOME

Critical to the discussion of outcome measures with respect to the Children's Unit is the realization that we are a short-term facility and that our exit criterion is not full habilitation. Affecting change significant enough to allow the child to enter a community or school district setting is our goal for each child. Therefore, the criteria for each individual child vary with respect to (1) the severity of the presenting problems, (2) the presence of appropriate intervention strategies that can be transitioned to other facilities while still maintaining the child's current level of social development and (3) the availability of a program that can meet current needs. Thus, a child who is transitioning from the Children's Unit to a relatively small school district often will need more specific training and possibly more extended attendance at the Children's Unit prior to being able to enter such a district program than would a child from a larger district where the options are more numerous.

Within this context, a total of 29 children with autism and 27 children with severe emotional disturbance have completed participation in our program. Table 10.6 lists the type of placement that the children transition to: programs within their home school districts, special classroom settings for which the home school district contracts with a local provider, and residential placement.

TABLE 10.6. Type of Placement for Preschool Program Children Upon Transition

	School District	Contracted Special Services	Residential
Autism	54%	42%	4%
ED	70%	30%	0%

Figure 10.3 presents pre- and post-data concerning language development. The graphs present the pre and post scale rank for each child in the two groups. As can be seen, the children with autism tend to be at only the gestural or vocal level of communication upon entry, while those with severe emotional disturbance tend to utilize words or phrases to communicate their needs and desires. The scale is a crude one and does not imply equal degree of change between rankings (communication level was assessed as follows: 0 = nonverbal, 1 = vocal, 2 = gestures, 3 = signs, 4 = word, 5 = phrase, 6 = sentence, 7 = conversational speech). However, the figure is illustrative of the significant degree of change obtained for most children with autism and the clear differences between the two groups.

Systematic Assessment Data

Each child's progress is tracked on a daily basis as described under the curriculum component of this chapter. Overall assessment is compiled into an annual report which provides the following data: the current classroom behavior management needs, the current instruction management requirements, the child's current educational needs including 10- or 12-month services, and current staff to child ratio in the range of staff to child ratio which is appropriate for this child. Current standardized testing results typically are reported including scores from the *Peabody Picture Vocabulary Test* (Dunn & Dunn, 1981), *Vineland Adaptive Behavior-Scales Classroom Edition* (Harrison, 1985), the *Slosson Intelligence Test* (Armstrong & Jensen, 1981), and additional testing as is appropriate for any individual child. A current overall grade level performance is assessed on reading, writing, and arithmetic readiness skills. Current status of classes of problem behavior, as well as the typical

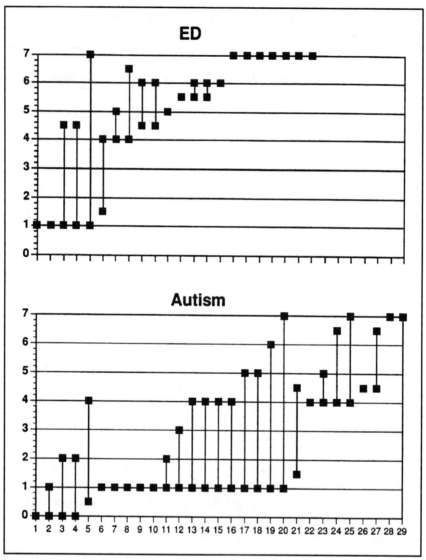

Figure 10.3. Pre- and post-language development for children with severe emotional disturbance and children with autism. *Note.* The y-axis scale is 0 = nonverbal to 7 = conversational speech.

antecedents of problem behaviors are reported, as is an assessment on the current level of communication development for each child.

A checklist indicating the degree of progress within the school year in the areas of a child's social and emotional development is completed as is a summary of the child's characteristics of learning rate and pattern. Continuing assessment of the specific IEP goals targeted for a given child in an area is reflected in a table completed for each child, wherein each curriculum area is assessed for the factors that continue to limit progress in this area. Finally, an absolute ability level within the area is provided by comparing a child's current status to that of age appropriate norms.

In addition to these types of assessments, a narrative description of child progress; behavioral, social, and emotional development; and anticipated goals, objectives, concerns, and progress for the coming year are included. This section also includes a description of the level of parent involvement and the parent program available to families.

In combination, these checklists, psychometric tests, behavioral observations, reports and other information such as rate of current progress, characteristics of learning rate and style, and current impediments to maintaining or accelerating progress are compared on an annual basis to the intake level-of-functioning report prepared when the child entered the program. The contrast or similarities between these two reports provide another means of assessing child progress and assist in determining the appropriateness of the child's continuing in the program or transition to an alternative program.

FUTURE EFFORT

Perhaps one of the greatest impediments to progress is that the solid, proven methods of intervention are costly and require highly trained individuals. It is therefore difficult to maintain the public's attention as well as assist parents to focus upon effective intervention methods while there is a seemingly constant bombardment of "new breakthroughs," often hyped by the media, which with time, investigation, and reflection are shown to be simply a passing fad or gross misstatement of actual efficacy. It is very easy to construct a long list of such cures and breakthroughs and it is a sad commentary that the list will continue to grow. This strikes to the heart of the issue confronting many parents: They are in great distress and there is a lack of consistent responses to their needs. Because of this, it is quite understandable that a parent would seek a "new treatment" even if it is still unproven.

Thus, one weakness of many programs is that they are either funded on soft research money and thus must focus on relatively short-term and narrow issues, or programs such as the Children's Unit are funded through the normal state educational funding mechanisms and thus are limited in the range of services that can be provided and the number of families that can be served. For instance, while it is clear that early intervention is extremely beneficial, funding for early detection programs is often minimal. Likewise, it is very clear that parents of children with autism often undergo high levels of stress. Nevertheless, it is very difficult for a true school program to acquire consistent funding to provide counseling, respite, and the broad range of services so important to the individuals experiencing chronic stress. While one would hope that cooperative efforts among the various agencies in addition to the school setting could result in achieving the type of broad base services necessary for families, such efforts are infrequent and often transitory, and the current outlook is not optimistic given the continuing economic pressures faced by state and local governments.

Thus, it is ironic that after several decades of intensive research efforts, we indeed possess most of the information and procedures necessary to significantly impact children with autism, but that it has occurred at a time of significant social and economic change, wherein the willingness or ability to appropriately fund such programs that use effective interventions is the exception rather than the rule.

REFERENCES

Armstrong, R. J., & Jensen, J. A. (1981). *Slosson Intelligence Test (SIT) for Children and Adults.* East Aurora, NY: Slossen Educational Publications, Inc.

Carrow, E. (1973). *Screening Test for Auditory Comprehension of Language— Test Manual.* Boston: Teaching Resources Corporation.

Dunn, L. M., & Dunn, L. M. (1981). *Peabody Picture Vocabulary Test–Revised, Manual for Forms L and M.* Circle Pines, MN: American Guidance Service.

Frankenburg, W. K., Dodd, J. B., & Fandal, A. W. (1973). *Denver Develop-*

mental Screening Test. Denver, CO: Ladora Project and Publishing Foundation.

Goldman, R., & Fristoe, M. (1969). *Test of Articulation.* Circle Pines, MN: American Guidance Service, Inc.

Harrison, P.L. (1985). *Vineland Adaptive Behavior Scales—Classroom Edition Manual.* Circle Pines, MN: American Guidance Service.

Lockshin, S. L. (1985). *Parent information series.* Unpublished manuscript.

Lockshin, S., & Romanczyk, R. G. (1982). *The IGS curriculum: Developing, implementing and evaluating a comprehensive individualized goal selection curriculum.* Paper presented at the Association of Behavior Analysis, Milwaukee, Wisconsin.

Romanczyk, R. G. (1984). A case study of microcomputer utilization and staff efficiency: A five year analysis. *Journal of Organizational Behavior Management, 6,* 141–154.

Romanczyk, R. G. (1986). *Clinical utilization of microcomputer technology.* New York: Pergamon Press.

Romanczyk, R. G. (1991). Monitoring and evaluating clinical service delivery: Issues of effectiveness of computer data base management. In A. Ager (Ed.), *Microcomputers in clinical psychology* (pp. 155–173). Chichester, England: Wiley Press.

Romanczyk, R. G., Colletti, G., & Brutvan, L. (1982). *The data based staff meeting: Structure and procedures.* Paper presented at the Association of Behavior Analysis, Milwaukee, Wisconsin.

Romanczyk, R. G., & Lockshin, S. L. (1982). *The IGS curriculum.* CBTA: Vestal, New York.

Romanczyk, R. G., & Lockshin, S. L. (1984). Short-term intensive services: The deficit oriented, focused model. In W. P. Christian, G. R. Hannah, & T. J. Glahn (Eds.), *Programming effective human services* (pp. 433–456). NY: Plenum Publishing.

Touchette, P. E., MacDonald, R. F., & Langer, S. N. (1985). A scatter plot for identifying stimulus control of problem behavior. *Journal of Applied Behavior Analysis, 18,* 343–351.

Chapter 11

LEAP Preschool

PHILLIP S. STRAIN and LINDA K. CORDISCO

The Early Childhood Intervention Program began in 1985 as part of the Department of Child and Adolescent Psychiatry of the Western Psychiatric Institute and Clinic, University of Pittsburgh. Under the direction of Dr. Phillip S. Strain, the program is now affiliated with St. Peter's Child Development Centers, Pittsburgh, Pennsylvania. The Early Childhood Intervention Program is a research, training, and development program that focuses on the needs of young children with disabilities and their families. The preschool program—Learning Experiences, an Alternative Program for Preschoolers and their Parents (i.e., LEAP)— is currently 1 of 10 programs affiliated with the Early Childhood Intervention Program.

LEAP Preschool began in 1982 as a federally funded (i.e., Handicapped Children's Early Education Program) model demonstration program serving young children with autism and typical children ages 3–5 years within an integrated preschool classroom. At the time of its inception, the LEAP program was one of the few early childhood programs in the country that was committed to inclusive practices for young children with autism and their families.

The LEAP program consists of three main program components: the integrated preschool, a behavioral skill training program for parents, and national outreach training activities. The integrated preschool consists of two classrooms, each serving 16 children (10 typical children and 6 children with autism) ages 3–5 years. The preschool program operates

3 hours a day, 5 days a week, for 12 months of the year. The preschool is co-sponsored by the Fox Chapel area school district and is located within a local early childhood center. Staff-child ratio for each classroom is 3 adults to 16 children; each classroom is staffed by two teachers and a classroom assistant. A full-time speech and language specialist provides services to children with disabilities and their families within the classroom and home environments.

In addition to the classroom program, families of children both with and without disabilities may participate in a skill training program designed to teach parents the basic principles of behavior management and effective strategies for teaching young children. The program is designed to reflect a family-centered approach, with activities being individualized for each family based upon desired outcomes for training. Additional services available to families include a monthly parent support group, referral services to various community agencies, and transition planning and follow-up activities. Two part-time family service coordinators are available to work with parents who participate in these activities.

The third program component includes national outreach training activities. LEAP Preschool is currently in its fifth year of funding (Early Education Program for Children with Disabilities) as a National Outreach Training Project. Training activities focus on seven key areas: child assessment activities, developing individual educational plans, instructional programming for the integrated classroom, behavior management, social skills training, transition planning, and working effectively with families. To date, 20 early childhood programs from 10 states have participated in outreach training conducted by the staff of LEAP Preschool.

Guiding principles that have shaped program development efforts over the past 10 years at LEAP Preschool have included the beliefs that:

1. all children (i.e., both children with and without disabilities) can benefit from integrated early childhood environments

2. young children with autism benefit most from early intervention when intervention efforts are conducted across school, home, and community environments

3. young children with autism make the greatest gains from early intervention when parents and professionals work together as partners

4. young children with autism can learn many important skills (e.g., social skills, language skills, appropriate behavior) from typical same-age peers

5. young children with autism benefit most from early intervention when intervention efforts are planned, systematic, and individualized

6. both children with and without disabilities benefit from curricular activities that reflect developmentally appropriate practices.

The LEAP program is currently supported by a variety of funding sources. These include subcontracts with local school districts and intermediate units for providing early intervention services, financial support from the program's sponsoring agency (St. Peter's Child Development Centers), and federally-funded research and training grants. Estimated direct service personnel costs per child (for children with disabilities) for the 1991–92 school year were approximately $25,000.

Early intervention services in Pennsylvania are mandated by an entitlement act known as the Early Intervention Services System Act. This act requires that a statewide system of coordinated, comprehensive, multidisciplinary, interagency programs be established and maintained by the Department of Health, the Department of Public Welfare, and the Department of Education to provide appropriate early intervention services to all infants, toddlers, and preschoolers with disabilities and their families.

POPULATION SERVED

Since 1982, 155 children have participated in LEAP's integrated preschool program. One hundred and seven of these children have been typical children, and 48 have been children with autism or pervasive developmental disorder. Children identified as "typical children" have been children who, at the time of admission, have had no known developmental or behavioral difficulties.

The majority of children with disabilities that have attended LEAP Preschool were diagnosed as having autism or pervasive developmental disorder prior to their referral to the preschool. LEAP admission requirements include independent evaluations by a licensed clinical psychologist or child psychiatrist confirming a diagnosis of Autistic Disorder or Pervasive Developmental Disorder, Not Otherwise Specified using the criteria of *DSM-III-R* (American Psychiatric Association, 1987) and/or the *Childhood Autism Rating Scale* (CARS) (Schopler, Reichler, DeVellis, & Daly, 1988).

Of the 48 children with autism or pervasive developmental disorder, four have been female and 44 have been male; 43 have been caucasian, four have been African-American, and one has been biracial (caucasian and Native American). Age at admission has ranged from 30 to 64 months (mean = 43 months). As measured by the *McCarthy Scales of Children's Abilities* (McCarthy, 1972), children's cognitive ability at admission has ranged from 6 to 119, with a mean score of 61. The *Sequenced Inventory of Communication Development* (Hedrick, Prather, & Tobin, 1984) expressive language scores at admission have ranged from 0 to 48 months, with a mean score of 22 months. Receptive scores have ranged from 4 to 44 months with a mean score of 23 months. Level of severity of autism as indicated by the *Childhood Autism Rating Scale* for children that have attended the preschool have ranged from 30 to 49, with a mean of 37.

ASSESSMENT PROCEDURES

The intake process at LEAP Preschool for children with autism typically begins with a referral call from a local school district or intermediate unit (i.e., an administrative unit that contracts with school districts within a designated geographic area to provide special education services) or from interested families who have been referred to the program from departments of pediatrics at local hospitals. Intake consists of a five-step process that includes: (a) an initial phone contact with the family, (b) an invitation to the family to observe the preschool program, (c) a referral for a formal evaluation (if one has not been recently conducted), (d) a family interview and home observation of the child, and (e) placement review and recommendations.

Information gathered during the initial phone contact with families includes: residence of family, age of child, diagnosis of child (if any), evaluations that have been conducted to date, early intervention services the family is currently receiving, and early intervention services that the family wants for their child and themselves for the upcoming year.

Interested families are then invited to come and observe the preschool program and meet with program staff. During their visit, families are provided with more in-depth information concerning the preschool program and the admission process. In addition, opportunities are available for families to talk with other parents whose children are currently attending the LEAP Program.

Following the observation at the preschool, families of children who have previously been evaluated and diagnosed as having autism or pervasive developmental disorder are asked to submit copies of all relevant reports to the preschool program. Families of children who have not been diagnosed are referred to their school district or intermediate unit or a private child psychiatrist for an independent evaluation (note: psychiatric evaluations are made available to interested families at no cost).

In addition to the formal child evaluation, a structured interview is conducted with families in their home or at the preschool. The purpose of the interview is to provide families with an opportunity to share information concerning their child's development related to communication, play, social, and self-help skills; reaction to change; sensory responsiveness; and adaptive behavior. Also, an informal play observation of the child is conducted in the home that focuses on play, language, social interaction skills, and adaptive behavior. Information gathered from these three main sources (i.e., formal evaluations, family interview, and child observation) are then reviewed and recommendations are made regarding the appropriateness of the placement for the child.

Following admission to the preschool, children with autism are tested by an experienced examiner every 3 months with the *Childhood Autism Rating Scale* and the *Learning Accomplishment Profile* (Sanford & Zelman, 1981); every 6 months with the *Sequenced Inventory of Communication Development*; and every year with the *McCarthy Scales of Children's Abilities.*

Other assessment measures used include ongoing direct observations of adaptive behavior and functional communication, play, and social interaction skills in school, home, and community settings. Families are also asked to complete a parent questionnaire (see Appendix A) of their child's strengths and needs across a variety of skill domains (completed once a year). Information concerning the child's medical and developmental histories is gathered from families during the intake process. Families are asked to submit copies of all pediatric and neurological evaluations that have been completed on their child. The school district that hosts the preschool provides annual hearing and vision screenings and requires that all entering children have a complete medical examination.

Information is also gathered, with parental consent, related to the family's perceived concerns, priorities, and resources related to enhancing their child's development. Families are provided with a variety of options for sharing this information, including discussing concerns and priorities during home visits or with the family service coordinator at the preschool, completing a family needs assessment (see Appendix A), or sharing information at the multidisciplinary team meeting and/or the Individual Education Plan (IEP) meeting. All interactions with families throughout the year are viewed by the staff as opportunities for families to share such information.

Assessment activities for families participating in behavioral skill training include gathering information from families related to family concerns and priorities for training, desired family outcomes, family members' skill competencies related to implementing behavioral strategies, childrearing beliefs and values, and family members' preferences related to use of behavioral strategies. Assessment information is gathered via informal discussions with families and direct observation of parent-child interactions in home and community settings.

PROGRAM STAFF

Each of the preschool classrooms is staffed by two full-time certified teachers (i.e., special education, early childhood education, or early childhood special education) and a full-time classroom assistant. A full-time speech and language specialist provides services to young children with autism within the classroom setting. In addition, the speech and language specialist consults with classroom teachers and families related to effective strategies for facilitating children's language during routine activities in school, home, and community settings.

Two part-time family service coordinators provide support to families related to accessing community resources and training related to the effective use of behavior management strategies in home and community settings. Both family service coordinators are also parents of children with disabilities.

A full-time assessment specialist conducts formal child assessments and gathers information for research activities via play assessments in home and school environments. In addition, this person is responsible for gathering information from families via phone interviews and written questionnaires.

Administrative staff include a part-time clinical supervisor who provides ongoing supervision to all direct-service staff, monitors all data collection related to individual goal plans for children with autism, and chairs all Individual Education Plan (IEP) meetings and progress update meetings with staff and families. A part-time program director oversees the day-to-day operations of the preschool program; handles all referrals, placements, and program transitions for children and families; chairs all administrative staff meetings; and coordinates research activities conducted in the preschool classrooms and national outreach training activities. A part-time office manager offers additional administrative support to the program.

Because the preschool program is associated with a nationally recognized research, training, and development program (i.e., the Early Childhood Intervention Program, St. Peter's Child Development Centers), numerous opportunities are available for staff development and training. These opportunities include attending monthly research symposia (sponsored by the Early Childhood Intervention Program); participation in federally-funded research, model program, and inservice training grant activities; and attending and presenting at state and national conferences. Supervision practices include a peer-observation and mentoring system and regularly scheduled observation and feedback sessions (data-based model) with the clinical supervisor.

Over the past 10 years, the preschool program has also served as a training site for numerous undergraduate and graduate students from Departments of Special Education, Early Childhood Education, Child Development, Educational Psychology, and Child and Adolescent Psychiatry. In addition, the preschool program functions as a training site for a federally funded national outreach grant for professionals working in the fields of early intervention and early childhood education who are interested in replicating the LEAP model.

CURRICULUM

The curriculum at LEAP Preschool reflects both a behavioral as well as a developmentally appropriate practice approach (Bredekamp, 1987) for teaching children with and without disabilities within an integrated early childhood environment. Learning activities are selected based upon the needs, interests, and developmental levels of individual children as well as the age span of children within each classroom. An integrated curriculum approach (i.e., designing learning experiences that promote children's skill development across multiple domains) is used to provide opportunities for learning related to all areas of development (e.g., social/emotional, language, adaptive behavior, cognitive, physical). Curricular activities are selected that encourage children's learning through active exploration with concrete materials and interactions with other children and adults.

The Creative Curriculum for Early Childhood (Dodge & Colker, 1988) is used as a guide for instructional planning. The physical environment of each classroom is arranged so that there are clearly defined interest areas (e.g., block area, house corner, table toys, art, sand and water, library) that support child-initiated, child-directed play. Weekly themes (e.g., dinosaurs, transportation, families) are used to help children learn about the world around them and to enable children to acquire information and concepts through planned activities that take place in each interest area. The classroom daily schedule (see Table 11.1) is designed to provide a balance of activities that include quiet/active, individual/small group/large group, child-directed/teacher-directed, large muscle/small muscle, and indoor/outdoor learning activities. Weekly instructional planning focuses on both general skill concepts to be emphasized with all children during both child-directed and teacher-directed learning activities (e.g., recalling a sequence of events, identifying functional use of objects, sharing toys with peers) as well as individual goals for children with autism (e.g., verbally requesting desired food items during snack time).

To best meet the needs of children with autism, the early childhood curriculum is supplemented with learning activities and instructional strategies specifically designed to facilitate the development of functional skills, independent play and work skills, social interaction skills, language skills, and adaptive behavior. Functional skills instruction focuses on teaching children with autism skills such as transitioning from

TABLE 11.1.   LEAP Preschool—Sample Daily Schedule

9:00–9:15	Arrival	Children select quiet table top activities such as puzzles, books, drawing, or manipulative toys.
9:15–9:30	Circle Time	Large group activity that focuses on finger plays, music/movement, socialization, and discussion of the day's activities.
9:30–10:15	Discovery Time	Children choose from activities in interest areas as well as participate in teacher-directed individual or small group activities.
10:15–10:30	Story Time	Stories related to the weekly theme are read to children in one or more groups.
10:30–10:45	Snack/Bathroom	
10:45–11:00	Quiet Work Time	Children select from a variety of choices requiring minimal clean-up such as table toys, drawing, books, and listening center.
11:00–11:15	Indoor/ Outdoor Play	Children participate in a variety of large muscle activities.
11:15–11:45	Center Time	Children choose from activities in interest areas as well as participate in teacher-directed individual or small group activities.
11:45–12:00	Circle Time and Dismissal	Children prepare to go home and then gather together as a large group to discuss the day's activities, plan for tomorrow, and sing favorite songs.

one activity to another, selecting play activities, following classroom routines, and participating in group activities.

Independent play skills are taught using instructional strategies such as peer modeling; task analysis; direct instruction; and prompting, fading, and reinforcement procedures.

Social interaction training focuses on teaching children with autism the necessary skills for developing friendships with same-age typical peers. Strategies used by classroom teachers for facilitating social interactions include structuring the environment to promote peer interactions (e.g., limiting play materials, structuring thematic play activities); peer imitation training (cf. Apolloni & Cooke, 1978); peer-mediated strategies (cf. Odom & Strain, 1984); teacher cueing, prompting, and reinforcement for peer interactions (cf. Strain, Shores, & Kerr, 1976); and socio-dramatic script training (Goldstein, Wickstrom, Hoyson, Jamieson, & Odom, 1988).

Language skills of typical children are facilitated within the preschool classroom by providing a variety of stimulating and enriching activities that encourage language in young children. A more intensive and systematic approach is used to develop age-appropriate language skills for children with autism. A variety of "milieu-teaching" procedures (Warren & Kaiser, 1988) (e.g., incidental teaching, mand-model technique, and time delay) are used to facilitate the language of children with autism within routine classroom activities. Direct instruction is also used as needed to teach targeted language skills during initial stages of learning.

The early childhood curriculum is also adapted as needed to meet the needs of children who display challenging behaviors. Intervention procedures include the development and implementation of strategies to prevent behavior problems (e.g., effective use of classroom rules, environmental arrangements, scheduling, activities, and materials) as well as the use of positive reinforcement procedures for increasing desired behaviors. Procedures for conducting functional analyses of behaviors and for implementing and evaluating individualized behavioral interventions are incorporated into daily curricular activities within the classroom.

Instructional strategies used by the classroom teachers reflect both a developmentally appropriate practice approach to early childhood education as well as a "best practice" approach to early intervention. Teachers facilitate all children's learning by: (a) providing opportunities for children to choose from a variety of activities, materials, and equipment; (b) increasing children's engagement with materials by assisting and guiding children; and (c) extending children's learning by asking questions or making suggestions that stimulate children's learning.

As needed, teachers modify instructional practices to best meet the needs of children with autism. The guidelines (Cordisco & Izeman, 1991) used by classroom teachers when making decisions about instructional strategies for young children with autism are shown in Table 11.2.

Individual children's progress (i.e., children with autism) towards identified goals and objectives is monitored on an ongoing basis. Skill

TABLE 11.2. Guidelines for Modifying Instructional Strategies

1. Instructional strategies for young children with disabilities should be as normalized as possible, i.e., they should approximate, whenever possible, instructional strategies utilized with same-age typical peers.

2. Instructional strategies should focus on teaching functional skills during naturally occurring routines and events in the classroom.

3. Instructional strategies should incorporate learning objectives into child-selected activities and teach the necessary skills (e.g., choice making, independent work/play skills) children with disabilities need to participate in activities.

4. Instructional strategies should be individually determined for the child, the task, and for where the child is in the learning process (i.e., stages of learning).

5. Instructional strategies should include teaching strategies for enhancing the probability of skill generalization.

6. Instructional strategies should be effective, that is they should result in children successfully learning desired skills.

acquisition is evaluated via assessments of how frequently or how long, how well, with what level of assistance (e.g., level of prompts), and under what conditions (e.g., materials, adults, activities, settings) children perform desired skills. In addition to assessment of skill acquisition, assessments of maintenance and generalization are conducted as a means of evaluating the effectiveness of instructional strategies.

INTEGRATION VERSUS SEGREGATION

Since its inception in 1982, LEAP Preschool has operated as a full inclusion program for young children with autism and their families. As
briefly described in the introduction, the philosophy of the preschool is
best reflected in the following beliefs:

1. *All children (i.e., both children with and without disabilities)
can benefit from integrated early childhood environments.* Over the
past 10 years, LEAP Preschool has served over 107 typical young
children and 48 children with autism or pervasive developmental
disorder. Results of research studies (Hoyson, Jamieson, & Strain,
1984) indicate that both typical children as well as children with
autism demonstrate significant developmental gains from entry to
completion of the preschool program. Follow-up data on children
with autism indicate that LEAP graduates continue to make significant developmental gains during the elementary school years.

2. *Young children with autism benefit most from early intervention when intervention efforts are conducted across school, home,
and community environments.* At LEAP Preschool, education of
young children with autism is viewed as a 24-hour-a-day process. A
child's "teachers" are defined as all primary caregivers who interact
with the child on a daily basis (e.g., teachers, parents, older siblings,
baby sitters, grandparents). Intervention strategies are jointly developed with primary caregivers and are implemented across school,
home, and community environments. Two part-time family service
coordinators are available to work with families in the home and
community to best facilitate the child's successful integration in
those environments. Families receive individualized behavioral skill
training related to both teaching their child new skills as well as
effective strategies for responding to their child's challenging behaviors in a variety of home and community settings (e.g., mealtimes,
bathtimes, bedtime, grocery shopping, restaurants).

3. *Young children with autism make the greatest gains from
early intervention when parents and professionals work together as
partners.* Parent involvement is frequently cited as an essential component for a successful integrated preschool program (Salisbury,
1990). Results of our own research suggest that children with autism

who attended LEAP's integrated preschool program and whose parents participated in behavioral skill training demonstrated greater developmental gains over time than a matched sample of children with autism who attended a segregated preschool program that did not offer behavioral skill training for families (Strain, Hoyson, & Jamieson, 1985).

4. *Young children with autism can learn many important skills (e.g., social skills, language skills, appropriate behavior) from typical same-age peers.* An integral part of instructional programming for LEAP's integrated preschool is providing daily opportunities for children with and without disabilities to play together and learn from each other. Typical children serve as peer models for children with autism during child-initiated play activities as well as teacher-directed small group activities. Children with and without disabilities are often paired together for partner activities (e.g., art and gross motor activities) as well as informal peer tutoring activities (e.g., "reading" a story to each other). Social interaction and communication skills are frequently taught by using typical children as intervention agents (e.g., Strain, Hoyson, & Jamieson, 1985). Typical children are also encouraged to engage in peer problem-solving activities related to adaptations and support that may facilitate a child's (with autism) inclusion into routine classroom activities (e.g., peers may be asked to identify how they could help a child learn that it's time to put the toys away and come to the snack table). Curricular activities are planned within each classroom that emphasize the positive value of diversity and the uniqueness of all children.

5. *Young children with autism benefit most from early intervention when intervention efforts are planned, systematic, and individualized.* An 8-step process of instructional planning is used to facilitate the successful integration of young children with autism. The process begins with an assessment of each child's strengths and needs across developmental skill domains as well as functional skills needed by the child to participate in daily activities within the school, home, and community environments. Based upon the results of assessment, instructional goals and objectives are identified for skill areas where the child demonstrates developmental delays or observed performance deficits. Any needed modifications for children related to materials and the environment, the early childhood curriculum, and instructional strategies are then identified by the in-

structional planning team (i.e., classroom teachers, therapists, parents, etc.). Individualized learning experiences for children with autism are planned for by identifying how goals and objectives and adaptive instructional strategies for individual children can be incorporated into child-directed play activities, routine classroom activities, and teacher-directed small group activities. Any needed modifications to the social context of the classroom (e.g., use of peer buddies, need for one-to-one instruction) are identified and planned. The final step in the process involves planning for ongoing evaluation of individual children's skill performance related to identified goals and objectives.

6. *Both children with and without disabilities benefit from curricular activities that reflect developmentally appropriate practices.* As discussed previously, the curriculum reflects an attempt to "integrate" both a developmentally appropriate practice approach to early childhood education as well as a behavioral approach to instructional programming for young children with autism. This eclectic approach has allowed us to develop a model program that is normalized for both children with and without disabilities as well as effective for children with significant learning and behavior challenges. Data on individual children's performance indicates that children with autism can learn important skills when provided with both child-directed and teacher-directed learning experiences within an integrated early childhood environment.

BEHAVIOR MANAGEMENT

Behavior management strategies used at LEAP Preschool support the use of preventative and positive approaches for managing challenging behaviors of young children with autism. A variety of classroom-wide preventative strategies are used to support children's engagement in positive prosocial behaviors. Such strategies include the effective use of: classroom rules, daily schedules, activities, instructional materials, and staff assignments. In addition, curricular activities are designed to provide children with autism numerous opportunities to make choices and exercise control over their environment, as well as teach important skills in the areas of play, social skills development, and communication.

Instructional planning teams that include the teachers and classroom assistants, the family service coordinator, speech therapist, parents, program supervisor, and other primary caregivers meet as needed to discuss concerns related to individual children's behavior in school, home, and community environments. When a specific behavior is identified as a concern, the conditions and circumstances that may predict when the behavior will or will not occur are identified, as well as hypotheses regarding the possible functions of the behavior. Individualized preventative strategies (e.g., opportunities for adult/peer attention, waiting activities, opportunities for choices, reduction of task demands) that may reduce the likelihood that the child will engage in the undesirable behavior are reviewed and discussed. Alternative desired behaviors and strategies for teaching these behaviors are identified, as well as intervention strategies to be used when the child engages in the undesirable behavior. Procedures are identified for promoting generalization and maintenance of desired behaviors across environments, activities, and persons, and for evaluating the effectiveness of intervention strategies.

PARENTAL AND FAMILY INVOLVEMENT

Policies and practices at LEAP Preschool related to working with families of young children with disabilities reflect a family-centered approach to early intervention (e.g., Dunst, Trivette, & Branch, in press). Specifically, support and services for families reflect the beliefs that:

1. support and services should be individualized, flexible, and responsive to the needs of families

2. program efforts should be family- versus child-focused

3. program efforts should support families as decision-makers and encourage parent-professional partnerships

4. intervention strategies should be in congruence with family values and beliefs

5. intervention efforts should build upon family strengths and resources and provide families with opportunities to learn new skills

6. both formal and informal sources of support should be utilized to address family concerns and priorities

In addition to the preschool program's philosophy related to working with families of young children with autism, special education regulations and standards related to early intervention in Pennsylvania require Individual Education Plans (IEPs) to include, with parental consent: a statement of family concerns, priorities, and resources; a statement of the major outcomes expected to be achieved with the family; criteria, procedures, and timelines for determining if outcomes have been achieved; a statement of the early intervention services necessary to address family concerns and priorities; and steps to be taken to support the transition of the child.

One of the primary services that is available to families participating in LEAP Preschool is the behavioral skill training program. This program focuses on teaching parents the basic principles of behavior management as well as strategies for teaching children new skills. Training activities include both didactic instruction (i.e., a behavior skill training curriculum for parents has been developed and field-tested over the last 10 years) as well as individual "practice sessions" in home and community settings. Practice sessions focus on family-identified desired outcomes for training, both for their child and themselves. Specific intervention strategies for achieving desired outcomes (e.g., child will remain seated at the dinner table and eat a variety of food items) are modeled (by the family service coordinator) for the family in the natural environment. Family members then "practice" these skills with their child with the family service coordinator providing encouragement and positive/corrective feedback. A variety of assessment measures (e.g., direct observation data, rating scales, parent reports) are used to evaluate the effectiveness of intervention programs.

Additional services available to families include: (a) a monthly parent support group that focuses on topics and issues identified by participating families; (b) referral to various community agencies such as respite care programs, recreational programs, health care services; and (c) transition planning and follow-up services (e.g., assisting families in identifying placement options for their children, visiting kindergartens and school-age programs, identifying information to be shared with "receiving" programs, identifying the nature and extent of follow-up support to be provided to the family and receiving program).

CHILD AND FAMILY OUTCOMES

With funds from the Handicapped Children's Early Education Program, National Institute of Mental Health, and local education agencies, we have shown, using a controlled comparison design, that the LEAP program yields the following short-term and long-term outcomes:

1. children in the experimental program (i.e., LEAP) generally do not qualify for an autism diagnosis after 2 years in treatment; the vast majority of comparative treatment children still qualify

2. both groups of children make developmental progress on intellectual and language measures, with experimentally-treated children consistently making better progress

3. on observational measures taken in school and home, the experimentally-treated children are generally more appropriate, social, and actively engaged (academically) than their counterparts

4. no negative and some positive outcomes (e.g., better social skills, fewer disruptive behaviors) have been noted for normally-developing children at the experimental program

5. gains for experimentally-treated children tend to maintain following program participation, with approximately one-half of the children now enrolled in regular education classes (oldest cohort in 5th grade); most parents enrolled their children in neighborhood kindergartens without any reference to their child's prior treatment history

6. few family outcome measures initially distinguish the two groups; however, experimental parents show substantial improvement 2 to 3 years *away* from treatment on measures of depression and stress.

To more precisely identify the peer instructional variables that are functional within the LEAP setting, a variety of substudies were conducted on the effects of specific peer behavior on children with autism. Other functional analyses were completed on the effects of specific parent behaviors on child appropriate behavior and compliance and the effects of group-based teaching strategies on children's skill acquisition (Cordisco & Strain, 1986; Strain, 1987; Strain, Hoyson, & Jamieson, 1985).

On the fundamentally important issue of long-term effects of LEAP involvement, it has been shown that:

1. the initial improvements made by LEAP children on measures of cognitive, communicative, and aberrant behavior reduction maintain over time

2. comparison group children make little developmental progress after treatment; however, they *do not* appear to regress

3. LEAP and comparison group children look quite similar on direct observational measures of appropriate behavior in the home, attesting to the legitimacy of the comparison program's parent training component

4. LEAP children are vastly superior to comparison group children on school-based direct observational measures of echolalic speech and appropriate behavior (attending, on-task)

5. LEAP children's social interactions with peers are far more frequent and positive (Strain & Kohler, 1988)

Our follow-up data on the experimental group children are particularly striking when cost-of-treatment issues are considered. Assuming continued regular class placement for our participants, the cost savings in special education dollars alone are approximately $51,000 for each child over a 12-year time period (i.e., 1st–12th grades).

MAJOR ISSUES FOR FUTURE EFFORT

After a decade of experience in developing and refining the LEAP model, two guiding themes have emerged to focus and shape our future directions. First, we have become acutely aware of the need to maintain a useful balance between model program development and remaining open to new information and innovations in the field. While overreaching beliefs and values about the nature of service delivery may not (possibly should not) vary greatly, strongly held beliefs can often lead to invariant methods. In a field where knowledge explosion is manifest, rigidity in method serves neither clients or programs well. At LEAP, we have relied, to a large extent, upon active inservice training and inhouse research generation to help keep us permeable to change. Our challenge for the future is to incorporate new knowledge in ways that preserve essential LEAP elements, while discarding that which is no longer state-of-the-art.

A second central theme for our future efforts involves a commitment to better understand, forecast, and improve on our outcomes for children and families. While it is true that many clients have shown great improvement during and after their LEAP experience, others have not. As yet, we do not know the variables that contribute to differential outcome. We do know something about variables that seem not to play a role. They include initial child level of functioning, family income and education level, and severity of autistic symptoms. It would also appear that differential provision of intervention is not occurring. Of course, any conclusions at this point are tentative, given the relatively small sample size for doing the necessary correlational analyses. As we gain more clients, and thus increase the N-size for complex correlational studies, we should have a much better grasp over the interaction between client characteristics and service outcomes.

REFERENCES

American Psychiatric Association. (1987). *Diagnostic and statistical manual of mental disorders* (3rd ed., revised). Washington, DC: Author.

Apolloni, T., & Cooke, T. P. (1978). Integrated programming at the infant, toddler, and preschool levels. In M. Guralnick (Ed.), *Early intervention and the integration of handicapped and nonhandicapped children* (pp. 147–165). Baltimore, MD: University Park Press.

Bredekamp, S. (Ed.). (1987). *Developmentally appropriate practice in early childhood programs serving children from birth through age 8.* Washington, DC: National Association for the Education of Young Children.

Cordisco, L. K., & Izeman, S. G. (1991). *Program design: Instructional strategies for young children with disabilities. Early Intervention Guidelines.* Harrisburg, Pa: Pennsylvania Department of Education, Bureau of Special Education.

Cordisco, L. K., & Strain, P. S. (1986). Assessment of generalization and maintenance in a multicomponent parent training program. *Journal of the Division of Early Childhood, 10* (1), 10–24.

Dodge, D. T., & Colker. L. J. (1988). *The creative curriculum* (3rd ed.). Washington, DC: Teaching Strategies, Inc.

Dunst, C. J., Trivette, C. M., & Branch, R. L. (in press). Supporting and strengthening family functioning: Toward a congruence between principles and practice. *Prevention in Human Services.*

Goldstein, H., Wickstrom, S., Hoyson, M., Jamieson, B., & Odom, S. (1988). Effects of script training on social and communicative interaction. *Education and Treatment of Children*, 2 (2), 97–117.

Hedrick, D. L., Prather, E. M., & Tobin, A. R. (1984). *Sequenced inventory of communication development—Revised Edition.* Seattle: University of Washington Press.

Hoyson, M., Jamieson, B., & Strain, P. (1984). Individualized group instruction of normally developing and autistic-like children: The LEAP curriculum model. *Journal of the Division of Early Childhood*, Summer, 157–171.

McCarthy, D. (1972). *Manual for the McCarthy Scales of Children's Abilities.* New York: The Psychological Corporation.

Odom, S. L., & Strain, P. S. (1984). Peer-mediated approaches to increasing children's social interaction: A review. *American Journal of Orthopsychiatry*, 54, 544–557.

Salisbury, C. L. (1990). *Policy and practice in early childhood special education series* (Available from: Research Institute on Preschool Mainstreaming, Allegheny-Singer Research Institute, Pittsburgh, Pa.).

Sanford, A. R., & Zelman, J. G. (1981). *The Learning Accomplishment Profile.* Winston-Salem, NC: Kaplan.

Schopler, E., Reichler, R. J., Devellis, R. F., & Daly, K. (1988). *The Childhood Autism Rating Scale* (CARS). Los Angeles: Western Psychological Services.

Strain, P. S. (1987). Comprehensive evaluation of young autistic children. *Topics in Early Childhood Special Education*, 7, 97–110.

Strain, P. S., Hoyson, M., & Jamieson, B. (1985). Normally developing preschoolers as intervention agents for autistic-like children: Effects on class deportment and social interaction. *Journal of the Division for Early Childhood*, Spring, 105–115.

Strain, P. S., Kohler, F. W. (1988). Social skill intervention with young handicapped children: Some new conceptualizations and directions. In S. L. Odom and M. B. Karnes (Eds.), *Early intervention for infants and children with handicaps: An empirical base* (pp. 129–143). Baltimore: Paul H. Brooks Publishing Company.

Strain, P. S., Shores, R. E., & Kerr, M. M. (1976). An experimental analysis of "spill over" effects on the social interaction of behaviorally handicapped preschool children. *Journal of Applied Behavior Analysis*, 9, 31–40.

Warren, S. F., & Kaiser, A. P. (1988). Research in early language intervention. In S. L. Odom & M. B. Karnes (Eds.) *Early Intervention for Infants and Children with Handicaps: An Empirical Base* (pp. 89–108). Baltimore, MD: Paul H. Brookes, Publishing Company.

APPENDIX II.A

Note. The material in this appendix is currently being used by LEAP. Other programs are welcome to adopt it for their own use.

ABOUT OUR CHILD . . .

Child's Name: _____   Date: _____

Name of Person(s) Completing This Form	Relationship to Child
_____	_____
_____	_____
_____	_____

We would like to invite your family to complete this form in preparation for your child's IEP meeting. This form is one way you can provide us with a better understanding of your child's strengths and needs. Your family may also choose to share this information with us at the IEP meeting without completing this form.

Child's Name: _____

Date: _____

Please check any that apply

Area	Some things our child knows or already does in this area are:	Some skills we would like our child to learn in this area are:	We are working on this at home	We would like classroom teachers to work on this	We would like more information about this	We would like to talk to other parents about this	We would like this as a topic at a parent meeting	We would like some training on strategies for teaching this
Play (skills such as sharing, taking turns, playing by self, playing with other children . . .)								
Language (skills such as communicating needs; following directions; listening skills; concepts such as in, on, up, down . . .)								
Dressing (skills such as taking clothes off, putting clothes on, zipping, buttoning . . .)								
Toileting (skills such as sitting on or standing at potty, toilet scheduled, toilet trained . . .)								
Mealtime (skills such as eating with utensils, eating more of a variety of foods, pouring juice, eating more slowly, table manners . . .)								

Child's Name: _____

Date: _____

Area	Some things our child knows or already does in this area are:	Some skills we would like our child to learn in this area are:	Please check any that apply
			We are working on this at home / We would like classroom teachers to work on this / We would like more information about this / We would like to talk to other parents about this / We would like this as a topic at a parent meeting / We would like some training on strategies for teaching this
Bathtime (skills such as sitting (staying) in tub, washing self, combing hair, brushing teeth . . .)			
Community Activities (skills such as shopping with family members, eating out in restaurants, riding in the car . . .)			
Cognitive (skills such as numbers, letters, colors, shapes, sorting . . .)			
Motor (skills such as running, jumping, playing ball, coloring, building with blocks . . .)			
Other (please specify)			

Child's Name: _____

Date: _____

Please check any that apply

Some behaviors we would like our child to do less often are:	We are working on this at home	We would like classroom teachers to work on this	We would like more information about this	We would like to talk to other parents about this	We would like this as a topic at a parent meeting	We would like some training on strategies for teaching this

Some of the things our child enjoys are (e.g., favorite song, activity, toy, snack, etc.)

_____

_____

_____

_____

_____

_____

Is there anything else about your child's strengths and needs that you would like to discuss at the IEP meeting?

_____

_____

_____

_____

_____

_____

OUR FAMILY WOULD LIKE . . .

Child's Name: _____   Date: _____

Name of Person(s) Completing This Form	Relationship to Child
_____	_____
_____	_____
_____	_____

LEAP Preschool is a program for young children *and* their families.* At LEAP, we recognize that all families have their own strengths and needs. This form is one way you can provide us with a better understanding of what your family's needs are and how we can work with you to meet these needs. If you choose to complete this form, you may want to periodically update this information, since your family's needs may change over time. You may also choose to share this information with us, at any time, without completing this form. All information you provide will be kept confidential.

DIRECTIONS: Please put a check ($\sqrt{}$) next to any of the items listed below that your family might: a) like some information about, b) want some assistance with, or c) care to discuss with a staff person or other parents at LEAP.

Note: If you indicate a need for a service that is not provided by LEAP (e.g., respite care), your Family Service Coordinator will work with you to identify how your family may be able to obtain these services.

Caring for Our Child

1. Ways to play or talk to our child _____
2. Ways to teach our child _____
3. Ways to respond to our child's behavior _____
4. Teaching others (e.g., relatives, friends, babysitters) how to care for our child _____
5. Finding day care for our child _____

6. Finding babysitter or respite care _____
7. Information about our child's disability _____
8. Information about other services for our child _____
9. Other: _____

_____ _____

Support for Our Family

1. Helping family members accept our child's disability _____
2. Talking about concerns and supporting spouse/significant other, family members, etc. _____
3. Finding time to spend with my spouse/significant other _____
4. Identifying ways to spend special time with each of our children _____
5. Spending time with friends _____
6. Finding more time for myself _____
7. Making it all work: household chores, child care family responsibilities, etc. _____
8. Planning/doing family recreational activities _____
9. Other: _____

_____ _____

*Note: The term "family" is used to describe all primary caregivers and others who assume a major role in the child's life.

Community Services We May Need

1. Finding physicians or dentists who are knowledgeable about young children with disabilities _____
2. Finding suitable housing _____
3. Information about food/nutritional programs _____
4. Options for transportation _____
5. Information about utilities assistance _____
6. Information about financial assistance _____
7. Information about GED, adult education programs, job training opportunities _____
8. Information about additional therapies, skill training programs, recreational programs, etc. for our child _____
9. Information about support groups (e.g., parent groups, AA, Parents Anonymous, etc.) _____
10. Information about individual or family counseling _____
11. Other: _____

_____ _____

Talking About Our Child

1. Talking about our child to our parents and other relatives   _____
2. Talking about our child's disability to our other children   _____
3. Knowing how to respond when friends, neighbors, or
   strangers ask about our child   _____
4. Explaining our child's disability to other children   _____
5. Talking to other professionals (doctors, teachers, therapists,
   etc.) about our child to get the information and help we want   _____
6. Talking to other parents of young children with disabilities   _____
7. Other: _____
   _____   _____

Planning for the Future

1. Information about special education laws and parents' rights   _____
2. Information about local, state, and national advocacy activities
   for children with disabilities and their families   _____
3. Information about evaluating our child for special education   _____
4. Talking with school district personnel   _____
5. Visiting school-age programs   _____
6. Identifying the best program for our child   _____
7. Identifying other services for our child   _____
8. Identifying skills that will help our child succeed in
   kindergarten or first grade   _____
9. Information about parent advocacy services   _____
10. Information about guardianship   _____
11. Information about family wills   _____
12. Information about residential programs   _____
13. Other: _____
   _____   _____

Please tell us any other ways we may be able to help and/or support your family:

_____
_____
_____